Separation
of
Church and State:
The Myth Revisited

Other books by the same author

Education in the Truth
1969

Philosophy of Education:
A Christian Approach
1977

Christianity and Democracy
1978

Separation of Church and State:

The Myth Revisited

Norman De Jong
Trinity Christian College

in collaboration with

Jack Van Der Slik
Sangamon State University

PAIDEIA PRESS
Jordan Station, Ontario, Canada

Canadian Cataloguing in Publication Data

De Jong, Norman
 Separation of church and state

Bibliography: p.
ISBN 0-88815-063-6.

1. Church and state - United States - History.
I. Van Der Slik, Jack R., 1936-   . II. Title.

BR516.D43   1985   322'.1'0973   C85-098226-X.

Copyright 1985 by Paideia Press Ltd. © All rights reserved. Published by Paideia Press Ltd., P.O. Box 1000, Jordan Station, Ontario, Canada L0R 1S0. No part of this publication may be reproduced, stored in a retrieval system, or transmitted in any form without the written permission of the publisher.

Cover design: Gerrit V.L. Verstraete, Christian Communications Centre, Toronto.

ISBN 0-88815-063-6
Printed in Canada.

CONTENTS

Dedication   viii
Acknowledgements   ix
Preface   xiii

Chapter I   **Introduction**   1
   Unraveling the Controversy   4
   Roman Catholic Perspectives   9
   Theological Dimensions   12
   End Notes   14

Chapter II   **Should Church and State Be Separated?**   15
   The Myth   17
   Our National Creeds   20
   The Constitutional Context   22

Chapter III   **State Creeds for State Churches**   25
   The Ecumenical Creeds   29
   Germany   30
   The Low Countries   30
   England   32
   Church Life in America   35
   Response to the Revolution   39
   Summary   43
   End Notes   44

Chapter IV   **The States Draft Their Constitutions**   47
   The Process   47
   The Contents   49
   Qualifications for Holding Office   53

Legislating Morality	55
Later Developments	56
Conclusion	58
End Notes	58

Chapter V Schools for Religion and Morality ... 61

Curricular Patterns	64
The Textbooks	66
Responsibility for Schools	68
Methods of Financing	73
Religious and Political Controversy	76
The Dartmouth Case	77
End Notes	79

Chapter VI Religious and Moral Leadership from Congress ... 82

The Northwest Ordinance of 1787	87
Washington's Leadership	91
Later Developments	92
End Notes	94

Chapter VII The Unholy Alliance: Religion and Politics in Virginia ... 97

The National Context	99
The Rise of the Baptists	101
The Legal Framework	102
Educational Qualifications	103
Theological Distinctives	104
Persecution	105
The Political Arena	107
The State Constitution	108
The General Assessment Bill	110
The Federal Constitution	113
Conclusion	117
End Notes	118

Chapter VIII The Constitution of the United States ... 123

The Convention: Disestablishment and Religious Freedom	126
Religion and the Bill of Rights	129
Framing the Religion Clauses	136
Religion, "Separation," and the Intent of the Framers	140
End Notes	142

Chapter IX **The Presidential Election of 1800: Thomas Jefferson's Second Revolution?**   147
   Jefferson's Victory: A Sketch of Events   149
   Religion and the Election of 1800   154
   The Revolution of 1800:
      A Religious Revolution?   163
   End Notes   166

Chapter X **The Theology of Pluralism**   169
   Pluralism Within Unity   170
   Their Common Faith   171
   The Rejection of Errors   177
   End Notes   179

Epilogue   181
Appendices   187
Bibliography   203

Dedicated to
Wilma
my wife of twenty-seven years,
who helped in innumerable
ways to bring this manuscript
to completion.

ACKNOWLEDGEMENTS

No book is the product of a single person operating in isolation. In most instances, books develop out of some context which includes sustained dialogue, probing questions arising from a scholarly community, or the continued surfacing of a societal issue which refuses to accept resolution. This manuscript is the result of such processes which were set in motion already during the autumn of 1979. At that particular juncture in my life, Jack Van Der Slik was serving as Academic Dean of Trinity Christian College, where I was newly installed as Professor of Education.

With a long-range eye on the upcoming Bicentennial of the United States Constitution, Jack encouraged me to begin a comprehensive research on the history of church-state-school relationships during our country's early national period. Through his assistance and recommendations, a National Endowment for the Humanities summer stipend was received. Through his constant interest and scholarly prodding, the research continued for two quickly passing years, with writing and re-writing interspersed whenever time permitted or the situation dictated.

The contribution of Jack Van Der Slik extends beyond that of encouragement and prodding. As the manuscript took shape, he carefully read and reacted to each chapter, pointing up omissions, potential errors in judgment, and examples of deficient or ambiguous phraseology. His most meaningful contributions came, however, in the texts of Chapters VIII and IX which he independently researched and drafted. Because of his skill and expertise as a political scientist, he was better able to unravel the political machinations which enveloped the constitutional convention of 1787 and the election of 1800, two events which we judged to be highly significant in the formulation and clarification of church-state relationships. His educated insights will become readily apparent as the reader digests those two chapters.

A second person who deserves a special word of thanks is Tim Breen, author of numerous books on early American history and Professor of History at Northwestern University in Evanston, Illinois. His pointed suggestions and precise directions to unknown sources were major helps to me, especially during the summer of 1980. His extensive knowledge of the period constantly sharpened my research efforts and focused my questions on the most relevant concerns. Many of the resources listed in the Bibliography would not have become known to me had it not been for his help.

Research would soon run amuck were it not for the assistance of library staffs. At the Northwestern University Library, at the Newberry Library in Chicago, and at Trinity Christian College, I encountered a parade of people who were willing and anxious to be of assistance, directing me in a variety of ways to the materials and sources necessary to the research.

The administration at Trinity Christian College have been particularly helpful and encouraging to us in our efforts at research, writing, and publication. To Gerard Van Groningen, Burton Rozema, and Charles Schoenherr, President and Vice-Presidents respectively, goes a special word of appreciation. Their confidence in our work gave new incentive to overcome each frustration. Many thanks also to Linda Bieze, for her timely information releases and promotional efforts, and to John Bakker and Randy Van Schepen for their creative efforts on the cover of this book.

Another class of assistants that I wish to acknowledge are those colleagues at Trinity Christian College who read and reacted to parts or all of the manuscript. Among those are Dr. Daniel Diephouse from the English department, Dr. Robert Eells, Dr. Steven Pointer, and Dr. Robert Rice, all from the history faculty, Dr. Burton Rozema, our Vice President for Academic Affairs, Hendrik Sliekers, our librarian, and Mr. Edward Vander Weele, my colleague in Education. Each one offered appropriate suggestions and needed encouragement. Their contributions are deeply appreciated.

Other helpful assistance, clarification of issues, and inspiration came from a variety of groups and professional organizations who invited me to present papers or speeches at their meetings. Among them are the Weaton College Fall Education Conference and its chairman, Dr. Paula S. Martinez, The Association of Teacher Educators in Christian Colleges (ATECC), The Conference on Faith and History, which invited me to present a paper at its biennial meeting in Ft. Worth, the North Baptist Christian School of Rochester, New York, and the adult education classes at both the Western Springs and Calvin, Oak Lawn Christian Reformed Churches.

A special word of appreciation goes to John Sparks, John Van Til, and Victor Vouga of the Public Policy Education Fund of Grove City, Pennsylvania, who read the entire manuscript, persuaded me to write an abbreviated version for one of their *Special Reports*, and promoted the sale of the book through their publications. Their endorsement has been a special inspiration to me.

The typists who contributed significantly to the production of the manuscript are Mrs. Debbie Vander Pol, Mrs. Ann Boerema, and my daughter, Amy Lynn De Jong. Their neat, accurate, and efficient work lightened my load considerably, allowing me the luxury of researching, writing, and rewriting without worry.

Last, but not least, a special thanks to my wife and children who supported, encouraged, and responded in numerous helpful ways. Not only did they grant me the largest desk and the quietest corner in our home, but they also faithfully read each chapter of the manuscript, evaluating each page for clarity and interest. Because of their reactions, I am confident that the book can be read with profit by adults, college students, and high school students.

None of the above persons are responsible for the errors, shortcomings, or failures of this book. I alone take full responsibility for those. Inevitably some will appear and become evident only after it is too late to correct them. It is my hope and prayer that such will not detract from the overall message of the book.

Norman De Jong, Ph.D.
Trinity Christian College
June 12, 1984

PREFACE

Incredible! Is that true? Established state churches in the U.S. well into the 19th century? Section 29 in every new township appropriated for the support of religion? Separation of church and state is contrary to the U.S. Constitution?

When I first began serious research into the topic of this book during the early spring of 1980, I thought myself to be an above average student of American history. I had an earned doctorate from a respected university and had taught at the college level for more than a decade. I knew how our country was formed and the degree to which Puritan influences had waned by 1776. I accepted almost uncritically the argument advanced by our courts concerning separation and spoke as a defender of recent Supreme Court decisions, albeit with some reservations.

But then came a series of surprises. Through funding from the National Endowment for the Humanities, I was able to spend the summer of 1980 pouring through the records and dusty old books in both the Newberry Library and in Northwestern University library. With the helpful suggestions of Professor Tim Breen from Northwestern's American History faculty, I was able to locate copies of all the earliest state constitutions, as well as the Journals of Congress, and volumes of materials which seemingly had lain unstudied for decades. What I found oftentimes was surprising and at times almost incredible. What I learned through those forays into the public record ran contrary to so much of what I had been taught by contemporary authors and my own professors. Unable to contain my own excitement and the joy of discovery, I shared my findings with family, friends, and students.

Typical Americans, they had all taken their required doses of American history in high schools and colleges, although not with the same persistence and enthusiasm that I had. Their confessions, that they had never encountered most of the information which now lay exposed on the public record, convinced me that contemporary history teaching is warped and slanted in favor of secularism. This conviction was reinforced in a variety of ways as I presented papers on this subject at a number of conferences around the country. Reactions were never of the impartial, ho-hum variety. Audiences were either enthusiastic and elated to find that Christian political activity was validated and justified by our founding fathers, or stridently opposed to further dissemination on finding their separation arguments seriously eroded.

One does not have to work with historians very long before one realizes that there is no such thing as neutrality. History writers are, like the rest of the human race, valuing, judging, and selecting individuals. They all have their value systems and priority scales, using them either consciously or subconsciously to focus on, cull out, and hold up for public examination that which they consider to be important. In every research effort and in every publication, the material that is glossed over and ignored far exceeds that which is extracted for dissemination. For some, wars with all the military maneuvers, strategies, battle lines, and body counts are important. For others, intellectual history and ideological revolutions are paramount. For still others, literary and social events are most worth noting. For generalists, the blending of many different dimensions of a country's history is the important end to be attained. Regardless of which perspective is pursued, each historian selects and ignores according to his or her predetermined set of values and priorities. That is not intended as criticism, but as a bland recognition that historians, too, are human beings.

But historians not only select on the basis of personally held value systems. They also make personal judgments about that which they encounter. A contemporary historian, writing about the elections of 1980, would have to deal substantively with the Moral Majority and other conservative groups who worked for the election of Ronald Reagan and the defeat of many liberal senators. To pretend that no judgments were being made about the worth or the rightness of such political activity would be to feign neutrality. One may have mixed reactions to the Moral Majority, endorsing some actions and condemning others, or one may even claim to "suspend judgment until all the facts are in," but judgments of "good" or "bad" and "true" or "false" will inevitably be made. Since it is the accepted business of historians to present the truth about the past, they unavoidably reject some theses and explanations as being false, while others are put into print for unquestioned acceptance as truth. Although the "good" and "bad" judgments are often studiously kept out of print, since the appearance of such would unmask the myth of neutrality, they are there for the careful reader to discern through the choice of words, the appending of labels, the type of evidences advanced, and the inferences gained by what was omitted. What is often practiced is the focusing on what is obviously true and undebatable. To say, for example, that the Constitution of the U.S. was drafted in 1787 or that George Washington was the first president of our country is not to present "neutral facts," but such obviously and undebatably true ones that almost no one will wage intellectual warfare against them. Only in that sense of "absence of warfare" can one talk in terms of neutral history. But, to deal only with *obvious truth* and undisputable data is to write trivial history and to ignore basic questions about which controversial opinions will inevitably arise.

Reading and writing history, then, is a serious and consequential business. One should not approach it glibly or with the confidence that the historian is telling the truth, the whole truth, and nothing but the truth. Bernard Bailyn earlier sensitized me to the importance of this through his stinging criticism of American educational historians. Writing his *Education in the Forming of American Society*, he noted that "the main emphasis and ultimately the main weakness of history written by the educational missionaries" of the early 20th century derived directly from the fact that they were apologists for secular public education. As such, "they had no capacity for surprise. They lacked the belief, the historian's instinct, that the elements of their world might not have existed at all for others, might in fact have been inconceivable to them" (pp. 9-10).

The element of surprise which triggered the writing of this book was the awareness one day that Congress not only specified in the Appendix to the Northwest Ordinance of 1787 that Section

16 be appropriated for education, but that Section 29 also be reserved "for purposes of religion." If that were true, something of deep significance for constitutional interpretation had been omitted from my education. If that had been delegated to the ash pile of insignificance, either by design or collective apathy, what other events and decisions might also lie there unnoticed, but capable of guiding us, if resurrected through the chaos of our confusing culture?

The purpose of my research, then, was to find answers to such basic questions as:

1. Was the Constitution of the United States, with its notable First Amendment, designed to erect a "wall of separation between church and state," as both the U.S. Supreme Court and numerous lower courts have contended repeatedly since 1947?
2. What was the status of religious life in the decades surrounding the drafting of the Constitution? Had it atrophied to a level of national impotence, as some recent liberal historians have claimed? Or were the various denominations powerful and effective forces in the shaping of America?
3. Was the election of 1800 really a national referendum on church-state separation and the "second great American revolution" as Jefferson repeatedly boasted in his later years? Or was Jefferson merely engaging in political rhetoric for the benefit of his constituency who wanted to believe what they heard?

Although one can never claim to have exhausted all possible sources of information, the evidence seems to be insurmountably in support of the contention that religious life and influence in the early national period were significantly different from what they are in the late twentieth century and that contemporary understandings of the past need both correction and revision. To read these pages, then, one may need to exercise a capacity for surprise. Hopefully that surprise, whenever it occurs, will result in only temporary incredulity, and the reader will thoughtfully reexamine the historical record.

The reader will note, too, that these pages are not without their bias, for all who analyze and write have a perspective from which they select and present their historical data. The bias is clear and straigtforward in Chapter II where I articulate the thesis that *church and state*, although not coterminous, *cannot be separate* because both, by definition, are essentially collections of people. At the same time, however, I defend the concept that church and state are analytically distinctive from each other, just as the fingers are noticeably different from the hand and yet cannot be separated from each other without doing irreparable damage to both.

The reader may also recognize in these pages implied social criticism and an historical apology for the cause of religious education. No excuses are made for that, since all education is unavoidably religious. Whether one teaches that there is no God, that God is restricted to a limited realm or that God is sovereign over all of life, each teaching is religious, for religion is primarily the expression of some attitude or relationship toward the divine. In that sense, an agnostic or an atheist is as religious as the zealot, even though their attitudes and relationships to God may be diametrically opposed.

What makes this history somewhat unique is that it consciously focuses on the religious dimensions of early American life. In doing so, it puts the spotlight not on the pulpit or on published sermons, where one would expect to find a spiritual emphasis, but on the political actions and public records in which a majority of the adult populace were represented. Numerous other historians have willfully chosen to ignore that religious dimension, preferring to believe that religion is a purely private, Sunday-only concern with which the historian has no legitimate interest.

The primary purpose of this writing, then, is to inform the American public of the historical record of church-state-school relationships in the early national era and thereby to permit more informed discussions and decisions as Americans seek either to expand or to restrain the influence of religion on public life. The purpose is not to outline any grand strategies or plans for action by which the protagonists in the on-going debates may martial their forces for eventual success in the ideological warfare that characterizes our increasingly pluralistic society. The objective is not either to cast aspersions on the orthodoxy of any one denominational grouping or particular faith, although Baptists may find that difficult to swallow. By their own proud admissions they have often claimed exclusive credit for bringing about the degree of separation that currently exists. Because of that claim, and its conflict with the thesis as stated in Chapter II, implied criticism should be expected. The criticism that comes to expression, however, should not be extended to all the different branches of the Baptist faith that exist in twentieth century America. What is intended is nothing more than an accurate and fair picture of what the Baptists of the late eighteenth and early nineteenth centuries did and said at the time. Since the primary sources for such information are the writings of the Baptist historians themselves, the record will stand or fall on the accuracy with which they described themselves.

The purpose, then, is to describe in detail, with warts and all, the religious mentality which governed the states at the time of our country's founding. One of the warts which becomes painfully visible is that of the strident anti-Catholic bias which permeated the colonies and continued well into the twentieth century. No Christian should be proud of that, but it must be acknowledged that America was intended, by almost universal assent, to be a haven and a home for Protestants. If time permitted, the tracing of that anti-Catholic bias could easily be told through such notable events as the New York public school debates of the 1840's, the anti-Catholic planks of the political parties in the 1850's, and the ignominious Pierce Case which reached the Supreme Court in 1925. Later records could also be examined to show that most of the litigation concerning government support for religious education reflects that continuing anti-Catholic bias. Since Frank Sorauf has so carefully detailed that in *The Wall of Separation*, the reader is referred to it for additional insight.

The picture of the United States in the early national era that comes to expression in these pages is not only complex, but also incomplete. I have looked primarily at the religious, educational, and political dimensions of public life, but have ignored many other facets. In attempting to sketch out for the reader the actions of the founding fathers, I have focused on the *public record* as it came to expression in denominational creeds, state constitutions, and legislation as it emanated both from the federal Congress and from the various state assemblies. Even there I have been forced to narrow our focus, putting much more attention on the actions in Virginia, Connecticut, and Massachusetts than on what might have occurred in Rhode Island, New York, or North Carolina. Because of that, much still needs to be done before the picture will be finished. That task is open to everyone, for to the extent that we all know and better understand our nation's history, to that extent we will be able to make wiser and better informed decisions concerning our present predicaments.

Norman De Jong
June 15, 1984

CHAPTER I

Introduction

In 1791, three scant years after the Constitution of the United States had been adopted, Congress approved and the several states ratified ten Amendments to that Constitution. The First Amendment read, in part:

> Congress shall make no law respecting an establishment of religion, or prohibiting the free exercise thereof—,

From these cryptic phrases, presumably understood and well-intentioned by all those who voted for their adoption, has come monumental confusion. At the time this Amendment was passed, the United States was composed of thirteen states and slightly less than four million people. Today the U.S. population has mushroomed to some two hundred and twenty million people spread over fifty states.

The situation to which this Amendment is supposed to apply has changed drastically in the almost two hundred years since its adoption. New states were carved out of the wilderness, new territories were acquired, waves of immigrants have landed on our shores, and technological inventions have modernized our nation to a point beyond the wildest imaginations of even an inventive Ben Franklin.

Through all of that change, the First Amendment has remained fixed and absolute. No one has waged a prolonged effort to amend, abolish or alter it.

No matter which magazines or newspapers one reads, or which television network one watches, it is only a matter of time, though, before one confronts the issue of "separation of church and state." The issue is like the air we breathe; it permeates the mind-set of twentieth century America. It surfaces repeatedly in scientific journals, denominational weeklies, daily newspapers, legislative chambers, and nightly news broadcasts.

To be an intellectual in America during the last third of the twentieth century is tantamount to being cognizant of the church-state controversy. Yet mere acquaintance is not adequate for reaching any clear comprehension of the issues or being near any resolution of the crisis, for the conflict is shrouded in myth and garbled by illogical debate. To complicate matters, it seems to have been cemented in place by sometimes devious and presumably illegal efforts to circumvent a frustrating and yet sacred doctrine. "Separation of church and state" has become an immovable plank in United States jurisprudence, yet an annoyance which we wish were not there.

Typical of the American attitude toward this emotionally charged issue is that expressed in a highly respected denominational weekly. In one column, positive suggestions are made as to ways by which the salary of the United States Senate's chaplain might be raised so as to perpetuate his prestigious position. On the same page, written by the same author, is a highly critical commentary on conservative Christians in Kentucky who were attempting to keep the Ten Commandments in their public school classrooms. By supplying their children with notebooks, on the covers of which were printed the Lord's Prayer and the Decalogue, the parents could maintain their religious commitments without any "infractions upon the issue of separation of church and state."

One need not be a genius to recognize a glaring incongruity between the two columns. By what stretch of reasoning would it be highly permissible and even desirable to pay the salary of a chaplain in the Senate chamber, while declaring it unconstitutional to post the Ten Commandments on a classroom wall in a remote village of Kentucky? Are the Protestant minister's prayers at the beginning of each Senatorial session somehow judged beneficial to the law-making process, while the laws of God, to whom the Senators pray, considered injurious to the young whose responsibilities include a learning of the laws? Is religion a prerequisite to the law-making, but a stumbling block to the law-abiding? Or is the difference merely one of age, being good for the elderly and evil for the youth?

INTRODUCTION

If "separation" requires that the school officials in Kentucky remove the Decalogue from the public schools of the state, then it would appear to be a matter of simple logic to separate the Senate chaplain from both his post and his tax-financed paycheck. If it is clearly unconstitutional to allow teachers and children to pray even inocuous, undenominational prayers in public school classrooms, then it would seem equally unconstitutional to fund the work of chaplains in all the branches of the armed services and to construct lavish chapels at the military academies. With similar exercises in straight reasoning we could question the legitimacy of putting "In God we Trust" on all of our currency while making it illegal to ascribe any creative powers to that God in whom we claim to trust.

These inherently contradictory practices are a source of confusion to millions of persons in our chaotic culture. Clarity, we hope, will come from our courts. Insight and wise counsel, we trust, will come from the legal professionals whose shingles dot the main streets of our towns and cities. When in doubt, we think, ask the lawyers. The lawyer who serves the school board, the one who is supposed to be the authority on all matters regarding the law, he will know the answer to our dilemma.

Regrettably, the typical lawyer is part of the delusion under which most of us operate. According to the Executive Director of the Christian Legal Society, ninety-nine percent (99%) of the lawyers in the United States know virtually nothing about the First Amendment to the United States Constitution. On the average, law school faculties and curricula spend no more than thirty (30) minutes of time studying the First Amendment, its genesis, or its implications. When compared with the rigorous and extensive requirements of a three year degree program, that thirty minutes is no more than a drop in the bucket or a flashlight on a moonless night.

Where the legal professionals should be angels of light they have become, instead, purveyors of myth and counselors of ignorance. While such an assessment may seem a bit too harsh, the conditions which have lead to such widespread ignorance by the supposed experts is certainly understandable. Practicing lawyers and law school faculties, not unlike the rest of society's professionals, gravitate to those dimensions of law where the most business is generated. They, consequently, address themselves much more intensely to such questions as tax law, contracts, probate, estate planning, divorce, and criminal prosecution or public defense. In our most crass and calloused judgments, we might even accuse them of majoring in monied issues. Since very little income will be earned by extensive research into the machinations and political make-up of the Constitutional Convention of 1787, we simply cannot expect the typical lawyer to focus his or her attentions on non-profitable analyses.

If we are to unravel the mysteries of the First Amendment, we will not be able to count on the legal profession as a source of illumination. In most, but not all, cases where the First Amendment is concerned, the lawyers move with the masses and merely pass on to their clients what they expected to hear. Their stock response, when in doubt, is that the practice of religion in the context of civil activity is "probably unconstitutional." The grounds, they assert, is "separation of church and state."

Unraveling the Controversy

To say that the United States is an enormously complicated nation would be to make an undebatable understatement. In all of its vastness and all its diversity it represents an intricate maze of puzzles to even the keenest historians, political analysts, and social critics. To understand it in its present form baffles the best minds, yet we expect our students to understand not only its present, but also its past. Lacking the quality of omniscience, we take only fleeting glimpses into the past and accept uncritically the views of those who are supposed to teach us.

Such cavalier approaches to history may suffice for those who have consigned the American past to the realm of irrelevance. But for those who wish to unravel the controversy surrounding "the separation of church and state," an in-depth analysis of both the present and the past is essential.

In order to interpret the First Amendment correctly, we need to know and do a great many things. Recognizing at the outset that simplistic analyses and solutions will not suffice, we need to commit ourselves to exhaustive research and clearheaded thought. At the simplest and most elementary level, we ought to look at the key words in that First Amendment. We need to note first of all that *Congress* is restricted in its actions. The amendment does not speak to the states, to towns, school districts, or any other branch of government. For some reasons, to be examined later in this treatise, Congress was singled out. Secondly, we should consider the fact that "separation of church and state" is not anywhere mentioned in the amendment. Such language, which was being bandied about in Virginia, apparently was unacceptable to those who approved the amendment. The words that were chosen are *establishment of religion*. What did such terms mean and imply in the context of 1787? Thirdly, we must give equal weight to the coordinae conjunction *or*. The amendment contains two equal parts. "Congress shall make no law—*prohibiting the free exercise*" (of religion) is very much a part of the amendment, even though it is often ignored.

A second effort which must be waged is that of attempting to understand the religious and political character of the United States at that crucial stage of the country at the time of its founding. Regrettably, there are those who wrap all the Founding Fathers in angelic robes and whitewash them so that not a trace of heresy remains. In some schools and churches the characterization of Adams, Franklin, Jefferson, Madison, and Washington is strikingly similar to that of Abraham, Moses, Joshua, and Solomon. Such unrealistic appraisals simply will not do, for even a cursory reading of the available literature will demonstrate numerous heresies and blatantly anti-Christian emphases. Some of the Founding Fathers were avowed Deists who loudly protested against the deity of Christ. To call such leaders Christians is totally unacceptable, for a Christian, by definition, is one who is committed to following Christ.

To make the above distinctions, however, is not to close debate. Simply because some leaders were not Christians is not to preclude the possibility that the United States was a Christian nation. We need to ask a number of additional questions in order to make that determination. For example, were a *majority* of the people Christians? Did they leave for posterity any substantial evidence as to their religious commitments? Are there any public documents, on which the general public had opportunity to vote, that would clearly indicate a decidedly pro- or anti-Christian stance? Did the state legislatures or the Congress take any official actions which would give us clear and convincing evidence?

For a variety of reasons, most of the details of early American life have been lost to the average person. The typical high school and college textbook, almost of necessity, reduces the early national period (1775 to 1800) down to about twenty or thirty pages. To pretend that such limited coverage is an adequate base for understanding that highly significant era is simply to condone superficiality. Much of the important data has lain buried in university libraries and archives because it has not complemented the value system of modern-day historians. We hope that this treatise serves to uncover a beginning measure of pertinent sources and spurs young historians to renewed interest in a lively past.

A third major concern that needs to be addressed is that of *interpretation* by the courts. Since World War II the courts in the United States have been relatively consistent in reading the First Amendment as though it required a *"wall of separation between church and state."* But what about all of the state and federal court decisions between 1788 and 1947? Did the courts address the issue? Were their decisions uniform or even remotely so? If "separation of church and state" is a post-World War II mentality, as some have argued, does not 160 years of established legal precedent count for anything?

On a related question, we need to ask whether the judges who hand down their legal pronouncements are morally and ethically bound to make their decisions on the basis of original intent (strict construction) or whether it is permissable to interpret on the ground of current sentiment.

There is considerable precedent for a "loose construction" approach to the constitution. Under the "broad powers" conveyed by the "elastic clause" (Article I, Section 8, last paragraph), justices have frequently been forced to rule on questions which the Founding Fathers could not have conceptually visualized. In other cases, the constitution has been amended to alter radically the tone and intent of the original 1787 document. The fifteenth amendment, for example, gave voting privileges to blacks and native Americans whereas the constitution itself had treated such minorities as less than equals and even qualified them as 3/5 of a person. Another example of flexibility can be seen in the passage of the prohibition amendment (18th) and the rescinding of the same by the twenty-first amendment some fourteen years later in 1933.

At the same time, however, the constitution has been an exceptionally stable document and can not easily be changed. Over 3,000 amendments have been introduced into Congress, but only 26 have become a part of the Constitution. Since there are clearly prescribed congressional and state ratification procedures which must be followed if changes are to occur, the American public ought not to give up on the principles of "strict construction" easily. The general public, then, ought to insist that the courts interpret the Constitution on the basis of "original intent" and not allow any radical alteration simply by the process of judicial fiat.

If the First Amendment no longer says what the majority of American people wish it to say, there are political and legislative procedures for instituting change. If the majority of voters should prefer that the "wall of separation between church and state" be the language of the Constitution, then there ought to be public debate and an open forum on the issue. To remove the confusion, the Constitution ought to say what the majority mean and mean what it says.

If there is genuine and deep-seated disagreement, as currently seems to be the case with the First Amendment, then all Americans who are concerned about the pervasiveness of secular humanism and the apparently negative rulings concerning public religious practice ought to expend more effort to eliminate current misunderstandings. Such efforts are constitutionally guaranteed, not only to those who wish to restrict religion, but also to those who wish to exert religious influence on public life. If it can be demonstrated, conclusively and beyond reasonable doubt, that the original intent of the First Amendment was merely to prevent Congress from establishing a *national* church, as the evidence seems to indicate, then those who wear the robes of the judiciary must be educated to rule accordingly.

Still another element that needs our careful attention is that word *religion*. Since the Constitution talks of *religion* and nowhere mentions *church*, we ought to clearly define the term. What does the word mean? If we look at the list of recent court cases in which the supposed "separation" was the issue, we will notice that religion has a very wide range of meanings and implications. A partial listing would include:

1. Prayer in public school classrooms;
2. use of university classrooms for Bible study;

3. the teaching of Transcendental Meditation;
4. Bible reading on public school premises, especially when done for devotional purposes, or when required by school authorities;
5. creationist explanations of life's origins;
6. bus transportation for U.S. citizens who choose to go to private and parochial schools;
7. textbook distribution to elementary and secondary students who attend private or parochial schools;
8. use of the Ten Commandments for teaching moral behavior, whenever these are displayed or identified as such;
9. the singing of Christmas carols and Easter hymns at appropriate seasons of the year;
10. tuition tax credits or vouchers for those who choose schools where their own religious values and beliefs are taught.

The list could easily be expanded, but it becomes apparent from all of the many court decisions since 1960 that the courts have adopted a very comprehensive meaning of religion. Not only have they tried, by judicial fiat, to exclude conventional rituals and symbolic acts from public schooling, but they have also espoused a very pronounced theological stance. On the one hand, the wide range of decisions encompasses many dimensions of religious life. On the other hand, the courts clearly appear to be suggesting that religion must be a peculiarly private matter. In making their many decisions, the courts have accepted and forced on the American public a theology which has historically belonged to the Baptists, Quakers, Mennonites, and other dissenters who have come out of the Arminian tradition. Historically it has been Arminian theologians who have argued that religion is strictly a private, individual matter between a person and God. In that tradition, most clearly typified by the Baptists in early Virginia and Rhode Island, *the state was evil* and had no business meddling in purely individualistic religious matters. Now, ironically, it is the liberal Protestants in America who seem to have cornered that theology for themselves, and it is the Baptists and other fundamentalists whose ox is being gored. In this strange reversal of religious alignments, the courts have unwittingly argued that religion is to be a purely private matter, thus assuming for themselves a theology which has Protestant

Evangelicals howling with a mixture of confusion and rage.

In making religion a purely private, individualized concern, the courts have also become committed to a thoroughly secular philosophy. By asserting that religion must be kept totally separate from public education, from government, from civic responsibility, and from science, the judiciary has adopted the religion of secular humanism. In its broadest sense, secularism refers to the dividing of life into two separate, mutually exclusive realms, the sacred and the secular. The sacred, presumably, is that domain where God has influence and legitimate place. For many persons, some well-intentioned but misguided Christians included, God is limited to the eternal or other-worldly realm. For them, God is transcendant, but certainly not imminent. God has nothing to do with the nitty-gritty affairs of this life. When Christ ascended forty days after Easter, He went to heaven and now awaits our autonomous decisions to join Him in eternity. Such theological stances have contributed to this sacred-secular dichotomy and give fuel to the current renderings of the Supreme Court.

But there is another, more significant level of secular thought. Through their rulings on the religious cases since the early 1960's, the courts have unwittingly carved whole-life experience into separate, disjointed elements. This flies squarely in the face of the world-and-life views and the philosophic monism held by Puritans, Calvinists, Presbyterians, and Lutherans. It also contradicts the wholistic philosophies of such notable thinkers as Alfred North Whitehead, John Dewey, Jacques Maritain, Jonathon Edwards, Lohn Locke, and a host of others. By reducing religion to a private matter unrelated to the rest of existence, they have misunderstood the unity of life. They have sought to rend asunder that seamless fabric of which Whitehead and Dewey so fittingly wrote.

Roman Catholic Perspectives

When the question of "separation" is looked at from the vantage point of Roman Catholicism, the issue takes on more complexity and confusion. Historically and traditionally the Catholic Church assumed that there could and should be no separation of church and state. Wherever the Catholic Church has been dominant, there have been strong bonds of support and cooperation between the ecclesiastical officials and governmental officials. This has been true in Italy, Spain, France, Ireland, Poland, Mexico, and many of the countries in South America. It was also quite obvious in the lands of Germany, The Netherlands, and England before the Protestant Reformation wrested control away from papal authority.

In response to the democratic revolutions which were occurring throughout the Western world, the Roman Catholic Church formally articulated its position in the Syllabus of Errors. Writing in 1864, Pope Pius IX clearly and forcefully stated the Catholic opposition to the "very modern and very erroneous notion of 'separation of church and state.' " Partially because of such pronouncements, Catholic immigrants to the United States were forced to endure huge doses of ridicule, suspicion, and political repression. Out of that hostility emerged the American Nativist Association and splinter groups within both the Democratic and Republican parties. In the minds of such radicals, Americans were, by definition, white Anglo-Saxon Protestants. Catholic immigrants were openly to be treated as persona non grata.

As a means to self-preservation and protection in a largely unfriendly nation, Catholics during the period from 1850 to 1960 established thousands of separate parochial schools. Though the case of Pierce v. Society of Sisters in 1925 temporarily threatened to prohibit the free exercise of their religion, the Supreme Court ruled against this blatantly political effort to squash the Catholic schools.

During the decade of the 1960's the role of the Catholic Church in American life took on some new and significant characteristics. Although collusion could probably never be proven, four concurrent events came together to bring about profound and disturbing changes for American Catholics. The first of these was the election to the U.S. presidency of a Roman Catholic Irishman by the name of John F. Kennedy. Next was the convening of the Second Vatican Council (1962-1965) in Rome, in which the ecclesiastical hierarchy came to endorse, for the first time, religious toleration and what they called an "amicable separation of church and state." A closely related event within the Catholic Church was a shifting of priorities away from parochial education to a dire shortage of both clerical teachers and financial support from the parishes. In that context, the decisions of the Supreme Court to ban both mandatory prayers (Engel, 1962), and compulsory reading from the Bible (Schempp, 1963) take on an aura of cooperation around what appears to be the mutually acceptable religion of civilized secularism.

For some Catholics, particularly those who no longer had the option of inexpensive parochial education, the prospect of sending their children to a "neutral" school, where neither the Catholic nor the Protestant religion might be made compulsory, was at least temporarily acceptable. For others, whose commitment to the reforms of the Second Vatican Council was less than enthusiastic, it simply meant greater financial burdens and new efforts to get governmental support for schools that ostensibly performed a public service. In most of their efforts, however, the Catholic coalitions have been rebuffed on the grounds that any tax supported aid to parochial education would create excessive entanglement and thus be unconstitutional.

The reforms of Vatican II have created a number of dilemmas for the Roman Catholic constituency. Arguing on the one hand for an "amicable separation of church and state," it appears to the neutral observer that a request for financial assistance from the state would represent a compromise with that position. Whether amicable separation also implies financial separation is a question that has not been satisfactorily answered. A similar dilemma has arisen in conjunction with the settlement of teachers' disputes. If the state is to be separate from the church, then the faculties in the church-operated parochial schools should not get entangled with the courts or the government's Fair Labor Relations Board in any attempt to resolve internal disagreements within the church. Yet such appeals have frequently been made, with the government officials willingly agreeing to hear their cases. Ironically, both the church officials and the government agree to such entanglement while each proclaims loudly the theme of separation. On the surface, at least, the Catholic Church would appear to be more consistent if it returned to its earlier position enunciated by Pope Pius IX in the Syllabus of Errors. Such candor, however, might prove politically unwise and release a new wave of hostility. Given the current mood in America, such pronouncements may prove to be wholly unpalatable.

Theological Dimensions

An integral part of both Protestant and Catholic theology is the concept of the Kingdom. Jesus Christ claimed repeatedly, and Christians of all ages have readily affirmed, that He was and is the King of the universe. When Christians acknowledge Christ as King, they are honoring not a limited monarchy, reduced by constitutional restrictions, but an absolute sovereign. They serve a risen Lord who demands undiluted allegiance all the while they live as citizens in a nation which imposes severe restrictions and limitations on that worship. In the words of Sidney Mead, a highly respected American religious historian, this creates an "unresolved intellectual tension" between their theological commitments and their democratic loyalties.[1] The net result is a dichotomized mind-set for the American-citizen-church-members.

The attempted separation of church-membership from state-citizenship creates other theological and intellectual problems as well. Paramount among those is the meaning and import of *pluralism*. In a religiously diversified nation like the United States, this question takes on tremendous significance. Does pluralism require toleration of antithetical beliefs and life-styles? Is the Christian to condone and preach toleration toward worldviews that flagrantly contradict his own? Is that what freedom of religion means? If so, what happens to the Biblically required concerns for truth and falsehood, for good and evil? Are the morally upright thereby required to approve immorality? Is the Great Commission, whereby men are mandated to "go and make disciples of all nations, baptizing—and teaching them to obey everything (Christ has) commanded,"[2] suddenly limited by judicial edict to "private conversations"?

Such questions are not easily answered. Theological questions of such magnitude need careful examination in the light of Scripture if the citizen-church member is simultaneously to honor his King and obey the civil authorities. What is needed is a "theology of pluralism" and a "theology of citizenship," both, of course, rooted in the Word, for that is the standard for all theology. Articulating such religious positions will not be easy and should not be superficially treated. As Mead has argued,

> practically every species of traditional orthodoxy in Christendom is in-

tellectually at war with the basic premises upon which the constitutional and legal structures of the Republic rest. And if this is the case, then every convincing defense of the one tends to undermine belief in the other.[3]

One can and should argue with Mead's "loving, lingering belief on behalf of a Jeffersonian worldview,"[4] but it will be difficult to refute his assertion that the theology of Deism was at war with the theology of Protestantism at the very time our Constitution was drafted.

The men who met in Philadelphia in 1787 did not leave their theology at home when they went to draft the Constitution. Neither did they put it in a "private box" where it could not affect their public thinking. On the contrary, they carried their intellectual and theological baggage with them and allowed it to direct their thoughts as they wrestled with political solutions to the questions of citizenship in their newly independent nation.

Jefferson, Madison, and Franklin were deeply religious men. They acknowledged God, openly and reverently, but their Deistic religious principles ruled out a *Trinitarian* Deity, a Christ who was God Incarnate, and a Holy Spirit whose irresistable grace could not be confined. Their religion was in diametrical conflict with that of the Puritans, the Presbyterians, the Dutch Reformed, and a host of other Christian groups.[5] In the eyes of each opposing group, the other was an infidel.

To recognize that the early national period in American history was a time of intense religious rivalry is not to complicate the matter. Quite the opposite. Theirs was a time of religious diversity and tension, just as ours is in the late twentieth century. To recognize the parallels between the 1780's and the 1980's is to simplify the matter, for such an awareness gives us not only better opportunity to understand their solution to their problems, but also new insight into how we might solve the problems we are experiencing some two hundred years later.

The federal Constitution, with its hurriedly attached Amendments, was a compromise between the religious commitments of the Deists and the orthodoxy of the Puritans. It was not an irreligious document constructed in a religious vacuum. For the Founding Fathers there was never a question as to whether the United States should be a *religious nation*. It was only a question as to whether there should be a *national religion*.

On the latter question the Congregationalists, Presbyterians, the Episcopaleans, the Baptists, and the Deists were willing to compromise. For them it would be acceptable to say:

Congress shall make no law respecting an establishment of religion, or prohibiting the free exercise thereof. —

End Notes

1. Mead, Sidney, *The Old Religion in the Brave New World*, Berkeley: University of California Press, 1977, p. 3.
2. Matt. 28:19-20.
3. Mead, p. 2.
4. Ibid., on book jacket, written by Edwin S. Gaustad.
5. For a detailed analysis of Jefferson's religious views, see Norman De Jong, *Christianity and Democracy*, Nutley, New Jersey: The Craig Press, 1978, Chapter III, pp. 30-40.

CHAPTER II

Should Church and State be Separated?

The subject of church-state relationships is probably not the regular fare for dinner table conversation or dormitory discussion. Although some of you may be able to recall an animated dialogue with your parents or a college professor about the Supreme Court decisions banning prayer and Bible reading from the public schools, I dare to conjecture that not many of you have recently analyzed the supposed separation of church and state.

Since January, 1982, the "separation" issue has again come to public attention as a result of a federal judge's ruling in the case designated as *McLean v. the Arkansas Board of Education*. After a nationally publicized trial, the court decided that Act 590, which required public school teachers to give "balanced treatment" to both creation and evolution, was unconstitutional. The law was ruled unconstitutional, Judge Overton declared, because it violated "the separation of church and state."

In late twentieth century America the vast majority of persons have come to assume that, of course, church and state should be separated. Ever since 1947, when Justice Hugo Black wrote the majority opinion for the Everson Case, the phrase "wall of separation between church and state" has become progressively ingrained into the fabric of American jurisprudence. During the 1960's that notion successively convinced a majority of the Supreme Court to outlaw prayer and Bible reading in the public schools, as well as the posting of the Ten Commandments on classroom walls. Since those early decisions in the Engel and Abingdon cases, the courts of the United States have become extremely skittish about any kind of government which permits or even vaguely promotes religious activity. Let me cite for you a few contemporary examples.

In Kent v. Commissioner of Education, the Massachusetts Court in 1980 ruled that prayers offered in the public schools, in which God was petitioned for release of the hostages in Iran, were unconstitutional. Even though the court sympathized with the content of the prayers under attack, the judges ruled that these prayers, too, failed their test of secular purpose because they were an appeal to the Deity. The religious aspect of prayer, they argued, lies in the addressee, not in the message. By implication at least, the Massachusetts court would have to approve a similar prayer made to the mayor of Boston or the President of the United States.

Another case, known as *Widmar v. Vincent*, has given a somewhat different twist to this whole church-state controversy. At issue were the regulations of the University of Missouri at Kansas City which prohibited religious worship or teaching in any of its buildings or on its grounds. To the delight of many Christian campus groups, the Supreme Court ruled against the University, rejecting their argument that the state had a "compelling interest in maintaining strict separation" from the church.

But not only public school classrooms and university campuses have come under the watchful surveillance of the ACLU and government officials. In some cities even your home is not a safe place for prayer and Bible study groups. In 1980, for example, Mayor Tom Bradley of Los Angeles stated that, "a Bible study would not be a permissable use in a single family residential area—since this would be considered a church activity." In a town near Boston, the building commissioner notified a clergyman that inviting more than four people to his home for a Bible study was a violation of the "Home Occupation" ordinance. In Atlanta, a zoning official stated that any kind of regular home Bible study which includes non-residents is illegal without a special use permit. Two Maryland residents were issued a citation for using their home for worship services without a use and occupancy permit.

Other similar examples could be cited, but it now appears in many parts of the country that not only must church and state be separated. In addition, the state must also see to it that church and home are prevented from excessive entanglement. If the present trend continues, as it very well might, it is conceivable that by the end of this century the only place where we will legally be allowed to pray to God and read His word will be in our church sanctuaries on Sunday morning.

The Myth

Without any careful analysis or serious academic and philosophic investigation, the vast majority of Americans has been taught to believe that church and state ought to be separated, with an impenatrable wall between them. This is what we have been taught within the last three decades, largely through the influence of the very courts which were designed to protect our liberties. What is deplorable is not only the unwise decisions of our highest justices, but that we as a nation have not been equal to the problem and have not raised a successful and conceptually solid protest against the shoddy, unacademic, and unenlightened thinking which perpetuates the whole notion. In addition, we have allowed the Supreme Court to overstep its bounds and to exercise a disproportionate influence in relationship to that of the Executive and Legislative branches. We have allowed the Supreme Court to become our national educator without serious challenge.

We complicate the matter and we perpetuate this assumption peculiar to the United States when we fail to know our nation's history well and when we no longer bother to pack our words with the clear meanings historically ascribed to them. If we no longer study history carefully and no longer use our dictionaries, we are as guilty as those men and women who sit on the bench and interpret the laws for us. We, as well as they, have put God into ever smaller and smaller boxes. We, too, perpetuate myths where intelligence and common sense ought to prevail.

In diagram form, according to the contemporary American myth, the relationship between church and state would look as follows:

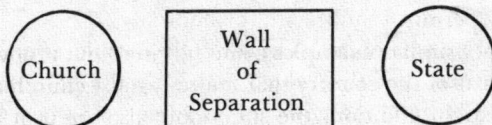

When confronting such an image, the least that we could do would be to ask for a definition of terms. What do you mean by the church? What do you mean by the state? We could also ask appropriate and necessary questions about "that wall of separation." *Who* put it in place? *Why* was it placed there? Was that presumed wall *intended* by the *founders* of our country? Does such language appear in our constitution or in any of our laws?

Such questions are legitimate and essential, but the answers to them will have to wait, at least for now. The first order of business, it seems to me, is a definition of terms, for if we don't know the meanings of the words we use, we have no business using them. When I check a dictionary I will soon find that the word "church" means: "The collective body of Christians; any body of worshippers; a religious society; the building in which worshippers gather." When I check the history of theology, of which "the church" is a vital and significant element, I find that our creeds, our catechisms, and our confessions all describe the "church" as the body of Christ, those people who are chosen of God, or the Bride of the Savior.

The "church" is and always refers to people. The church is God's people, your parents and mine, you and I. *We* are *the church*. Pastors, elders, deacons, organists, ushers, and choir members all help to make it up, but they, too, are people.

When I check with Webster concerning the "state", I find a similar kind of answer. The "state", says the dictionary, is a "political body; any body of people occupying a common territory." When I check books on political science or civics, I find there, too, that the state is identified as people who live in a specified territory and who are responsible to the same laws and the same government. Illinois, for example, is a *state* only because it is inhabited by a number of people who agreed to band together and live together with a common set of laws and common officers to make and enforce those laws. Before there were people in this territory there was no state. If we all left for California, the state of Illinois would no longer exist. We are the state, you and I collectively, just as you and I are the church.

But some may object. The state, they would assert, is not the average citizen, but that which makes up the government. The mayor of Chicago, the governor of Illinois, the city Council of Wheaton, and the justices who sit in Springfield, they are the state. Such an argument should have some credence, but we ought not to stop with those few individuals, for there are numerous offices and officers who help to comprise the state. We should add to that list all of the legislators and their assistants, all the policemen, the sheriffs, the meter maids, the firemen, the public health staff, the probation officers, the security force at the jails, the highway repair crews, and a host of others besides. In any listing, though, we ought not to forget the teachers, administrators, secretaries, and bus drivers of our public schools, for they are legally and historically agents of the state.

However long the above list of officers and state might become, one fact ought to be readily obvious. We are still talking about *people* whenever we talk about the government. Your relatives, your neighbours, you and I make up the government. The state is not a disembodied monster or a super-human entity which resides lifeless beneath some silver dome or crimped into a manilla folder in some bureaucratic jungle. No, the government and the state, as Webster so clearly points out, is a collection of persons, of which you and I are part.

If you and I are the church, and if you and I are also the state, then it would seem apparent that you cannot be separated from *you* and *I* cannot be separated from *myself*. We *as citizens* cannot be separated from us *as the church*, even if we attempt to commit ourselves to a sustained program of intellectual schizophrenia.

In reality, the church cannot be separated from the state. This presumed wall of separation between church and state is a figment of someone's imagination, a thought which remains a thought and cannot become an actuality. But let me also assert loudly and clearly that the two are not synonymous. The two terms cannot be equated, even though you and I are significant parts in both. Let me illustrate with another diagram.

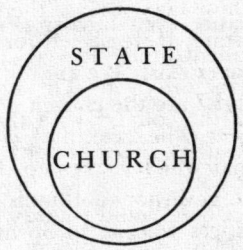

In the above illustration, the church is within the state, a part of it, but not equal to it. The state includes all those who live in it, both those who are members of the church and those who are not. Within the church are only those who are the elect of God, the called-out ones who are redeemed by the blood of Christ. That is *reality*. The church is within the state, but not identical to it.

On a parenthetical note, we might wish that every citizen of the state were also a member of the church. If we really took seriously the Great Commission, we would be doing much more to expand the church. The *ideal* situation would exist when everyone of our fellow Americans came to know the Lord and to live for Him. But that will not realistically happen, and a further discussion of it at this juncture would take us far afield.

Our National Creeds

Before we close our minds, though, to that possibility of a church that is almost coterminous with the state, let us conjecture something for just a minute.

Suppose that the President of the United States, in his constitutional concern for "our general welfare," looked across this vast land and took note of all the strange religions, heresies, if you will. Suppose, further, that after much serious discussion and many prayers, the President, with the full backing of Congress, called and convened a special national Synod to resolve the matter. (I should remind you here that it is quite proper to pray in the White House and in the halls of Congress, even though it is illegal in the classroom.) To continue, though, assume that the President and the Congress selected the best Biblical scholars in the country, paid all their expenses, and employed them for as long as necessary. Their task would be to draft a creed or a confession that was a comprehensive, accurate summary of Scriptural teaching so that all the citizens might be able to distinugish the true from the false religion. Conjecture even farther. Presume that Congress then took their document under serious study, debated it, and finally approved it by majority vote. They then had it printed and circulated throughout the country with the strong endorsement that everyone accept it as their personal confession of faith. Strange scenario, is it not?

Would you subscribe? Would you say, "Yes, I am willing to accept such a creed?" Most of us, I presume, would have some difficulty with such a procedure. Some of our churches, in fact, might even distribute petitions to impeach the President. Certain denominational leaders might even go so far as to put on their political shoes, march on Washington, and demand that those citizens whom we elected to office stop assisting us with the work of the Great Commission. That would be ironic, but strange things do happen in this mixed bag we call America.

In the event that you haven't guessed it by now, most of the historic creeds of the Christian church were formed in exactly the fashion just described. The earliest example of such a national and international statement of faith is the Nicene Creed, drafted at the request of the Roman Emperor Constantine in 325 A.D. We, along with almost the whole Western branch of the Christian church since that time, accept it and proclaim it as ours without so much as a twinge of conscience.

Since the Reformation, an almost identical procedure was followed in the drafting of the Lutherans' Augsburg Confession and their Formula of Concord, the Anglicans' and the Episcopalians' Thirty-Nine Articles, the Belgic Confession of Faith, the Germans' Heidelberg Catechism, and the international Canons of Dort drafted at the Synod of 1618-1619. The last major synod of such a sort, called into session by the English Parliament, produced the Westminster confession as well as the Larger and Shorter Catechisms.

When we willingly and knowingly adopt any one or any number of these creeds, we are saying, in effect, that it is and has been historically permissable for a king or a president or a legislature to utilize their offices for the general welfare of the church. We are implying that part of the duty of elected and appointed officials is to guard the gospel and to protect those citizens who are the called of Christ.

Should any have doubts about such assignment of responsibilities, let me quote from one of the creeds that many of us profess to believe.

> "God, the Supreme Lord and King of the world, hath ordained civil magistrates to be under him over the people, for his own glory and the public good; — it is his (i.e. the civil magistrate's) duty to take order, — ,that the truth of God be kept pure and entire, that all blasphemies and heresies be suppressed, — and all corruptions — in worship — (be) prevented."

Since this portion of the Westminster Confession was derived judiciously from Romans 13, I Peter 2, and a variety of Old Testament passages, to claim that it is no longer appropriate to our age would be to play the game of situational theology. To do that is to selectively believe and obey only those Scriptural passages which conform to our particular culture.

It may sound peculiar to our culturally conditioned hearing, but according to the Westminster and other confessions, it is the duty of our mayors, our governors, our legislators, and our President to protect the church and to guard her sanctity. By a quaint combination of political pressures and unfounded judicial precedents, that right and responsibility have been stripped away from our nation's public school teachers.

The Constitutional Context

Without going into an exhaustive historical analysis, let me also assert that it was not the Founding Fathers' intention to attempt the impossible separation of church and state. When Congress and the thirteen states drafted the Constitution and then adopted the first Amendment, they simply and clearly stated that "*Congress* shall make no law respecting an establishment of religion, or prohibiting the free exercise thereof."

It should be noted clearly that *Congress* was thereby prevented from designating an *established church*; for that was to remain the prerogative of the separate states. In Massachusetts, New Hampshire, and Connecticut the established state church was the Congregational. In Virginia it was the Protestant Episcopal. In a number of others it was more broadly specified to be the Protestant Christian religion, with almost all the states specifying in their constitutions the religious requirements for holding office. In the Delaware state constitution, for example, it was stipulated that any person who aspired to state office would have to make the following oath:

"I, ..., do profess faith in God the Father, and in Jesus Christ His only Son, and in the Holy Ghost, one God, blessed for evermore; and I do acknowledge the holy scriptures of the Old and New Testament to be given by divine inspiration."

In such a religious environment Congress saw no difficulty in appropriating tax monies for the training of ministers, paying the salaries of missionaries to the Indians, or the publication of the first American Bibles. In the summer of 1787, during the very same time that the Constitution was being drafted, Congress set aside section 16 in every township for the support of avowedly Christian public schools. In addition, but unbeknown to most Americans, Congress also stipulated that section 29 in every township be set aside *for the support of religion*. Congressional leaders saw themselves not as secular politicians, but as moral and spiritual guides to the new nation, the officially constituted leaders of American Christianity. Their duty, as they so clearly enunciated it in the Northwest Ordinance of 1787, was to promote and protect religion, morality, and knowledge.

When, then, was the "wall of separation" erected?

For all practical purposes, the "wall of separation" was not put firmly in place until 1947. In that year Supreme Court Justice Hugo Black, instead of going back to the Constitution, dug the phrase out of a letter written by Thomas Jefferson on January 1, 1802. For Jefferson it was a campaign promise to a selected group of political supporters. For us it has now become an intellectual nightmare and a seemingly immovable plank in American jurisprudence.

For those Christians who teach in the public schools of our land, the Supreme Court has effectively accomplished what Congress is expressly prohibited from doing. Congress was explicitly warned to make no law "prohibiting the free exercise" of religion, yet today we are denied the right, in our classrooms, to pray for the President or for the release of hostages held in Iran. From 9 o'clock to 3 o'clock, Monday through Friday, we are told to ignore and deny the God who made us. In our classrooms and on the school grounds we may not talk to Him and we may not read His only infallible guide for life and behavior.

The American Civil Liberties Union is pleased.

I wonder if God is.

CHAPTER III

"State Creeds for State Churches"

The first official census of the newly formed United States was taken in 1790, some 14 years after the Declaration of Independence, but only 2 years after the Constitution was ratified. A rather simplified counting procedure for determining representation in the House of Representatives, that first census has left historians guessing at the precise sociological, ethnic, and religious make-up of the American people during the formative years of our nation's history.

Some facts, however, are incontrovertible. Of special significance is the fact that the thirteen English colonies were not limited to English immigrants. Although the Anglicans in Virginia and the Pilgrims in Massachusetts were of English stock, they were soon joined on these shores by the Dutch in New York who were of Reformed persuasion. Later, in 1630, the Puritans established their colony in Massachusetts, representing another brand of dissenters from the heartland of England. Over the years these first immigrants were joined by thousands of Presbyterians from Scotland, Lutherans and Calvinists from Germany, French Huguenots, Moravian Brethren, Roman Catholics, Baptists, Quakers, and a handful of Mennonites. The thirteen colonies were, without a doubt, religiously diverse and international in origin. Many came to escape the religious and political suppression which they had experienced in their homelands. Here, they hoped, they could find the freedom to live out their religious and political convictions according to the dictates of their conscience. The Puritans, for example, wanted to establish their "city on a hill," a model Christian community, unrestricted by their Anglican monarch and their Anglican-dominated Parliament whom, the Puritans contended, had become too loose in their practice and too liberal in their theology. Later, when the Puritans gained ascendancy in the homeland and when Oliver Cromwell became ruler, the tables were turned and it was the Anglicans who sought escape to the colonies.

Apart from the founding of Georgia, which was established as a prison colony, one of the primary reasons for colonization was religious freedom. That was not the only reason, certainly, for many historians have also uncovered economic, demographic, political, and sociological reasons strong enough to push people out of their villages of birth and their family circles, and into a new, unsettled land.

When "freedom" is defined as "absence of restraint," as the term has been within the Enlightenment tradition, then it is assumed that the immigrants who came to the English colonies in North America came to escape from religion. It is assumed, then, that the Puritans, the Arminians, the Lutherans, and the Reformed all came to escape the harsh restrictions and restraints imposed on them by their homeland. Having arrived safely in this country, they could practice their religion however they wished or be free to practice it not at all. Given a century or more of such unbridled freedom, it could be expected that religious practice and conviction would gradually atrophy to a level of national impotence.

But such an analysis is a cruel hoax. The colonists who came to these shores came not to escape from the restraints of religion, but, more often than not, to practice the faith of their fathers in its most rigorous, and orthodox form. The Pilgrims and the Puritans, for example, came to these shores as a protest against the licentious, unorthodox, and liberal tendencies which they had seen creep into their beloved mother church in England. These people, and many others who followed them, were called Dissenters. They, like most splinter groups, dissented not as liberals against a conservative organization, but as conservatives against institutions which, in their judgment, had become excessively liberal.

To even think of freedom as the "absence of restraint" would have been anathema to most Puritans, for such a conception of freedom would have smacked too much of the radical Enlightenment theology which was to gain prominence during the latter decades of the 1700's. True freedom for the Puritan could be found only in total commitment to Jesus Christ, for the Scriptures said, "You shall know the truth, and the truth shall make you free."[1]

Ever since the days of the Enlightenment there have been concerted attempts to besmirch and blacken the religious character of the American colonists. To read some accounts of the Roger Williams episode in Massachusetts, for example, would be to conclude that the Puritans were the most cruel and oppressive tyrants who ruthlessly banished a religious dissident to the wilderness for doctrinal deviance. However, to read the extant record of the prolonged discussion which took place over a period of years and then to read the charter for the new Providence Plantation which was granted to Williams' followers is to get a quite different flavor of the incident. The prolonged and seriously studied issues which Williams raised was not a flamboyant exercise in autocratic behavior, but an extension of the controversy between Arminians and Calvinists which presumably had been settled some years earlier at the international Synod of Dordtrecht in 1618-1619. The conclusion reached jointly in Massachusetts and in England in 1636 was that the differences were irreconcilable and that the best solution was to grant the Williams' followers their own territory where they could live out their own religious convictions without having to compromise them in the context of a Calvinist community.

Whether one collects historical data from the perspective of Providence Plantation or from the perspective of Massachusetts Bay Colony makes a pronounced difference in the historian's recording of events. Similar differences of interpretation occur when the historian relies heavily on the writings of a Cotton Mather, or when he trusts implicitly in those of a Thomas Jefferson. Whereas Mather prized religious commitment highly, Jefferson, in his *Notes on Virginia,* critically characterized the Anglican clergy as indolent, immoral, and unconcerned about spiritual growth. Jefferson, convinced in his own mind that religious establishment was irreversibly evil, could find almost nothing positive to ascribe to the Anglican clergy of his native Virginia.

Such twentieth century religious historians as Sidney Mead and Franklin Littell have tried to convince their readers that American Christianity reached a level of national impotence during the time between 1775 and 1790. Arguing that the First Great

Awakening had died a natural death well before the War of Revolution, and that the Second Great Awakening was still a quarter century away, they have concluded that religious influence was at an all-time low during the very period when the national government was formed. Their research, however, is suspect, for both of them ascribe inordinate authority to the writings of Jefferson and rely too exclusively on his analysis. Similar complaints can be charged to the editors of *Church and State*, who also ascribe excessive credibility to Thomas Jefferson.

More reliable and better documented statistics can be found in William Warren Sweet's *The Story of Religion in America*. He reports the following denominational tally of churches:[2]

Congregational	658
Presbyterian	543
Baptist	498
Anglican	480
Quaker	295
Reformed (German and Dutch)	251
Lutheran	151
Catholic	50

What becomes readily apparent from the above figures is the wide diversity of religious affiliation within the thirteen original states. While the Congregational and the Anglican churches traced their roots directly to England, the bulk of the Presbyterian, Reformed, and Lutheran congregations were more continental in their sources and emanated from different religious heritages. The Baptists, as we shall see later in Chapter VII, were religious dissenters who broke from the Puritan and Congregational traditions, largely as a result of the theological dissonance created by the Great Awakening.

Within the New England states there was relative homogeneity of religion, with Congregationalists obviously dominant in Massachusetts, New Hampshire, and Connecticut. Rhode Island was predominantly Baptist from the outset, just as Virginia was Anglican in origin. Pennsylvania, by contrast, was described by Ben Franklin as being composed of one-third Quakers, one-third Germans, with the remainder including English Anglicans, Scottish Presbyterians, Moravian Brethren, French Huguenots, Dutch Reformed, and Swedish Lutherans.[3] In New York there was also a strong mixture of religious and national loyalties, with Dutch Reformed, French Huguenots, Quakers, and Presbyterians vying for control with the established Anglicans who clustered around New York City.

The Ecumenical Creeds

Although there was far more agreement than disagreement among the denominations, each group had its own set of theological distinctives and its own set of creedal formulations. Binding all the Christian traditions in a common faith were the ecumenical creeds which outlined the primary doctrines of the Christian faith. Among them were the Apostles, the Nicene, and the Athanasian creeds which were jointly held by all Protestant denominations, the Roman Catholics, and the Greek Orthodox.

The Apostles Creed is of indefinite origin, but the Nicene Creed was drafted by the Council of Nicea in 325 A.D. In that year the Roman emperor Constantine called together 318 bishops and commissioned them to resolve the doctrinal dispute which had been caused by the teachings of Arius.[4] Emperor Constantine was totally supportive of the church and its concerns, paying all the expenses for the Council from the Roman treasury. In addition, he built churches, constructed shrines for martyrs, and financed the copying of Bibles to replace those that had been burned by his anti-Christian predecessors. In making appointments to government office he gave priority to Christians and often invited the clergy to become involved in affairs of state.[5]

A creed is a confession of faith for *public* use and is always the result of religious conflict. Arising out of controversy, it is almost always polemical in character, intended as a response to perceived heresy and an attempt to formulate what a group believes in contrast to what should not be believed. The Athanasian and the Nicene Creeds were all of that, intended to quell the Arian controversy and to assert the orthodox explanation of the Trinity. Constantine apparently understood that clearly, claiming to be "a bishop of the church for external affairs"[6] and believing that God had called him to be as concerned for the spiritual well-being of his people as for their physical.

When the Protestant creeds were formulated in response to the Reformation, the three ecumenical creeds were all reaffirmed and required as the first standards of orthodoxy. The fact that these had been drafted by the government of Rome caused no stir whatsoever, for official state involvement was wholly acceptable to almost everyone and was to continue in the post-Reformation era.

Germany

The fundamental and generally accepted creed of the Lutheran churches is the Augsburg Confession. In keeping with the tradition initiated by Constantine some 1200 years earlier, the Diet of Augsburg was called together by Emperor Charles V. In the wake of the Reformation, a doctrinal debate had developed between the followers of Luther and those of Rome. It was the duty of the German princes to resolve this controversy, Charles reasoned, so he called the Lutheran princes together in 1530 and commissioned Melancthon to draft a summary of Lutheran beliefs. The resulting Augsburg Confession was signed by seven German princes and deputies from two cities, cementing a long symbiotic relationship between the civil and ecclesiastical officials.[7] When Luther read the Apology, he responded, "It pleases me very well, and I know of nothing by which I could better it or change it."[8]

Elsewhere in Germany, the followers of John Calvin also were confronted with the challenge of publicly articulating their faith. In Heidelberg, the capital of the Palatinate, Frederick III ordered Ursinus (a professor at Heidelberg University) and Olevianus (the court preacher) to prepare a manual for catechatical instruction. When they had finished their task, Frederick reviewed and approved the Catechism himself and then had it published in 1563. The Elector himself took the responsibility for dividing the Catechism into 52 sections (Lord's Days) and required that each Sunday one Lord's Day be taught so that the "whole counsel of God" might be explained to the churches each year. That practice, put into place by a German state in 1563, has continued in most Reformed-Calvinist churches down into the twentieth century.

The Low Countries

In the countries of The Netherlands and Belgium the religious and political controversies were much more intense than elsewhere in Europe during the late sixteenth century. Under the severe oppression of Spanish Catholic rule, Grotius estimated that the number of Protestant martyrs in Holland, under one reign, exceeded 100,000 persons. The most terrible persecution came under the Duke of Alva, who put to death more Protestants in one province of The Netherlands than did all the pagan emperors of Rome in the first three centuries after Christ.[9]

In that context, the Dutch Calvinists could understandably have appealed for separation of church and state. Instead, Guido de Bres wrote the Confession of Faith in 1561 and was himself martyred a few years later. Drafted as a protest against the cruel oppression of the Spaniards, it also was intended to prove that the Dutch Calvinists were law-abiding citizens and supportive of the government's contention that it had a responsibility to direct and regulate religious life. The Confession was quickly adopted and approved by the Synod of Emden (1571), a national Synod of Dort (1574), and another national Synod at Middleburg (1581). In 1619 the Synod of Dort adopted both the Belgic Confession and the Heidelberg Catechism as the official state creeds for The Netherlands. Throughout the seventeenth and eighteenth centuries these creeds were subscribed to by both the Dutch and the German Reformed congregations which had migrated to America.

Against such a backdrop of Spanish suppression, the Dutch Calvinists drafted one of the clearest apologies for church-state interaction that the Protestant faith has ever articulated. In Article XXXVI of the Confession of Faith, the persecuted Netherlanders proclaimed to their Spanish masters:

> We believe that our gracious God, because of the depravity of mankind, has appointed kings, princes, and magistrates; — to the end that the dissoluteness of men might be restrained, and all things carried on among them with good order and decency. For this purpose He has invested the magistracy with the sword for the punishment of evil-doers and for the protection of them that do well.
>
> Their office is not only to have regard unto and watch for the welfare of the civil state, but also that they protect the sacred ministry, and thus may remove and prevent all idolatry and false worship, that the kingdom of antichrist may be thus destroyed and the kingdom of Christ promoted. They must therefore countenance the preaching of the Word of the gospel everywhere, that God may be honored and worshiped by everyone, as He commands in His Word.[10]

After the forced departure of the Spaniards, the situation in The Netherlands did not long remain tranquil. Already in 1604, doctrinal controversy began surfacing at the state University of Leyden, where Jacob Arminius expressed disagreements with Calvinist theology. The controversy soon shook the entire country and quickly spread to France, Switzerland, Germany, England, and Scotland. Because the conflict centered on questions of free will, limited atonement, and the sovereignty of God, and not on matters of church-state relationships, Lutherans tended to side with the followers of Arminius.

In order to quell the controversy, the Dutch national assembly (the States-General) called for and convened the Synod of Dort in 1618. This international Synod convened on November 13, 1618 and remained in session until May 9, 1619. The Synod consisted of 84 members plus 18 commissioners. Fifty-eight of the delegates were Dutch Calvinists, hand-picked by the national assembly to ensure that orthodoxy was protected, for that was the mandate of those who ruled by divine appointment. James I of England also handpicked his delegates, as did the rulers from France, Germany, and Switzerland. The expenses of this national synod amounted to more than 100,000 guilders, which was paid by the national government of The Netherlands.

When the international collection of theologians finished its discussions and drafted its report, the States-General unanimously adopted the five points of Calvinism (The Canons of Dort), the Belgic Confession, and the Heidelberg Catechism as the officially approved creeds for the Dutch nation. At the same session, the government deposed some 200 clergy who insisted on following the teachings of Arminius. For the forseeable future at least, the States-General had guaranteed a complete triumph for orthodox Calvinism over deviant Arminianism.

England

The Protestant Reformation in England had an even more political quality to it than did those in Germany and the Low Countries. Already in 1571 the English Parliament passed a bill which required all English priests and teachers of religion to subscribe to the Thirty-nine Articles, which had become the official creed of English Protestants. In 1573 an injunction was issued at Oxford University requiring all students to subscribe to the Thirty-nine Articles before they might be granted a degree.[12]

The Reformation in England was as much a national

political movement as it was an ecclesiastical movement. It demonstrated less theological precision and produced no reformers of the stature of Luther and Calvin, but produced a greater power of practical organization and implementation. It infused the political process and contributed to some of the greatest literature ever produced. Because of the political involvement of kings and princes, England became the chief strong-hold of Protestantism in Europe and the pioneer of both Christian civilization and constitutional liberty.

In 1628 Charles I, in order to quiet the Arminian-Calvinist controversy which had resurfaced in England, republished the Thirty-nine Articles and reasserted their status as the official national creed for Englishmen. The Arminians were pleased with the King's moderation, but the Calvinists and Puritans objected to what they perceived as a "soft" reply to the Arminian heresy. In response to such official laxity, some Puritans chose to emigrate to America where they could establish their own bastian of orthodoxy at Massachusetts Bay. Others chose, meanwhile, to remain behind to build a political base from which they could establish Puritan supremacy and thereby "remove and prevent all idolatry and false worship."

Part of the Puritan displeasure with the official government leadership had been occasioned by King James I's issuance some years earlier of his famous *Book of Sports*. With the full weight of his regal office behind him, he decreed that Sunday evenings be devoted to dancing, leaping, fencing, and other recreations, while reserving the earlier part of the Sabbath for strict religious observance. To lead the way, the court set the example by sponsoring balls, plays, and masquerades on Sunday evenings. The Puritans considered such action to be blatant desecration, but the king argued that such activity was necessary to "make the bodies more able for war."[13]

The Thirty-nine Articles of the Anglican church have remained basically unchanged since Elizabethan days, although there were minor deletions made by William of Orange in 1688 and 1689 to appease the non-conformists. It was this creed, drafted and mandated by kings, queens, and princes, that the Anglicans carried with them to the American colonies and to which they adhered, even after they changed their name in post-Revolution days to that of the Protestant Episcopal Church.

Increased religious and political turmoil came to England with the Puritan Revolution of 1642 and the rise to power of Oliver Cromwell. As a majority of Presbyterians and Puritans were elected to Parliament, discontent with the religious leadership of the monarchy increased, as did questions concerning the adequacy of the Thirty-nine Articles. Accordingly, on June 12, 1643 the English Parliament issued an ordinance commanding "that an assembly of divines should be convened at Westminster, in London, on the first day of July following, to effect a more perfect reformation of the Church of England in its liturgy, discipline, and government on the basis of the Word of God."[14]

The Westminster Assembly was thus created by state authority, as were its products, the Larger and Shorter Catechisms. Not only did Parliament call the divines into session, but it personally selected most of the members, set the agenda, paid all the expenses, and gave final approval to the creeds which were drafted.

In such a context, church-state interaction was assumed, but it was also formally addressed and carefully articulated. After studious deliberation, the Westminster Assembly concluded that:

> God, the supreme Lord and King of all the world, hath ordained civil magistrates to be under him over the people, for his own glory and the public good; and to this end hath armed them with the power of the sword, for the defense and encouragement of them that are good, and for the punishment of evil-doers.[15]

The Assembly further argued that Christians should "accept and execute the office of a magistrate, when called thereunto, — (and) ought especially to maintain piety, justice and peace, according to the wholesome laws of each commonwealth."[16] The civil magistrate, they went on to say,

> has authority and it is his duty to take order, that unity and peace be preserved in the church, that the truth of God be kept pure and entire, that all blasphemies and heresies be suppressed, all corruptions and abuses in worship and discipline prevented and reformed, and all the ordinances of God duly settled, administered and observed.[17]

Wholly consistent with such creedal pronouncements, the Westminster Assembly defined the church as "all those throughout the world that profess the true religion, together with their children."[18] The family of God, they insisted, should not divorce itself from politics and the affairs of government, but should become actively involved in them. Since man's chief end in life was "to glorify God, and to enjoy him forever."[19] his religious convictions could not be confined, but had to permeate all his activities, whether they be dubbed public or private.

The denominational creed-making period closed at about the middle of the seventeenth century, with the foregoing statements of faith continuing to serve the mainline Protestant denominations through America's early national period and on into the twentieth century, with only minor revisions. Later evangelical denominations, such as the Baptists, Quakers, Methodists, and Moravians all acknowledged the leading doctrines of the Reformation, but differed on such matters as anthropology, the sacraments, church polity, and discipline. In the estimation of Philip Schaff, "their creeds are modifications and abridgements rather than enlargements of the Old Protestant symbols."[20]

Church Life in America

The church-state patterns which were prevalent in Europe also found their way to America. When the Revolutionary War broke out in 1776, nine of the thirteen colonies had established, state-supported churches. The Congregational church, which was an outgrowth of Puritan theology, was officially established in the New England colonies of Connecticut, Massachusetts, and New Hampshire. Elsewhere in the colonies the Anglican Church had become formally entrenched, with the governments of Delaware, Georgia, Maryland, New York, South Carolina, and Virginia designating the Church of England as the established body.[21]

In Virginia, the Anglican church had been established from the earliest days of the colony and was supported in its various activities by taxes and levies. In Maryland, though, the situation differed. Because of a rebellion involving some of the Catholic population in that colony, the Anglican church was made the official established church there in 1689. After that date, all tax monies were directed to the established church, with Catholics denied the right to vote. In Georgia and South Carolina the basic unit of colonial, and the later state, government was the parish. All the parishes, or congregational districts, were designated as the basic units of government, with a specified number of church members elected from each parish to form the colonial assembly. To further cement this church-state relationship, the parishes bore the names of Anglican saints. When the Georgia state constitution was later adopted, this practice was continued with the stipulation that "the representatives shall be of the Protestant religion."[22] In addition to serving as the basis for electing representatives, the 8 parishes became the official organs for such other government officers as fire fighters, militia, justices of the peace, and street maintenance supervisors.[23]

Although the majority of the colonies were thoroughly accustomed to having established state churches, the religious and ethnic diversity in the colonies of New Jersey, North Carolina, and Pennsylvania did not permit one denomination to become dominant. As will be noted in the next chapter, this diversity did not prevent these colonies from a broader type of religious establishment, with the Protestant-Christian religion being the only acceptable form.

Unique among the thirteen colonies was Rhode Island. Originally settled by Roger Williams and his followers, it was first named Providence Plantation. Because of the intervention of the Puritan Commonwealth from 1642 to 1660, the people in Providence received little attention and encouragement from England. When Charles II was restored to the throne, however, new efforts were made to formally recognize and establish this group of dissenters as the colony of Rhode Island. In 1663 Charles II issued a special charter in which he designated Benedict Arnold as Governour and named 12 Assistants, one of whom was Roger Williams.[24] The Charter granted extremely broad power and authority to the Governour of the Rhode Island Company, almost to the point of making him a self-perpetuating dictatorship and the colony a completely self-governing body. Recognizing that "some of the people and inhabitants—cannot—conforme to the publique exercise of religion, according—to the Church of England," Charles II stipulated that it was his royal will 'that all and everye person—may freelye and fullye have and enjoye" his religious and civil liberties to the fullest.[25]

When the Continental Congress requested in 1776 that each state draw up a constitution for its own governance, the people of Rhode Island refused to comply. Having been granted "full libertie in religious concernements" and the right to "worshipp as they were persuaded,"[26] they chose instead to remain under the Charter of 1663 and did not draft their first state constitution until 1842. Their "livelie experiment" was granted complete religious toleration by the King of England, yet it was this group alone which demanded separation of church and state in the years preceding the War of Revolution.[27] Leading the Baptist cause in Rhode Island was Isaac Backus, who also made frequent forays into Massachusetts after 1774 to register protests against the establishment of the Congregational denomination in that state. It was not until 1774 that Backus and his Baptist supporters mounted their offensive against the established church, arguing not along theological lines, but on the grounds that there should be no taxation without representation.[28]

Throughout the colonies there was a very mixed reaction to the Revolutionary War and the Declaration of Independence. Among the most active in supporting the war for independence were those who originated from countries other than England. The Scotch-Irish who largely comprised the Presbyterian denomination had a long history of hostility to England and thus supported the War of Revolution. Prominent among the Presbyterian leadership was Reverend John Witherspoon, the president of the College of New Jersey and the only minister to sign the Declaration of Independence.

The Dutch Reformed churches supported the Revolution with almost as great unanimity as did the Presbyterians, although the majority of their congregations were located in the New Jersey and New York area where the British army was most active. As a result of their pro-Independence efforts, many of the Dutch congregations had their property destroyed and many of the pastors were separated from their parishioners. The German Reformed and the Lutherans were also favorable to the patriot case, although there was also some pro-British sentiment among them.

The strongest support for the War and for Independence came from Congregationalists in Massachusetts and from the Baptists. Many ministers among the Congregationalists served as recruiting agents, chaplains, officers, and militia. Many of them "made resistance and at last independence and war a holy cause,"[29] using their pulpits, their pens, and their salaries to support the cause. The Baptists, meanwhile, also supported the patriots, but used the Revolution as a way of promoting religious liberty and thus gaining freedom from the established churches of the colonies. Given wide latitude for both civil and religious liberty in Rhode Island, and welcomed to Virginia with offers of inexpensive homesteading land, they nevertheless turned against British rule enmasse and fought ardently for independence.[30]

Among the Anglican church membership there was considerable division. Because of deep roots in the mother country, there were many Anglicans in New York and in the southern states who wished to remain loyal to England. Those who let their Tory sympathies be known were often threatened, harassed, and put in confinement. After the Declaration of Independence was signed, the difficulties of the loyalist clergy were increased and in many places their churches were closed.

The most tragic chapter in the War of Revolution, however, was experienced by the Methodists and those who conscientiously objected to war. Although the rapidly growing Methodists were considered dissenters from the Church of England, there were widespread Tory sentiments in their ranks. In Maryland especially the Methodists suffered great hardships at the hands of the patriots, with many of their preachers fined, jailed, beaten, or tarred and feathered.[31] In Pennsylvania, where the conscientious objectors had largely settled, the Quakers, Moravian Brethren, and the Mennonites were given a measure of protection as long as the British controlled Philadelphia. When the tide of war turned in 1778, however, large numbers of Quakers were deported to Winchester, Virginia, where they were placed in concentration camps.[32]

The War of Revolution and the Declaration of Independence, then, produced significantly different reactions among the denominational groups who made up the American populace. In the case of the Scotch, the Irish, the Dutch, and the Germans the primary motivations for supporting the war were the latent national rivalries which became legitimized. In the case of the Baptists, the Congregationalists, the Anglicans, and the Methodists, all of whom traced their ethnic roots to England, the reaction to war was much more diverse and complex. Political representation and taxation were often cited as causes for independence. It was the Baptists alone, however, who made of the war an excuse for attempting to separate the church from the state. In Massachusetts and Virginia particularly, the Baptists used the war as an opportunity to push a cause which offered increasing promise of success as the drive for independence intensified.

The War of Revolution and the Declaration of Independence presented peculiar problems for the established churches in the colonies. Political independence was assumed when Virginia initiated the drive to push for separation from England, but what about the severing of religious ties? Could the six states which had established the Church of England in their territories also cut the ecclesiastical bonds? Were the bishops who had been appointed by England now to be deposed, or could they remain in office? Were the church properties to be transferred to the newly independent states? Should the established churches now suddenly be disestablished. If so, what rules should govern this obviously complex procedure? Could the citizens who had professed their faith in the Thirty-nine Articles, the Westminster Confession, or the Belgic Confession, with all their creedal statements about church-state interaction, continue to believe what they had been taught? Or did independence from England require a transformation in theology?

Response to the Revolution

Answers to the above questions were the simplest and easiest in the New England states, where the embarrassing questions about membership in an English church did not have to be raised. The Baptists in Rhode Island had enjoyed religious liberty since 1663 and simply chose to live under the guarantees of their charter, although they now considered themselves to be totally separated from the powers that granted the charter. The Congregationalists in New Hampshire, Connecticut, and Massachusetts saw no theological or ecclesiastical significance to independence, so elected to maintain their established church practices until 1817, 1818, and 1833 respectively. Because their established churches were Congregational rather than Anglican, they considered their religious ties to be colonial and not imperial. Political connections in these states were with the colonial governments rather than with the mother country.

In Connecticut the colonial practice of "election sermons" was continued until at least 1818. These "election sermons" took on a variety of forms, but the most publicized occasions occurred annually at Yale College, where the legislators and other elected officials were convened and told what God and the church membership would expect from the lawmakers in the coming year. Each year a different pastor was selected for this important gathering. In 1784 Rev. Joseph Huntington preached on the theme of "National Justice." In 1785, Samuel Wales, Professor of Divinity at Yale, spoke on "The Dangers of Our national Prosperity." The next year Levi Hart, a pastor from Preston, Ct., was selected. In 1787, Elizur Goodrich addressed his sermon, "The Principles of Civil Union and Happiness Considered and Recommended."[33] In harmony with the teachings of Romans 13, the Christians saw their elected officials as servants of God, with authority established by Him.

The American Congregational churches periodically adopted and reaffirmed their doctrinal commitment to the Westminster Confession and required all professors at Yale to assent to it until 1823. Demonstrating their affinity with the Puritan movement in England, the Congregationalists called the Synod of Cambridge in 1648 and adopted the creed and the catechisms which had been drafted only 5 years earlier at the Westminster Assembly. In 1680, 1708, and 1865 the Congregationalists reaffirmed their commitments in Synods held at Boston and Saybrook.[34] In order to ensure that this religious heritage was transmitted to their children, the Shorter Catechism was standard curriculum in all the schools of New England.

In New Hampshire the impact of the established church took on more strident tones. From colonial days, the right to vote was limited to members of the established church. In other words, a Congregational membership card was the required ticket to the polling place. In 1792 a constitutional convention was held and this matter debated, but the decision was to continue restricting the franchise as in the past. In 1804, however, the Freewill Baptists were granted religious toleration, and one year later the Universalists were added to the list. When an effort was organized in 1850 to grant Catholics the right to vote, the measure was overwhelmingly defeated.[35] In 1877, during the height of the post-war civil rights movement, a state convention debated whether to omit the word "Protestant" from the Bill of Rights, but the move lost again.

Because of the unanimity with which the Scotch-Irish Presbyterians had supported the American cause of independence, its response to questions of ecclesiastical separation was much simpler than that of other denominational groups. At their annual Synod of 1786, for example, the Presbyterian church adopted a statement which said,

> The Presbyterian Church in America considers the Church of Christ as a spiritual society, entirely distinct from the civil government, having a right to regulate their own ecclesiastical policy, independently of the interposition of the magistrate.[36]

Two years later, at another Synod, the Presbyterian delegates again brought up their creeds for review. In the Larger and Shorter Catechisms they deleted the words "tolerating a false religion" from among the list of sins forbidden by the second commandment.[37] The Westminster Confession also came up for reexamination, with the attention focused on Chap. XXII, Section 3. Whereas the original document had stipulated that it was the duty of magistrates to keep the truth of God pure and to suppress all blasphemies and heresies, the Synod significantly altered this section to read:

> ... as nursing fathers, it is the duty of civil magistrates to protect the church of our Common Lord, without giving preference to any denomination of Christians above the rest, in such a manner that all ecclesiastical persons whatever shall enjoy ... full, free and unquestioned liberty.[38]

In making this unilateral change in the creed which had been drafted by the English Puritans, the Presbyterian church in the U.S. continued to recognize government officials as protectors of the church, and admitted that the universal, catholic church of which the Apostles Creed spoke encompassed more than their own denomination. By claiming, however, that the Church of Christ was only "a spiritual society, entirely distinct from the civil government," they manufactured a dualism which would hamper the work of their own members, whenever they took on the work of government or assumed a public function. In attempting to formulate a theology for disestablishment, the Presbyterians moved well beyond the needs of the hour and reduced religion to the level of a private, spiritual exercise. This not only brought a new spirit to Presbyterianism, but created a spiritual-secular dichotomy more in harmony with the Baptists than with their Puritan and Calvinistic heritage.

The most traumatic effects of the war for independence were those experienced by the Anglicans. By religion, by national origin, and by tradition they were inextricably linked with the enemy. But the enemy was their mother. Now cast in the role of rebellious children, they claimed that their conflict was with King George, who was the head of the English state. But King George was also the head of the English church. Long conditioned by their history of religious and civil unity, the Anglicans, who combined Tory sympathies with patriotic fervor, experienced an especially difficult period of adjustment between 1775 and 1800. Already in 1779, while the war was still raging and the outcome uncertain, the Anglicans in Virginia introduced a bill in their legislature which provided for the continued establishment of their denomination. Dropping their Church of England title, they unofficially referred to themselves as Episcopalians. In order to gather support, they also provided for the official incorporation of other denominations, provided that they subscribed to the following articles of faith:

1. there is one Eternal God and a future state of rewards and punishments,
2. that public worship is essential,
3. that Christianity was the true religion,
4. that the scriptures were divinely inspired, and
5. that every man has the duty of bearing witness to the truth.[39]

In making provision for the official sanction of other denominational groups, the legislature maintained their prerogative of recognizing only the Christian religion and, by implication, refusing the stamp of approval to those who could be considered heretical. For Virginia, at least, such a move represented a compromise between establishment and toleration. As will become evident in Chapter VII, the decision was unacceptable to the Baptists, who pushed instead for complete separation.

By 1784 the Anglicans had officially changed their name to that of the Protestant Episcopal Church in the United States of America. At their first General Convention meeting in Philadelphia the following year, they considered adopting a constitution and such other changes as were deemed necessary to conform "to the American Revolution and the Constitutions of the respective States."[40] At subsequent annual conventions they argued and debated the contents of their creeds and the provisions of their still unsettled constitution. Finally, on July 28, 1789, the first Triennial Convention of the Protestant Episcopal Church met to ratify their constitution. Selecting the site for symbolic significance, they approved their basic document for church governance in the State House in Philadelphia, using the very same room where the federal constitution had been signed a short time before.[41]

Complicating the picture for the Protestant Episcopals was their long commitment to the Thirty-nine Articles, the creed of their mother church, from whom they had declared their independence. Locked in a political struggle in Virginia over separation of church and state, the Episcopaleans continued to debate the content of their creeds and maintained their established church position wherever possible.[42] Finally, in 1801, at Trenton, New Jersey, the battle-weary Protestant Episcopals met to concede the disestablishment of their church in the United States. Mollifying their decision, though, they formally adopted the Thirty-nine Articles of the Anglican church as their own, thus acknowledging the ties which had previously bound them in ecclesiastical union. Tailoring their creed to reflect the political changes which had occurred, they rewrote Article XXXVII to read:

> The power of the civil magistrate extendeth to all men, as well clergy as laity, in all things temporal; but hath no authority in things purely spiritual. And we hold it to be the duty of all men who are professors of the gospel, to pay respectful obedience to the civil authorities.[43]

Summary

Throughout the newly independent states adjustments to the new nationalism had to be made. Churches in most denominations felt a compulsion to establish some sort of constitution or guidelines for ecclesiastical polity by which they could govern themselves. The Dutch Reformed churches, for example, preserved the church order of the Netherlands state church, but added seventy-three Explanatory Articles."[44] The Moravian Brethren established their own Society for Progagating the Gospel among the Heathen, thereby admitting that their London-based operations were no longer appropriate. The Baptists, meanwhile, intensified their fight for separation of church and state, all the while escalating their attacks on the heresies espoused by Universalists, Shakers, and Methodists.[45]

The prevailing opinion in Western Christendom, both in Europe and in the new United States, was that society ought to be distinctively Christian and should be maintained and protected by the offices of the civil magistrates. Government officials were called to their positions by God and had clear responsibilities to serve Him in their callings. For most Americans, this divine mandate of governors, legislators, and mayors was uncritically accepted. For many, too, such divine mandates clearly implied the necessity of state regulation and state establishment of churches.

Historically the record was clear. State creeds and state churches were necessary for the preservation of a Christian state. Of course the mayors, governors, and legislators were to be concerned for orthodoxy and purity of practice, for one had no business aspiring to public office if he had not clearly demonstrated his willingness to be God's servant here on earth. Those who sat in the state house on Monday were expected to be in their pew on Sunday. To be a Christian statesman was not a matter of disjointed allegiances, but the accepted order of the era.

End Notes

1. John 8:32 — Taken in context, it was obvious to the Puritan that the "truth" was not mere propositional statement, but completely incarnate in Christ.
2. Sweet, William Warren, *The Story of Religion in America*, Revised edition, New York: Harper & Bros., 1950. p. 172. For a similar set of statistics, see Humphrey, Edward Frank, *Nationalism and Religion in America*, 1775-1794, Boston: Chipman Law Publishing Co., 1924, p. 13. Such figures, although helpful in indicating the total number of churches throughout the thirteen original states, do not give all the information the historian needs. The size of the churches, the number of members, and the meaning of "membership" are questions about which there is still much conjecture.
3. Cremin, Lawrence A., *American Education: The Colonial Experience, 1607-1783*, New York: Harper & Row, 1970. p. 259.
4. Schaff, Philip, *The Creeds of Christendom With a History and Critical Notes*, Vol. 1, 6th ed., Grand Rapids: Baker Book House. 1931, p. 25.
5. Robert, Frank C., *To All Generations: A Study of Church History*, Grand Rapids: Christian Reformed Board of Publications, 1981, pp. 55-6.
6. Ibid., p. 56.

7. Schaff, p. 225.
9. Ibid., p. 503.
10. "Confession of Faith," *Psalter Hymnal, Doctrinal Standards and Liturgy,* Grand Rapids, Mich.: Publication Committee of the Christian Reformed Church, 1959, p. 19.
11. Schaff, p. 514.
12. Ibid., p. 618.
13. Ibid., p. 779.
14. Ibid., p. 730.
15. Westminster Confession, Chap. XXIII, Sect. 1. Quoted in Clark, Gordon H., *What Do Presbyterians Believe?* Philadelphia: Presbyterian and Reformed Pub. Co., 1965, p. 206.
16. Westminster Confession, Chap. XXIII, Sect. II.
17. Westminster Confession, Chap. XXIII, Sect. III
18. Ibid., Chap. XXV, Sect. II.
19. Westminster Shorter Catechism, Question and Answer 1.
20. Schaff, p. 10.
21. Sweet, *The Story of Religion in America*, pp. 189-190.
22. Constitution of Georgia, 1777, Art. VI, quoted in Poore, Benjamin P., *The Federal and State Constitutions, Colonial Charters, and Other Organic Laws of the United States,* Vol. I, Washington: Government Printing Office, 1877, p. 379.
23. Littell, Franklin H., *From State Church to Pluralism: A Protestant Interpretation of Religion in American History,* New York: The Macmillan Co., 1962, p. 19.
24. Charter of Rhode Island, 1663, quoted in Poore, Vol. II, p. 1600.
25. Ibid., p. 1596.
26. op. cit.
27. Sweet, *The Story of Religion in America,* p. 190. See also Humphrey, *Nationalism and Religion,* p. 363.
28. Humphrey, p. 363.
29. Sweet, p. 177.
30. For a more detailed description of the Baptist involvement see Chapter VII. For a more comprehensive treatment of this subject, see Mark Noll's *Christians in the American Revolution,* Christian University Press, 1977.
31. Sweet, pp. 183-4.
32. Ibid., p. 185.
33. Humphrey, pp. 349, 446-9.
34. Schaff, pp. 835-9.
35. Littell, p. 33.
36. Humphrey, p. 272.
37. Ibid., p. 280.
38. Ibid., p. 276.

39. Lohrenz, Otto, *The Virginia Clergy and the American Revolution, 1774-1799*, Ph.D. Dissertation, University of Michigan Microfilms, 1956, p. 305.
40. Schaff, pp. 650-3.
41. Humphrey, p. 228. It should be noted here that Schaff suggests that they approved their constitution already in 1785. He lacks credence, however, because he lacks specifics and then goes on to suggest that the dispute continued on for some years.
42. Chapter VII will detail this struggle in Virginia, but will cast little light on the debate in other states. What went on in Delaware, Maryland, North and South Carolina and Georgia is unknown to this author. That research remains to be done, probably by someone else.
43. Schaff, p. 653.
44. Humphrey, p. 301.
45. McLaughlin, Wm. G., "Isaac Backus and the Separation of Church and State in America," *American Historical Review*, LXXIII, June, 1968, p. 1398.

CHAPTER IV

The States Draft Their Constitutions

The Process

As the relationships between England and her American colonies became more and more brittle, an increasing number of colonists began talking about independence. In some quarters the talk was secretive and guarded, for any public statement declaring independence from the mother country would be met with opposition. In South Carolina, however, patriots were hard at work drafting a constitution. In New Jersey and Virginia, too, the public mood was strongly in favor of independence.

Breaking their colonial status and conducting a revolution for the sake of independence were exercises which had to be engaged in without the benefit of prior experience or well-illustrated precedents. To fight a war was one thing, but to initiate an experiment in self-government was something quite novel. Setting the pace and establishing a precedent for others to follow was South Carolina. In March, 1776, four months before the Continental Congress would formally sign the Declaration of Independence, a "provincial congress" in South Carolina composed and adopted a constitution for their newly independent state. Formally ratified by the congress which drafted it, the document was posted and distributed for information, but never submitted to the people for ratification.[1]

On the recommendation of the Continental Congress, the patriots in New Jersey secretly began drafting a similar document for themselves. Meeting behind closed doors and shifting sites from Burlington to Trenton to New Brunswick, a hand-picked convention committee put together a state constitution. Begun on

May 26, 1776, it was ready for approval on July 2, two days before the historic signing in Philadelphia. Following the example of South Carolina, the New Jersey constitution, too, was quickly published and posted for all to read.[2]

When the Continental Congress signed the Declaration of Independence on July 4, 1776, each of the thirteen colonies became independent states. Since Virginia, South Carolina, and New Jersey had already made their separate proclamations, Congress put out a call requesting the remaining states to draft constitutions by which they could govern themselves.

The first state to respond was New York, which had a constitutional convention chosen and read to work by July 10. Meeting in White Plains, the New York delegates found their work arduous and subject to significant compromises in order to satisfy the various political elements which made up their population. Continuing in session until April 20, 1777, the New York constitution was adopted with only one negative vote. Unique among all the states, the New York convention insisted on incorporating into their constitution the entire Declaration of Independence, including the long litany of political grievances against the King of England.[3]

Pennsylvania was also quick to respond, with its state convention assembled at Philadelphia on July 15, 1776. Expressing a great deal of respect for their political traditions, the constitutional delegates closely patterned their constitution after the charter of 1701, using almost identical language in many of the articles. By September 28 the document was complete and ready for publication. As in other states, the Pennsylvania constitution of 1776 was posted without ratification by popular vote.[4]

The Continental Congress' call for state constitutions met with a different response in Connecticut. Instead of writing a new document, the General Court simply appended an introductory paragraph to the charter of 1662, in which they declared,

> That the ancinet Form of Civil Government, contained in the Charter from Charles the Second, King of England, and adopted by the People of this State, shall be and remain the Civil Constitution of this State.[5]

In many respects the response of Connecticut was similar to that of Rhode Island, mentioned previously in Chapter III. Like the Baptist followers of Roger Williams, the inhabitants of Connecticut had been granted a large measure of self-government by the

English crown and had found their machinery of government to be very satisfactory. Of special significance to Connecticut, however, was their purpose for existence, which had been articulated by their forefathers and approved by Charles II. "The only and principal End of this Plantation," they said, was to "win and invite the Natives of the Country to the Knowledge and Obedience of the only true GOD, and the Savior of Mankind, and the Christian Faith."[6] When the Connecticut General Assembly adopted the charter of 1662 as its "new" state constitution, they demonstrated unusual tolerance and respect for their mother country, but also reaffirmed that their primary reason for existence was to evangelize the Indians.

Other states were not as hasty to respond. In Maryland and Delaware, conventions were not assembled until late August. In North Carolina, a special congress, "elected and chosen for that particular purpose," convened for the first time on November 12, but finished its work before Christmas. In New Hampshire the political divisions were the most pronounced and the results the most complicated. The initial response in that state was similar to most, with a convention hurriedly drafting a constitution in 1776 and posting it for public information. Two years later, however, a new, revised constitution was submitted to the voters at their town meetings. The revised version was rejected, and a new one submitted in 1781. The town meetings again expressed their displeasure, forcing still more revisions. Finally, on October 31, 1783, the resulting constitution was approved by a majority of the town meetings and scheduled to take effect on June 2, 1784.[7]

Similar political disagreements occurred in Massachusetts. Their first constitution was not drafted until 1778, and then was rejected by a majority of the voters. In response, the people of Massachusetts elected delegates to a constitutional convention which began meeting in Boston on September 1, 1779. Finally, on March 2, 1780, the convention completed its deliberations and submitted its constitution to the voters for ratification. The approved document was ratified by "more than two-thirds of those who voted."[8]

The Contents

The constitutions which the newly independent states drafted were a reflection of their concerns, interest, and values. Virginia, which led the move for independence, was also the most articulate in expressing its revolutionary ideology in its state constitution. Prefacing their basic government document with a Bill of Rights, they proclaimed for all to see and read:

> Section 1: That all men are by nature equally free and independent, and have certain inherent rights . . . namely the enjoyment of life and liberty.
>
> Section 2: That all power is vested in, and consequently derived from, the people; that magistrates are their trustees and servants, and at all times amenable to them.
>
> Section 3: That government is, or ought to be, instituted for the common benefit, protection, and security of the people, nation, or community; of all the various modes and forms of government, that is best which is capable of producing the greatest degree of happiness . . . , and that when any government shall be found inadequate or contrary to these purposes, a majority of the community hath an indubitable, inalienable, and indefeasible right to reform, alter or abolish it.
>
> Section 4: That no man, or set of men, are entitled to exclusive or separate emoluments or privileges.[9]

Such rhetoric had stirred the Virginians to declare their independence. It had little to do, however, with the daily operation of state government or the established Anglican church. Politically it gave hope and promise to the Deists, the Baptists, and those who considered themselves part of the Enlightenment. Practically, though, those committed to establishment of religion were still in power and would remain so until 1800.

Of the nine states which had an established state church prior to independence, New York took the most pronounced action to disestablish the Anglican church. In their constitution, they stipulated that "all such of the said statutes and acts . . . as may be construed to establish or maintain any particular denomination of Christians or their ministers . . . are hereby abrogated and rejected."[10]

Delaware also took steps to separate the state officially from the Anglican church. Far from being anti-religious, as shall be seen later, they decided that there should be "no establishment of any one religious sect" in their state in preference to any other.[11]

The states which did not have an established church prior to 1776 continued their anti-establishment tradition. New Jersey specified that "there shall be no establishment of any one religious sect in this Province, in preference to another."[12] Pennsylvania similarly declared that no man "can be compelled to attend any religious worship, or maintain any ministry, contrary to, or against, his own free will and consent."[13]

When the constitutional process was concluded, and each state had made its decisions about their basic governing policies, a majority of the states continued the tradition of established churches with which they had grown up. The divisions were as follows:[14]

No	Yes	Until
Rhode Island	Georgia	**
New Jersey	South Carolina	1790
Pennsylvania	Virginia	1800
North Carolina	Maryland	1810
Delaware	New Hampshire	1817
New York	Connecticut	1818
	Massachusetts	1833

In the European tradition, establishment of religion usually meant that one denomination was given special, privileged status and became the sole recipient of state tax monies. Other religious affiliations were labelled as dissenters and were either tolerated or declared to be illegal. Those who refused to conform to the practices and rituals of the established church were subjected to harassment, fines, imprisonment, and even destruction of persons and property. Such harsh treatments were well-known to many of the colonists, causing them to incorporate into their constitutions public statements guaranteeing religious toleration. New Hampshire, for example, while continuing their practice of establishment, asserted that "every individual has a natural and inalienable right to worship GOD according to the dictates of his own conscience."[15] Such rights had limited effect, however, for those whose religious commitments took them outside of mainline Protestantism were denied the right to vote. The majority in New Hampshire decided that to be a citizen with suffrage one had to be a Protestant.

New Jersey, too, while expressing opposition to establishment, was careful to point out that "no Protestant . . . shall be denied the enjoyment of any civil right, merely on account of his religious principles."[16] Giving the widest meaning to the word toleration were the states of New York, North Carolina, and Pennsylvania. New York not only promised that "the free exercise and enjoyment of religious profession and worship, without discrimination or preference, shall forever hereafter be allowed," but also asserted that one of the state's duties was "to guard against spiritual oppression and intolerance."[17]

The words "establishment" and toleration" took on different meanings in New Hampshire, South Carolina, and Maryland. Although Maryland officially continued the special status of the Church of England until 1810, their constitution of 1776 set forth a long statement "establishing the Christian religion." In order to effect such a broad establishment, they decreed that the legislature might "lay a general and equal tax, for the support of the Christian religion, leaving to each individual the power of appointing the payment of the money . . . to the support of any particular place of worship or minister, or for the benefit of the poor."[18] South Carolina, too, continued the special status and privileges of the Church of England, and also declared that, "The Christian Protestant religion shall be deemed, and is hereby constituted and declared to be, the established religion of this state."[19] Also granting proportionate shares of the tax revenues to other denominations, South Carolina went further and carefully dictated in their constitution what the acceptable parameters of orthodoxy would be. (For a complete text of this article, see Appendix C.) New Hampshire, also, while empowering "the several towns, parishes, bodies corporate, or religious societies" to levy taxes "for the support and maintenance of public protestant teachers," insisted that no person "shall ever be compelled to pay towards the support of the teacher . . . of another denomination."[20]

To the dismay and consternation of the Baptists, the constitution which was adopted by popular vote in Massachusetts was one of the most pronounced in its continuance of the established Congregational church. In the initial draft of their constitution, it was stipulated that, "The free exercise and enjoyment of religious profession and worship shall forever be allowed to every denomination of Protestants in this state."[21] This document, however, was rejected by a large majority. When the delegates revised their fundamental government policy and presented it for ratification, the language and the practices were made more stringent. The second draft stated that it was "the duty of all men in society, publicly and at stated seasons, to worship the Supreme Being, the great Creator and Preserver of the Universe."[22] Toleration was granted to those who chose to worship God in a manner other than that of the established Congregationalists, provided, though, that they did "not disturb the public peace or obstruct others in their religious worship."[23] Massachusetts, like New Hampshire and South Carolina, also stipulated a form of the voucher system, leaving it to the discretion of the individual citizen as to which public teacher, religious sect, or denomination should be the recipient of his share of the taxes levied. Legally there was no discrimination among the Protestant denominations, but practically there was a matter of conscience for the Baptists, who had to choose whether to accept the monies that were rightfully theirs. With such language inserted, the constitution was approved by more than a two-thirds majority. Clearly the Puritan tradition still adhered to the belief that it was the duty of the civil authorities to protect the purity of the Church of God, as their creeds stipulated. (For a more complete presentation of Massachusetts' constitution, see Appendix D.)

Qualifications for Holding Office

The newly independent states that emerged from the War of Revolution were thoroughly and almost exclusively Protestant. Nowhere was this more apparent than in the criteria for holding public office. After 1776, most of the states decreed that one had to be a member of the Protestant faith in order to be eligible for any government position. Georgia, Maryland, Massachusetts, New Hampshire, New Jersey, North Carolina, and South Carolina specified in their constitutions that all office-holders must be of "the Protestant Religion," with the latter state repeating that phrase no less than four times in its 1778 constitution. Pennsylvania, in spite of its reputation for toleration, ruled that each member of the legislature, before taking his seat, shall make and subscribe to the following declaration:

> I do believe in one God, the creator and governor of the universe, the rewarder of the good and the punisher of the wicked. And I do acknowledge the Scriptures of the Old and New Testament to be given by Divine inspiration.[24]

It was left to Delaware, however, to draft the most concise and most obviously Trinitarian criteria for their magistrates. Their constitution said that,

> Every person who shall be chosen a member of either house, or appointed to any office or place of trust, before taking his seat, or entering upon the execution of his office, shall take the following oath, or affirmation, if conscientiously scrupulous of taking an oath, to wit:
>
> I, A B, will bear true allegiance to the Delaware State, submit to its constitution and laws, and do no act wittingly whereby the freedom thereof may be prejudiced.
>
> And also make and subscribe the following declaration, to wit:
>
> I, A B, do profess faith in God the Father, and in Jesus Christ His only Son, and in the Holy Ghost, one God, blessed for evermore; and I do acknowledge the holy scriptures of the Old and New Testament to be given by divine inspiration.[25]

Although the strong positive relationship between church membership and civic participation was thus guaranteed, some states tried to make certain that there was no unbiblical cross-over of official functions. Cognizant of the uniqueness and importance of the ministerial office, Maryland specified that no "minister, or preacher of the gospel, of any denomination - shall have a seat in the General Assembly or the Council of this State."[26] The rationale for such limitations on ministerial privilege had been originally drafted by South Carolina, which had constitutionally declared,

> Whereas the ministers of the gospel are, by their profession, dedicated to the service of God and the care of souls, and ought not to be diverted from the great duties of their function, therefore no minister of the gospel or public preacher of any religious persuasion, whilst he continues in the exercise of his pastoral functions, shall be eligible to

the office of governor, lieutenant-governor, or to a seat in the senate or house of representatives.[27]

The argument advanced by South Carolina also found acceptance in the neighboring states of Georgia and North Carolina, with both of them adopting similar but abbreviated measures. Among the religiously diverse population of New York, the rationale found widespread agreement, appearing in their 1777 document in almost identical form.[28] Such decisions were not intended to demean the office of minister, but to recognize its importance to the community and its high calling as one of God's special functions within the state.

Legislating Morality

States which insisted on rigid religious tests both for voting and for holding public office were not averse to legislating the morality of their citizens. Those who were willing to profess publicly their faith in Christ and who recognized the divine authority of the Bible were also concerned about the behavior and conduct of those whom they were assigned to govern. In Virginia, for example, it was the duty of the sheriff to levy fines against those who failed to attend worship services regularly. Pennsylvania stipulated that "Laws for the encouragement of virtue, and prevention of vice and immorality, shall be made and constantly kept in force, and provision shall be made for their due execution."[29] New Hampshire was even more precise, specifying that it was "the duty of the legislators and the magistrates . . . to inculcate the principles of humanity and general benevolence, public and private charity, industry and economy, honesty and punctuality, sincerity, sobriety, and all social affections, and generous sentiments, among the people."[30]

It was Massachusetts, however, which most clearly articulated the inextricable relationship between religion, morality, and knowledge. Since "the happiness of a people and the good order and preservation of civil government essentially depended on" those three coherent elements, the legislature was to require "the several towns, parishes, precincts, and other bodies—politic or religious societies to make suitable provision . . . for the institution of the public worship of God and for the support and maintenance of public Protestant teachers."[31] As will become apparent in Chapter V, this section of the Massachusetts' constitution was adopted by the Continental Congress as a model for the Northwest Ordinance of 1787.

The primary means to teaching moral behavior were the schools which were already in operation. Impressing on young children the various demands of God was the most direct way to ensure that the young people would mature into knowledgeable, God-fearing members of both the community and the church. Recognizing this clearly, most of the states made some constitutional provision for the continued support of publicly-financed schools. Because economic repercussions were painfully present during and after the war, though, both Pennsylvania and North Carolina specified that such instruction should be accomplished "at low prices."

Later Developments

Because of a protracted boundary dispute with New York State, Vermont was not admitted to the union until February 18, 1791. The people of Vermont had requested statehood long before, however, and had completed their constitution already in 1777. One of the longest and most detailed of all the state constitutions, it had been drafted and ratified by a constitutional convention which was in session for only 7 days. With sections borrowed wholesale from the constitutions of Pennsylvania and other states, the Vermont document was a unique blending of Enlightenment thought and orthodox Protestantism. Although reaffirmed by the state legislature in 1779 and 1782, it underwent substantial revisions in 1786 and again in 1793. Reflecting its Pennsylvania source, the Vermont constitution required religious oaths for all officeholders, mandated legislation preventing vice and promoting virtue, and stipulated the Protestant religion as a necessary prerequisite for full civil rights.

Because of westward expansion, other states soon were added to the union, with Tennessee admitted in 1796 and Ohio in 1802. Although Tennessee's constitution declared "That no religious test shall ever be required as a qualification to any office,"[32] they violated their own statute by also stating, "No person who denies the being of God, or of a future state of rewards and punishments, shall hold any office in the civil department of this State."[33] Ohio, on the other hand, followed the examples of Maryland,

Massachusetts, New Hampshire, and South Carolina, and decreed that "each and every denomination of religious societies in each surveyed township" must be granted "an equal participation, according to their number of adherents, of the profits arising from the land granted by Congress for the support of religion."[34]

Tennessee should have contained provisions in its constitution similar to those of Ohio, for Congress had specified, at the time of admission, that the new state's government "shall be similar to that which is now exercised in the territory of Ohio," and that the inhabitants "shall enjoy all the privileges, benefits, and advantages set forth in the ordinance of the late Congress."[35] Tennessee, however, reflecting the states-rights attitude and the individualistic philosophy which was being propagated by Jefferson and the Republican Party, chose to ignore the Congressional demand once it had been granted statehood. Similar attitudes prevailed, particularly in the South, as political factions became more pronounced. Georgia and South Carolina, in 1789 and 1790 respectively, had revised their constitutions to reflect the growing democratic sentiments and had deleted the requirements that their office-holders be of "the Protestant religion."

George Washington, in his Farewell Address in 1796, was convinced that the Democratic Societies formed by Jefferson would "destroy the government of this country" and "become potent engines, by which cunning, ambitious and unprincipled men will be ennobled to . . . usurp for themselves the reins of government."[36] Convinced that "religion and morality are indespensible supports" for political prosperity and the "great Pillars of human happiness,"[37] Washington enjoined all the states to respect and cherish them and to retain the religious requirements of their constitutions.

A majority of the states paid close heed to Washington's advice, although new states like Alabama and Arkansas drafted constitutions which sounded more like textbooks on individualism and states-rights than instruments of national unity. Although some of the discriminatory features of the early state constitutions gradually disappeared during the nation's first half-century, resistance to any change was particularly stubborn in the northern and New England states. In 1835, when North Carolina amended the requirements for holding civil office from "Protestant" to "Christian," the voters approved by a margin of 26,771 to 21,606.

Pennsylvanians actually intensified their discriminatory regulations in 1838 by adding the phrase "white freemen" to the criteria for voting, while retaining all the religious qualifications of earlier constitutions.[38] As late at 1864, the constitution of Maryland still required that office-holders must profess "belief in the Christian religion, or of the existence of God, and in a future state of rewards and punishments."[39] New Hampshire clung even more tenaciously to its requirement that legislators be of the Protestant religion, not deleting that criterion until 1877.

Conclusion

The makers of the Revolutionary constitutions, while promising religious liberty, never assumed the state to be wholly neutral in matters of religion. Conditioned by centuries of creedal allegiance, and not yet entangled in secular dichotomies, they usually took for granted a consensus of opinion in support of the Protestant faith and the authority of Scripture. Recognizing a spreading allegiance to Enlightenment philosophy and to free will theology, some of the states made bold pronouncements about freedom of conscience and individual liberty, yet in their governing practices they found it agreeable to levy taxes for the support and encouragement of religion and morality.

When Alexis de Tocqueville toured the United States and wrote his *Democracy in America*, he noted:

> There is no country in the whole world in which the Christian religion retains a greater influence over the souls of men than in America, and there can be no greater proof of its utility, and of its conformity to human nature, than that its influence is most powerfully felt over the most enlightened and free nation of the earth.[40]

End Notes

1. Poore, Benjamin, *The Federal and State Constitutions*, Vol. II, pp. 1615-28. This practice of adopting a constitution in convention, and not submitting it to the people for ratification, was common throughout the colonies. Although South Carolina modified their constitution in 1778, 1790, and in 1868, it was not until the later date that the people were given opportunity to vote on it. Popular sovereignty was simply not acceptable to those in leadership positions.

THE STATES DRAFT THEIR CONSTITUTIONS 59

2. Ibid., p. 1310. The New Jersey constitution was a model of stability and remained unchanged until 1844. It did not contain any reference to schools or education, which deficiency was corrected in 1844.
3. Ibid., p. 1328.
4. Ibid., p. 1541.
5. Constitution of Connecticut—1776, Par. 1, quoted in Poore, Vol. I, p. 255. All subsequent quotations from state constitutions are from Poore, Vol. I or II.
6. Op. cit.
7. Poore, Vol. II, pp. 1279-80.
8. Ibid., Vol. I, p. 956.
9. Virginia Bill of Rights—1776, quoted in Poore, Vol. II, pp. 1908-9.
10. Constitution of New York—1777, Art. XXXV.
11. Constitution of Delaware—1776, Art. 29.
12. Constitution of New Jersey—1776, Art. XIX.
13. Constitution of Pennsylvania—1776, Art. II.
14. The date for disestablishment in Georgia is uncertain, but probably does not extend past 1790. In all of the states the process was rather slow and gradual, with different actions undermining different aspects of establishment. In states like South Carolina the primary effect was the removal of a tax base for Christian, Protestant ministers. In Virginia it meant the gradual granting of ecclesiastical privileges to the Baptists.
15. Constitution of New Hampshire—1784, Part I, Article I, Section V.
16. Constitution of New Jersey—1776, Art. XIX. This Protestant requirement, which also applied to the holding of any civil office, was not removed until 1844.
17. Constitution of New York—1777, Art. XXXVIII.
18. Maryland, Constitution of 1776, Art. XXXIII.
19. Constitution of South Carolina—1778, Art. XXXVIII.
20. Constitution of New Hampshire—1784, Part I, Art. I, Sec. VI.
21. Humphrey, *Nationalism and Religion*, p. 365.
22. Constitution of Massachusetts—1780, Part the First, Art. II.
23. Ibid.
24. Constitution of Pennsylvania—1776.
25. Constitution of Delaware—1776, Art. 22.
26. Maryland, Constitution of 1776, Art. XXXVII.
27. Constitution of South Carolina—1776, Art. I, Sec. 23.
28. Constitution of New York—1777, Art. XXXIX.
29. Constitution of Pennsylvania—1776, Sect. 45.

30. Constitution of New Hampshire—1784.
31. Constitution of Massachusetts—1780, Part the First, Art. III.
32. Constitution of Tennessee—1796, Art. XI, Sec. 4.
33. Ibid., Art. VIII, Sec. 2.
34. Constitution of Ohio—1802, Art. VIII, Sec. 26.
35. "An Act for the government of the territory of the United States south of the river Ohio—1790," quoted in Poore, Vol. II, p. 1667. The reference is to the Northwest Ordinance of 1787, which will be explained in greater detail in Chapters V and VI. All new states were required, by Congress, to follow the rules established for the Ohio Territory.
36. Washington's Farewell Address, Sept. 19, 1796, *The Writings of George Washington*, Vol. 35, p. 225.
37. Ibid., p. 229.
38. Poore, Vol. II, p. 1560.
39. Whitehead, *The Separation Illusion*, p. 18.
40. De Tocqueville, Alexis, *Democracy in America*, trans. by Henry Reeve, Vol. I, New York, p. 285.

CHAPTER V

Schools for Religion and Morality

In 1647 the Massachusetts General Court passed a law which required towns of more than fifty families to provide a schoolmaster, and communities of more than one hundred families to establish a Latin grammar school. Predicated on the conviction that there was eternal hostility between God and Satan, and that education was essential to the triumph of the Lord's side, the law was dubbed "The Old Deluder Satan Act." Since the skill of reading was prerequisite to Biblical knowledge, and Biblical knowledge was essential to Godly living, the Puritans' "city on a hill" could not expect to overcome the wiles of the devil if ignorance prevailed. Other New England colonies passed similar legislation, with the exception of Rhode Island, where there was concern that public schools might lead to coercion in matters of private conscience. Thus began the public educational system in America.

Throughout the colonial period, schools became increasingly necessary and important, although the patterns varied considerably among the southern, middle, and New England colonies. For a variety of cultural and economic reasons, the southern colonies were slow to establish public schools. In the New England colonies, most towns complied with state legislation, increasing the literacy rate for men from 60% in the early colonial period to 90% by 1775.[1]

Since the Puritans had dissented so sharply from the Church of England, they could no longer expect their ministers and community leaders to be trained in their mother country. They thus had to establish an institution of their own for that purpose, founding Harvard College in 1636. But even with their own seminary at the college, cracks appeared in the theology of New England and questions were raised about "half-way covenants" and the meaning of "visible saints." In 1701, consequently, a group of ministers in Connecticut, convinced that the preparation of pastors required their personal supervision, established Yale. Some years later, the Connecticut Assembly, expressing a fear "that corrupt and pernicious Principles may be instilled into Youth, by the setting up of publick Seminaries . . . , which are not under the Inspection of the publick Authority of the Government,"[2] decreed that no other college or public school might open without a special license from the General Assembly. By such action, the Assembly asserted that its responsibility included not only the training of the clergy, but also the role of watchdogs for orthodoxy in the warfare with satan.

One of the most pressing concerns in the Puritan mind was the discernment between Truth and Falsehood and the accompanying conflict between good and evil. Since their creeds daily reminded them that the only reliable guide to truth was the infallible Scriptures, the first reason for developing reading skills was that the individual might be able to read the Bible. Without a thorough knowledge of God's revealed will, one could not fulfill his obligations to the covenant or attain the visible sanctification which God required. In colonial New England, the generally held assumption was that formal education was a function of the government officials, but religious considerations played the central role in the licensing of public schools, which were expected to inculcate truthful information about God and the world which He had created. Cooperation between ministers and civil authorities was clearly illustrated by a 1701 Massachusetts' law which required "the approval of a new school-master in any town by the local minister and at least two others of the neighboring clergy."[3]

But such a spiritual priority for education was not unique to the colonies of Massachusetts and Connecticut. Farther to the south in Maryland, with its Anglican establishment, "the criterion of an academic education was the ability 'to read distinctly in the Bible."[4] When the English established William and Mary College in Virginia in 1693, they expected it to prepare leaders for the southern colonies, and required that it be a thoroughly Anglican institution. In order to preserve orthodoxy, as the Anglicans perceived it, the Church of England specified that even though a clergyman might receive his pastoral training at the college in Virginia, he had to be approved and licensed by the Bishop in London. When the Dutch settlers finally were granted a charter in 1770 for Queen's College (Rutgers Univ.), they argued that "the people of the Reformed Faith and Discipline were very numerous, and were desirous of a learned and well-qualified ministry, and therefore desired a college not only for the usual reasons, but especially that young men might prepare for the ministry."[5] (For the text of Rutger's Charter, see Appendix B). Columbia and Princeton, too, were founded especially for the purpose of training ordained clergy. Princeton, which was originally called the College of New Jersey, was established by Presbyterians, and graduated 120 ministers during the period from 1758 to 1789. The most brilliant president of the College of New Jersey was the Rev. Jonathon Edwards, who died shortly after taking office in 1757. Another illustrious leader of the institution was Rev. John Witherspoon (1767-1795), who was known better to his own generation as a leading Presbyterian preacher and theologian than as a signer of the Declaration of Independence.

One of the effects of independence was the cutting off of the supply of ministers and educated leaders from the continent. During the war itself, both King's College (now Columbia) and William and Mary were closed by the patriots because the institutions were too obviously English in their sympathies, but both were reopened after the war was over. The result was that new colleges had to be established quickly throughout the states. Although serious financial difficulties hampered efforts during the first two decades after the war, the number of colleges increased from 9 in 1775 to 48 by 1820.[6] One of the first denominational groups to organize a college after the war was the German Reformed church in Pennsylvania. Opened in 1787 to train their own pastors, teachers, and public servants, they named it Franklin College, in honor of Benjamin Franklin, who was the largest individual contributor to its endowment.[7] Expressing their deepest longings in a liturgical prayer, they said,

> Since it has pleased Thee chiefly, by means of the Germans to transform this State into a blooming garden, and the desert into a pleasant pasturage, help us not to deny our nation, but to endeavor that our youth may be so educated that German schools and churches

may not only be sustained but may attain a still more flourishing condition.[8]

The primary purpose of most colleges, then, was to train pastors for the churches which occupied central place in most communities. Yet, as the population increased and the rift between England and America widened, there was an increased demand for other types of public servants to meet the needs of the people. Although nearly 50% of Harvard's graduates before 1690 had entered the ministry, more and more young men during the eighteenth century chose such careers as medicine, government service, teaching, and business. Recognizing the legitimacy and necessity of such studies, denominations which had established schools to perpetuate and advance their particular way of life often found that an inevitable broadening of the school's clientele for economic reasons inexorably broadened the school's purposes.[9] This expansion of the colleges' programs and offerings did not necessarily affect their religious commitments, however, for those with a grounding in Calvinistic theology realized that ministers were not the only servants called by God to Kingdom service. The College of New Jersey, for example, persuaded Witherspoon to come to this country and to take over the presidency because of his reputation as a "powerful protagonist of Presbyterian orthodoxy" and as an advocate of education for public service.[10] As president of the college, he sought on every possible occasion "to unite together piety and religion—to show their relation to, and their influence one upon another—and to guard against anything that may tend to separate them, and set them in opposition one to another."[11]

Curricular Patterns

The expansion of programs and the broadening of purpose, although experienced widely on the college level, did not significantly affect the public elementary and high schools. When the city of Boston, on October 15, 1789, passed an ordinance revamping "The System of publick Education," they decreed,

> That it be the indispensable duty of the several School-Masters, daily to commence the duties of their office by prayer, and reading a portion of the Sacred Scriptures, at the hour assigned for opening the School in the morning; and close the same in the evening with prayer.

> That the several School-Masters instruct the children under their care, or cause them to be instructed in the Assemblies' Catechism, every Saturday, unless the parents request that they may be taught any particular catechism of the religious Society to which they belong.
>
> That they frequently address their pupils on moral and religious subjects; endeavoring to impress their minds with a sense of the being and providence of God, and the obligations they are under to love, serve, and pray to Him, . . . and that they caution them against the prevailing vices, such as sabbath-breaking, profane cursing and swearing, gaming, idleness, writing obscene words on the fences, etc.[12]

Recognizing, too, that religious education was organically united to basic learning skills, they decreed that the *Holy Bible, Webster's Spelling Book,* or the first part of his *Institute,* be used in all the city's Reading Schools. The spiritual dimension of public education was further demonstrated in the graduation exercises of a Massachusetts Grammar School, as reported in the *Connecticut Courant* on September 29, 1818. After describing such elements of the program as the sacred music, the appropriate prayers, and the Oration on the Utility of Bible Societies, the paper editorialized,

> How happy is that Society, when faithful parents and pious teachers can live to see religion and science rising together—'when their sons are as plants grown up in their youth; and their daughters as corner stones polished after the similitude of a palace.'[13]

In all levels of schooling the curriculum was predominantly religious in character. At the primary level the basic material used was the *Hornbook*, which contained the alphabet and the Lord's Prayer. As the student moved up to higher levels, he was introduced to the Bible and the Westminster Catechisms, by means of the *New England Primer.* Those who graduated to the grammar or secondary schools expanded their studies to include the Greek and Latin languages, as well as the classics. Because the Calvinistic creeds had declared that God revealed Himself first of all through the world and universe which He had created, and secondarily through His inscripturated Word, those who came out of that Calvinistic tradition might not limit themselves to a study of the Bible. The whole creation was a textbook through which man might come to know God, yet the created world was fallen and distorted by the curse of sin. The Scriptures, therefore, as John

Calvin had argued, were the spectacles by which man might come to know the world aright.

In that tradition, the classics were simply other sourcebooks for the laws of nature, inferior to, but not in conflict with the greatest sourcebook, the Bible. A knowledge of the classics would heighten and intensify the doctrines which the child had earlier encountered in the catechism and in the primary textbooks. Unlike the dualists of either the Thomist or Anabaptist traditions, the Congregationalists, the Presbyterians, and the Reformed viewed the great writings of the past as tools to aid in understanding the complex world which God had made. The ability to read the Greek Classics in their original language, though, was a secondary benefit accrued from pursuing another primary objective. The grammar school student had to learn the Greek language, first of all, so that he might be able to study the Bible in the original, thus avoiding the errors and nuances of translations and versions which had come down through the ages.

Exerting pressure on the grammar schools, from the top down, were the colleges, which required reading skills in both Greek and Latin as prerequisites for admittance. Harvard College, for example, published new entrance requirements in 1770 and stipulated that all future candidates for admission would be examined "in any part of the following Books—The Greek Testament, Virgil's Aeneid, and Cicero's Select Orations."[14]

The Textbooks

Next to the Bible, the most influential and widely used book in New England during the colonial era was *The New England Primer*. Reflecting its strongly Puritan perspective, the early editions contained the Lord's Prayer, the Apostles Creed, a picture and story about the martyrdom of John Rogers, prayers for children, William Cotton's Catechism, and poems calculated to impress spiritual truths on young minds.[15] Published originally in 1690, it was used widely in all of the colonies except those in which the Church of England was officially established. When Ginn and Co. issued a Twentieth Century Reprint, they advertised it as "one of the greatest books ever published" and claimed that "it reflected in a marvelous way the spirit of the age that produced it."[16] Its history has been written by Paul Leicester Ford, who estimated that 3,000,000 copies were printed.

As the colonies moved through the era of independence from England, the *Primer* continued its popularity and received even broader acceptance throughout the colonies. In 1781 it was revised somewhat and labelled as "A Neat and Beautiful Edition."[17] Two years later Noah Webster published a complementary text, which he called *The First Part of a Grammatical Institute of the English Language,* but which came to be popularly known as *The Speller* or simply *The Institute.*[18] Because of its orthodox religious perspective and its utilitarian value, the *Institute* received strong endorsements from the Rev. Ezra Stiles, the Governor of Connecticut, the President of Yale, and the mayor of New Haven. It was also adopted later by the University of Georgia and declared to be the only acceptable or approved language text for all the schools in Georgia. In 1839 a Baltimore newspaper stated that the annual sale of Webster's *Speller* had reached 600,000 copies, making it the most popular textbook of the time.[19]

From the start of the American Revolution to 1843, Noah Webster was the most prominent educator and the best loved author in the United States. In many respects, he stood as the prime exemplar of the early national era. Combining patriotic fervor with traditional orthodoxy, he wrote to a friend in 1783, "America must be as independent in literature as she is in politics — as famous for arts as for arms — and it is not impossible, but a person of my youth may have some influence in exciting a spirit of literary industry."[20] In his "Preface" to *An American Selection of Lessons in Reading and Speaking,* he complained that none of the existing language texts was "calculated particularly for American Schools . . . In America it will be useful to furnish schools with additional essays, containing the history, geography, and transactions of the United States . . . A love of our country, and an acquaintance with its true state, are indispensable — they should be acquired in early life."[21]

In 1790, Webster published an intermediate text called *The Little Reader's Assistant,* which was designed to bridge the gap between the *New* England Primer and his own *Speller*. Two years later a competitive book, *The Child's Companion*, was published by Caleb Bingham and was advertised as filling the same need. Continuing the Puritan perspective of the *Primer,* it was designed to "impress upon their minds the importance of RELIGION and the Advantages of GOOD MANNERS."[22]

Continuing his concern for Christian education, Webster published an updated version of the New England Primer in 1795. Described as being larger than the common size *Primer*, "it contained the Catechism, Religious Dialogue, Dr. Watts' Cradle Hymn, Prayers, Verses and Spiritual Songs for children, a variety of Stories, with upward of fifty lessons for spelling and reading." The publisher advertised it as "a proper key to Mr. Webster's Spelling Book."[23] In 1816, the acknowledged leader of American educators exerted his influence on the legislature of Massachusetts and persuaded them to establish Amherst College for the expressed purpose of providing a school "for indigent young men entering the ministry."[24] Still later, in 1833, Webster busied himself with editing the Bible. Not a new translation, but a grammatical revision designed to conform to American usage, it was endorsed by the faculty of Yale and recommended for use in all the public schools.

Responsibility for Schools

When contemporary educators attempt to assign responsibility for education in the early national period, they frequently try to superimpose their own twentieth century thought patterns on that era. Although the terms public, private, and parochial were used in the late eighteenth century, they did not connote the radical disjunctions which those terms convey in the late twentieth century. None of the words conveyed the implications of neutrality, secular knowledge, or sectarian emphasis. When the city of Boston in 1789 mandated their "System of publick Education," they harbored no notions of a separatistic state divorced from the church or from the home. Neither did they envision the body politic as operating within a carefully defined sovereign sphere which had exclusive jurisdiction only within its own limited realm. Such twentieth century concepts would have sounded totally foreign to eighteenth century citizens.

In the New England of 1789, towns were defined as geographic regions or communities of people with predominantly homogeneous characteristics. Families of common faith, common ethnic origin, and common ancestry banded together and formed a network of relationships with common needs and shared values. In most New England towns those homogeneous qualities could best be summed up by the term Puritan or Congregationalist. Other communities could best be described as Baptist or Lutheran or Episcopal, with little integration occurring as long as population was sparse and new land plentiful.

As one moved into the states of New York or New Jersey, one could find similar demographic patterns established by the Dutch Reformed, the French Huguenots, or the Scottish Presbyterians. In Pennsylvania the typical ethnic conclave might contain primarily Quaker, Moravian, or German Reformed families. As one moved further to the south, the typical pattern in the coastal areas of Virginia was that of Anglican communities, while the back country was inhabited primarily by Baptists and Presbyterians. The most heterogeneous mixtures of ethnic and religious cultures that could be found in the newly united states were those in cities such as New York, Philadelphia, and Charleston, but even there communities of like interests quickly emerged and interspersing of religious convictions was rare.

For a Congregational church member to assume some feigned attitude of neutrality when he was elected to the General Court of Connecticut or to the Continental Congress would have been unthinkable, or at least unacceptable if ever attempted. Even in Rhode Island and Virginia, where the Baptist theology of separation was gaining increasing adherents, the Baptist electorate adamantly expected their elected representatives to espouse the theological commitments of their constituency. To make laws or to condone decisions which were contrary to their most deeply held beliefs would have been adequate grounds for rejection at the next election.

From the total gamut of issues which could be addressed, one that needed immediate attention was that of locating responsibility. Where should the locus of authority lie? Who should be responsible for ensuring that every child received the essential rudiments of instruction? Who should have the prerogative for determining the extent and the character of that education? And who should be charged with guarding the quality of that instruction, making certain that truth and not falsehood was taught? The answers to such questions varied widely, for the United States was truly pluralistic since its earliest colonial days. The answers that emanated from New England were different than those in the middle states and even more different yet than those in the southern states. Because education was given highest priority among the Congregationalists of New England, we shall look at those answers first.

Since the earliest enactments in Massachusetts, it was the decision of the lawmakers that education was a corporate responsibility. Eschewing individualism, the General Court mandated that towns of more than fifty families had to provide a schoolmaster and communities of more than one hundred families were required to provide a Latin grammar school. The loss of any child to the wiles of that old deluder Satan was to be the concern of every family, for all persons were called to a life of sanctification within the Body of Christ. Within that corporate context, individual fathers were still judged to be accountable, resulting in a law which stipulated that "once a week at least, every father was supposed to teach his children from a catechism."[25] As was noted earlier, the local pastors were assigned the responsibility for approving teachers, thereby guarding the truth of what was taught, since it was the minister who had the most advanced training in matters of religious discernment. Throughout the colonial and early national period, it was the state, too, which legislated the curriculum to be taught, specifying the daily use of the Bible and such textbooks as the *Primer*, complete with all its Puritan contents.

Such legislation did not pose any threats of lawsuits or charges of excessive entanglement between church and state. Those who comprised the Body of Christ were, or should be at least, the very same persons who were citizens of the town of Boston or the state of Massachusetts. All people, whether they be Anglicans, Baptists, or Congregationalists, were called to be obedient to the commands of God. Those who articulated those laws and codified them in eighteenth century form were simply doing their duty as Christians who were called to public service.

Nowhere is the alliance of church, state, and school more clearly typified than in the Massachusetts Constitution of 1780. It was the duty of the legislature, they said, to "require the several towns, parishes, precincts, and other bodies—politic or religious societies to make suitable provision, at their own expense, for the institution of the public worship of God and for the support and maintenance of public Protestant teachers of piety, religion, and morality." (see Appendix D). That same symbiotic relationship was evident in the regulations concerning the government of higher education, which specified that the "governor, lieutenant-governor, council, and the senate, . . . with the President of Harvard College, . . . together with the ministers of the Congregational churches in the towns of Cambridge, Watertown, Charleston, Boston, Roxbury, and Dorchester . . . shall be the overseers of Harvard College."[26]

In Connecticut the legal responsibilities for education were almost identical to those of Massachusetts. Schools were mandated by state legislation, with communities or congregations of believers expected to take the initiative. Since the pastors were usually the leaders of the communities, they also became the leaders in the schools. Since the church was the state, and the state was the church, it was not at all unusual for schools to be organized by church societies, supervised by ministers, and funded by state-collected taxes. In New Haven, the City Meeting adopted a plan in 1790 whereby all the separate congregational schools were combined under one special committee, consisting of four members from each church society in the city. This committee's responsibility included the coordination of curriculum and the organization of efforts for the most efficient use of resources. One of its first activities was the planning of a central library of 1000 volumes which might be circulated among the member schools.[27]

The church-run school was also the most prevalent form of institutionalization in the middle states of Delaware, Maryland, New Jersey, New York, and Pennsylvania. Since these states were more religiously diverse than those in New England, the establishment of a state-wide common school system was not seriously attempted. Although most of the states did articulate constitutional requirements for education, the implementation of those laws was left largely to the discretion of the various religious communities throughout the states. This pattern has led many educational historians to conclude that "parochial" schools were predominent in the middle states, a description which is not inaccurate, but which fails to make important comparisons with the New England states, where religious societies were also the most significant organizing forces. What distinguished the two regions was the religious homogeneity in New England and the religious heterogeneity in the middle states. In both regions, the primary control over schools rested with church societies who exercised a collective or corporate responsibility for the education of their youth.

The general pattern in the Southern states was significantly different. Missing in this region was the commonly accepted idea of corporate responsibility. The size of the plantations, the type of agriculture, the presence of large slave populations, and the diminishing influence of the established Anglican church all contributed to a pattern of personal responsibility and individualistic effort. Wealthy plantation owners often hired private tutors for their children and then sent them to Europe for advanced schooling. When foreign affairs prevented it, students were sent to such southern colleges as William and Mary, Hampden-Sydney, or the University of Georgia. Corporate responsibility was exercised only in providing education for the poor, with that limited usually to the elementary level and apprenticeships.

At the college level, the question of narrow denominational allegiance and control became an increasingly thorny issue in the decades after the United States became independent. In Connecticut, legislation in effect since the early 1700's had given Yale a monopoly on higher education. Holding fast to its traditional orthodoxy and denying entrance to other than Congregationalists, Yale became the object of strident attacks during the early 1820's. Yale was accused of being too rigid in its theology and of denying admission to Episcopaleans, who petitioned the legislature for a license to establish their own college. The controversy was finally settled, against Yale's wishes, by the granting of a charter to Washington exclusively for students from Episcapalean churches.[28] Denominaltional differences were thereby protected, but the influence of Yale was eroded.

Throughout the first half of the nineteenth century, college administration was reserved almost exclusively to the clergy. Even state schools, such as the State University of Vermont, which was established at Burlington in 1794 and was open to every youth, "whatever his religious faith," had ministers selected as their presidents. Union College in New York, so named by the State Regents "because it represented all religious sects,"[29] had as one of its first presidents the Reverend Jonathan Edwards, a graduate of Princeton and son of the great revivalist. While toleration for

SCHOOLS FOR RELIGION AND MORALITY

diverse faiths was demonstrated in such institutions, there was no desire or thought of establishing irreligious or neutral education. What gradually occurred in these ecumenical schools, however, was that the separate churches gradually surrendered their striking power and control over public education and allowed the locus of authority to shift to elected or appointed boards. In pluralistic states like New York, this transfer of responsibility became more apparent.

Methods of Financing

Questions of control were often inextricably tied to sources of funding, for he who paid the piper often called the tune. Yet, in communities where the lines between church and state were almost indistinguishable, those responsible for public education exercised a great deal of ingenuity and some measure of doctrinal license in raising funds.

One of the least orthodox methods of fund-raising was that of the lottery. When the Anglicans of New York decided to establish King's College, they succeeded by collecting 3500 pounds through a lottery. Just prior to the American Revolution, Harvard College conducted a lottery for several months, hoping to realize enough profit to support their operation. From then until 1791, when the General Court of Massachusetts found it almost impossible, because of war debts and devaluation of currency, to make their annual grants to the college, Harvard frequently resorted to lotteries as a source of revenue. With that practice widely accepted, the college again sponsored lotteries in 1794-96 to collect money for a new building.[30]

Another means of gathering revenue was through the formation of scholarship funds and solicitation from individuals. In 1813 Yale organized a Benevolent Society to raise funds for "assisting young men of character and talent, . . . who have promise of future usefulness to their country and the Church of Christ."[31] This foundation was soon expanded to become the American Education Society, with branches in other states. By 1819 it was giving aid to 200 students in various colleges and universities. Two years after Yale initiated its fund, Harvard established a Society to assist students who were studying for the ministry. Membership in the Society was contingent on the payment of $5.00 per year, with ordained clergy only having to pay $2.00.

The Baptists who governed Rhode Island College also experienced financial difficulties during the post-war years. Opposed in principle to using tax monies for religious education, they commissioned their president, James Manning, to draft an appeal to the King of France, soliciting the King's aid in establishing a collection of books and in funding a French professorship. In 1784 Manning sent the request to Benjamin Franklin, and asked that he endorse it before forwarding it to the French court. Franklin complained that he never received it, so a duplicate request was sent to Thomas Jefferson in 1786, who promptly endorsed it and promised to present it personally to the King.[32]

One of the most prevalent means of supporting schools was that of land-grants by the states. With unsettled land plentiful and cash sometimes scarce, schools were often given large endowments which paid handsome dividends in subsequent years, if managed wisely. In 1794, the state of Maine donated "six towns of land" toward the establishment of Bowdoin. In 1800, the State Legislature of New York appropriated 6,000 acres of land and $10,000 in cash for support of Union College in Schenectady. In 1821 the Massachusetts legislature voted that $10,000 per year, for 10 years, be appropriated for Harvard College.

The state which was the first to establish a permanent tax fund for financing public schools was Connecticut. As early as 1785 a notice appeared in New Haven newspapers announcing that "The several School Districts in New London who are entitled to receive a proportion of public monies, are desired to bring their lists on levy 1784, to the committee for dividing said monies."[33] In 1798 a Legislative Act was approved in the Assembly, specifying the criteria for eligibility to draw money from the state education fund. To be eligible, the law said, "a School Society must have a Committee of School Visitors, not more than 9 in number, who should visit schools at least two times per year, in groups of two."[34] With monies accrued from the sale of public lands, the State School Fund became so large by 1810 that a legislative committee could no longer administer it, so a commissioner of public education was appointed. In 1816 the legislature formulated a policy for distribution of the excess monies in the fund, which had grown to $145,014. Stipulating that the monies must be spent for the "general cause of Religion and Literature," the legislature apportioned the monies as follows:[35]

>   1/3 to go to Presbyterians and Congregationalists
>   1/7 to Episcopaleans
>   1/8 to Baptists
>   1/12 to Methodists
>   1/7 to Yale

In 1818, when Connecticut ratified a new state constitution, they gave special place to education. They not only reaffirmed their commitment to the purpose and support of Yale College, but also specified that,

> The fund called the school fund shall remain a perpetual fund, the interest of which shall be inviolably appropriated to the support and encouragement of the public or common schools throughout the State, and for the equal benefit of all the people thereof.
> ... no law shall ever be made authorizing said fund to be diverted to any other use than the encouragement and support of public or common schools among the several school societies, as justice and equity shall require.[36]

In spite of the generous dispersal policies adopted by the legislature, the balance in Connecticut's school fund kept growing, reaching a total of $1,756,233 in 1825. Another state which considered education to be a corporate responsibility and established a state school fund was Massachusetts. In their 1780 constitution they had declared that religion, morality, and knowledge were the pillars on which civilization was built. Through the levying of taxes for the support of "public Protestant teachers," Massachusetts was able to finance not only "public schools," but also academies and "private schools." Operating according to legislation similar to that of Connecticut, the "Abstract of the Massachusetts School Returns for 1837" revealed the following data:

Number of towns reporting	294
Number of public schools	2,918
Average attendance in winter	111,520
Taxes collected and paid out	$465,228
Monies raised privately	$48,301

Number of Academies or Private Schools	854
Aggregate of Scholars	27,266
Amount paid as tuition	$32,826
Amount from local funds	$189,536

An analysis of the above report suggests that schools were small, enrolling an average of 38 students at the elementary level, and numerous, averaging almost 10 schools per town reporting. Costs, too, were low, averaging less than $5.00 per student at the elementary level and slightly more than $8.00 per student at the secondary level. According to the dictates of the Massachusetts' constitution, taxes for schools had to be raised primarily at the local level, avoiding thereby the problems experienced by Connecticut, which had accumulated excessive surpluses in its state school fund.

Religious and Political Controversy

During the first two decades of the nineteenth century, Connecticut was aflame with controversy and hostility between "democrats" and "federalists." The members of the Democratic-Republican party were followers of Jefferson and Madison, while the Federalists came from the tradition of Washington, Hamilton, and Adams. Although the Democrats had captured the presidency in 1800 and retained it through the next three decades, the majority of voters in Connecticut continued their allegiance to the Federalists.

Because of the religious inclinations of Jefferson and Thomas Paine, most Federalists considered "democrats" to be heretics and infidels, with newspapers and politicians hurling epithets at each other. Occasionally the debate took on humorous tones, as it did on April 1, 1817, when the Yale student newspaper reported that the Democratic Party had contributed $20,000 to the college.[37] A more typical tone was expressed in the *Connecticut Courant*, in which the editor complained,

> The democrats have attacked our State officers—our Clergy, our College and our Missionary Society, and have now come down to our schools—"Schools in which Ignorance is taught as a Science." This is indeed laying the ax at the root, for if they succeed in prejudicing the majority of the people of this state against the sources of knowledge and religion, the tree of federalism must indeed fall.[38]

The hostilities which had clouded the school picture in Connecticut during the first two decades of the nineteenth century, gradually dissipated during the 1820's. In 1825, a Democrat, Seth P. Beers of Hartford, was appointed to be commissioner of the state school fund, a post which he retained until 1849. Whereas the Democrats had voted against the apportionment of surplusses to the various denominational groups, and had also been instrumental in removing the Congregational church from establishment status in 1818, one of their recognized party leaders was responsible for administering the state tax fund which financed parochial education. Some of this shift in attitude was attributed to the Supreme Court's famous Dartmouth decision, handed down in 1819.

The Dartmouth Case

The controversy which had swirled through the country during the early 1800's finally worked its way up to the United States Supreme Court. What was judiciously decided in 1819, though, had its roots in the original Connecticut Charter of 1662, which had been retained as the "new" Constitution of 1776. From the very beginning of its statutory existence, Connecticut had declared that its primary reason for existence was to "win and invite the Natives of the Country to the Knowledge and Obedience of the only true GOD, and the Savior of Mankind, and the Christian Faith."[39]

Dartmouth College was originally founded by Rev. Eleazor Wheelock in 1751 as a means of implementing that missionary mandate. Begun as an Indian Charity School in Lebanon, Connecticut, it was chartered by that colony's General Court and placed under its jurisdiction. In 1763, Rev. Wheelock petitioned the Assembly for funds to support his work and the more than twenty Indian youths who were studying to become missionaries to their own people. The Assembly reacted favorably and promised to release tax funds for this purpose, as well as to recommend the cause to all of Connecticut's churches for their support. (For more detail, see Connecticut's Missionary Mandate, Appendix A).

In 1770, New Hampshire took a special interest in Rev. Wheelock's program and enticed him to move his school to Hanover, New Hampshire. The governor offered a 3300 acre tract of land "freely given for the use of the college." In a letter of response dated August 23, 1770, Rev. Wheelock promised,

> I hope soon to be able to support by charity a large Number not only of Indian youths in Moor's charity school, which is connected and incorporated with the College, but also of English youths in the College, in order to their being fitted for missions among the Indians.[40]

Rev. Wheelock had also received support from the Society for the Propagation of the Gospel, which was based in London, but that source of funds was cut off by the advent of the War. In 1778, Wheelock appealed for money from Congress and was granted $925.00 for expenses occurred in "supporting a number of Indian youths at his school."[41] For a number of years thereafter, appropriations for Dartmouth College and Rev. Wheelock's Indian mission efforts were regularly approved by Congress.

As the War of Revolution drew to a close, the program at Dartmouth attracted increasing attention. In 1781, the question was raised as to whether other students might enroll, but the answer was an emphatic "No," with the explanation that this school was reserved for evangelizing Indians and for training missionaries to the Indians. By 1787, enrollment at Dartmouth had increased to 1309 students and a new three-story building (150' by 50') had been erected, which was described as being "most elegant" and the largest in all of New England. With its reputation spreading, monetary support increased. In 1789, the government of the state of Vermont made a generous donation of 23,000 acres "of wild land," in "consideration of its contiguity to that State." The same year the state of New Hampshire made a grant of 41,000 acres "of valuable land, adjoining the Connecticut River, near Hanover," and followed that in 1796 with another grant of 24,500 acres.[42]

The historic Supreme Court case, known as Dartmouth v. Woodward, had its immediate roots in a political squabble within the Legislature of New Hampshire, which had come under the political dominance of the Democratic-Republican Party. As part of a political power struggle with the Federalists, the Democrats tried to wrest control of Dartmouth College and to change its direction. The Democratic governor, with the support of the legislature, appointed a new Board of Trustees for the college and disbanded the existing Board. The college, in defiance of the governor, continued to operate as a college without state funds while the case was slowly working its way through the lower courts.

Meanwhile, the State Legislature loaned $4,000. to William Woodward, their newly appointed Treasurer of the College, to pay his legal expenses.

When the Supreme Court, under Chief Justice Marshall, finally handed down its 5-1 decision on February 2, 1819, it was clear that the Democrats had lost and that the old Board of Trustees had won. The Supreme Court ruled against Woodward and ordered him personally to pay a $20,000. indemnity to the college. The original charter, which had articulated the college's purpose of evangelizing Indians and training missionaries, was guaranteed. Ruling in favor of Dartmouth were Justices Marshall, Washington, Livingston, Johnson, and Story. Justice Duval was the lone dissenter.

One of the clear implications of the Dartmouth decision was that charters and contracts were to be considered inviolate, but there was also a strong assertion that colleges and schools were to be granted immunity from political changes within the electorate. The Supreme Court said, in effect, that the Constitution of the United States would protect the right of a college to consider its primary purpose of propagating religion without interference from dissenting political or religious factions and that it had the right to receive state tax funds for such purposes. Shortly after the decision was handed down, the legislature restored the funds to Dartmouth, allowing the enrollment to increase to 220 students by the next year.

End Notes

1. Moran, Gerald F. and Vinevskis, Maris, "The Puritan Family and Religion: A Critical Reappraisal," (Unpublished Paper, Newberry Library) 1980. p. 24
2. Butler, Vera M., *Education as Revealed by New England Newspapers Prior to 1850.* New York; Arno Press, 1969. p. 43
3. Greene, *Religion and the State,* p. 121
4. Walsh, Lorena S., "Till Death Us Do Part: Marriage and Family in Seventeenth Century Maryland," *The Chesapeake in the Seventeenth Century* (Tate and Ammerman, editors). Chapel Hill: Univ. of North Carolina Press, 1979. P. 148
5. Humphrey, *Nationalism and Religion,* p. 285.
6. The colonial colleges and their establishment were as follows:

College	Date	Denomination
Harvard	1636	Puritan
William and Mary	1693	Anglican

Yale	1701	Congregational
College of New Jersey	1746	Presbyterian
Dartmouth	1751	Society for the Propaga- of the Gospel
King's	1754	Anglican
College of Philadelphia	1755	
College of Rhode Island	1765	Baptists
Queen's	1770	Dutch Reformed

7. Humphrey, p. 306
8. Ibid., p. 314
9. For the most comprehensive defense of this thesis, see Lawrence Cremin's, *American Education: The Colonial Experience,* p. 265 & ff.
10. Cremin, p. 299
11. Ibid., p. 300
12. Butler, *Education as Revealed by New England Newspapers,* p. 495
13. Ibid., p. 286
14. Ibid., p. 22
15. Brown, Arlo A., *A History of Religious Education in Recent Times,* New York: The Abingdon Press. 1923. p. 38
16. Ibid., p. 37
17. Butler, p. 422
18. Webster intended to publish a three-book series, with the first part on spelling, the second on grammar, and the third on reading.
19. Butler, p. 417. By contrast, Thomas Dilworth's *A New Guide to the English Tongue* sold only 300,000 copies in the course of thirty years.
20. Letter, Webster to John Canfield, Jan. 6, 1783. Quoted in Cremin, pp. 568-9.
21. Webster, Noah, *An American Selection of Lessons in Reading and Speaking,* Fourth Edition, Hartford: Hudson and Goodwin, 1788. p. i.
22. Butler, p. 422
23. Ibid., p. 412
24. Ibid., p. 109
25. Morgan, *The Puritan Family,* p. 98
26. Constitution of Massachusetts— 1780, Chapter V. Butler reports in *Education as Revealed by New England Newspapers,* p. 30, that later in 1780 the number of Congregational ministers was raised to 15 and continued at that level until at least the 1850's.
27. Butler, pp. 366-9
28. Ibid., pp. 72-3

29. Ibid., p. 138
30. Ibid., pp. 24-7
31. Ibid., p. 70
32. *The Papers of Thomas Jefferson*, Vol. 10, pp. 462-3. The effort was unsuccessful, and it appears from correspondence that Jefferson's appeal was less than enthusiastic.
33. Butler, p. 351
34. Ibid., p. 355
35. Ibid., p. 356. It should be noted here that the fractions do not equal one whole, suggesting a problem in the newspaper's reporting. The newspaper account, edited by Butler, also stated that the balance was left in for accumulation purposes. The vote in legislature is reported as 103 in favor, with 90 opposed.
    Constitution of Connecticut—1818, Art. VIII, Sec. 2
37. Because this was reported on April 1, it can be assumed that this was an April Fools' joke, especially because of the longstanding objection of the democrats to Yale's established position.
38. *Connecticut Courant*, March 26, 1816. Quoted in Butler, p. 371
39. Constitution of Connecticut—1776, Par. 1
40. Butler, p. 81
41. *Journals of Congress*, Dec. 18, 1778
42. Butler, pp. 84-89

CHAPTER VI

Religious and Moral Leadership from Congress

On September 5, 1774, the Continental Congress first convened in Philadelphia to discuss the colonies' escalating troubles with England. The delegates were far from united on what course to follow, but one of their first official acts was to pass a Resolution, "That the Reverend Mr. Duche be desired to open the Congress, tomorrow morning with Prayers, at the Carpenter's Hall, at 9 o'clock." The next morning, Rev. Duche, an Anglican clergyman, "read several prayers in the established form, and read the Psalter for the seventh of September, which was the 35th and 36th Psalms."[1] In commenting on this first worship service in the halls of Congress, John Adams noted,

> I never saw a greater effect upon an audience. It seemed as if Heaven had ordered that Psalm to be read on that morning. After this, Mr. Duche, unexpectedly to everybody, struck out into an extemporary prayer, which filled the bosom of every man present.[2]

From the very first meeting, Congress had a chaplain and always recognized the Sabbath as a special day by adjourning and suspending all official business. The duties of the chaplain included opening each session with prayer, conducting funeral services, preparing and delivering sermons for days of fasting, prayer, humiliation, and thanksgiving, and a variety of other spiritual assignments. Particularly during the distressing days of the Revolutionary War, Congress designated special days for expressing dependence on God. On July 12, 1775, Congress proclaimed the next July 20 as a "day of public humiliation, fasting and prayer so that we may with united hearts and voices unfeignedly confess and deplore our many sins and offer up joint supplications."[3]

Congress did not limit itself, however, to a foxhole theology. During the war, four separate days of fasting and humiliation were designated, but there were also special times for thanksgiving and praise. December 18, 1777 and November 28, 1782 were observed as days of corporate gratitude for the successes of the colonial militia. Similar times of praise and rejoicing were proclaimed on December 11, 1783, after the peace was signed with England, and on November 26, 1789, when the Constitution was finally ratified. In making one of its earlier Prayer proclamations, Congress acknowledged that "it becomes all public Bodies, as well as private Persons, to reverence the Providence of God, and look up to him as the supreme Disposer of all Events," and recommended "to all the States, as soon as possible to appoint a Day of solemn Fasting and Humiliation, to implore of Almighty God the Forgiveness of the many Sins prevailing among all Ranks."[4]

There is little hint of denominational prejudice in the worship activities and proclamations of the Continental Congress, for most of the major religious groups were well represented among the delegates. The Presbyterians were represented by the notable Rev. Witherspoon, the Lutherans by Rev. Muhlenberg, and the Baptists by Reverends Manning and Ward. John and Samuel Adams were noted as Congregationalists, while the Anglicans were represented by Washington, Randolph, Duane, and Jay.[5] John Jay, who was later to distinguish himself as one of *The Federalist's* authors, was also very active in drafting the constitution of the Protestant Episcopal Church, and served on its standing Committee of Correspondence for many years. In a time of military urgency they had learned to tolerate and even respect each other, but such a spirit was restricted to those of the Protestant faith. During the war itself Congress provided Anglican, Presbyterian, and Congregational chaplains for the military companies, but extended little support to those of the Catholic faith. Congress further demonstrated its anti-Catholic bias when it enumerated the various acts of Parliament which were considered injurious to the colonies. In that litany of complaints, the denunciation of the Quebec Act was particularly vigorous because it permitted the establishment of the Catholic religion so close to American borders.[6] Toleration knew its bounds, for most of the delegates saw themselves not only as political leaders, but as spiritual guides to the new nation, the officially constituted leaders of American Protestantism.

Typical of the times and the denominations which they represented, Congress also took time to legislate on matters of morality. On November 28, 1775, Congress approved "Rules for the Regulation of the Navy," in which they mandated,

> If any shall be heard to swear, curse, or blaspheme the name of God, the Commander is strictly enjoined to punish them for every offense, by causing them to wear a wooden collar, or some other shameful badge or distinction, for so long time as he shall judge proper. If he be a commissioned officer, he shall forfeit one shilling for each offense, and a warrant or inferior officer six pence.[7]

In similar vein, on October 12, 1778, Congress adopted the following resolution:

> Whereas true religion and good morals are the only solid foundation of public liberty and happiness: Resolved, that it is hereby earnestly recommended to the several states, to take the most effectual measures for the . . . suppression of theatrical entertainments, horse racing, and such other diversions.[8]

But not all Congressional action met with glorious response or universal approbation. Since their earliest gatherings, Congress had displayed an interest in Indian missions, partially with an eye toward strengthening American influence among the various tribes, whose interests were also being catered by the British. On April 10, 1776, Captain White Eyes, a Delaware chief, was invited to address Congress and was appropriately introduced. After the formal courtesies were dispensed with, the President added, "We are pleased that the Delawares intend to embrace Christianity. We will send you, according to your desire, a minister and a schoolmaster, to instruct you in the principles of religion and other parts of useful knowledge."[9] Congress then proceeded to pass legislation authorizing the salaries of a minister and a blacksmith to be sent to the Delaware tribe. The response among the tribe, however, was negative, for the resolution did not specify that the pastor would be from the Moravian church. Without that assurance, the tribe instructed Chief White Eyes to reject the offer.

The war with England caused a variety of difficulties which came to Congressional attention and became objects of their concern. Students were prevented from studying in the mother country, and English ministers were deterred from filling colonial pulpits. In addition, the supply of King James Bibles was cut off, leaving no source for resupply as copies became worn, tattered, or lost. On October 26, 1780, Congress, amidst other pressing concerns, addressed the issue. In typical states-rights fashion, they passed a resolution recommending to the states "that they take proper measures to procure one or more new and correct editions of the Old and New Testaments" and "that such states regulate their printers by law so as to secure effectually the said books from being misprinted."[10]

Three months later, Robert Aitken of Philadelphia wrote to Congress, informing the members that he had completed a printing of the Bible and asking them for an official endorsement. Congress responded by appointing a committee consisting of Mr. Duane, Mr. McKeon, and Rev. Witherspoon to examine his work and to report back. The committee, in turn, sought the advice of Rev. Dr. White and Rev. Mr. Duffield, joint chaplains of the Congress at the time. The final response was that Congress "highly approved the pious and laudable undertaking of Mr. Aitken," commended him for "his care and accuracy in the execution of the work," and recommended his edition of the Bible to the inhabitants of the United States.[11]

From the very outset, Congress articulated a sense of religious authority and attempted in every possible way to construct a well-ordered society built on the convictions of Protestant Christianity. Most of the state constitutions limited civil office and voting privileges to Protestants, thus assuring a Reformation mentality in Congress. That mind-set took a poorly disguised turn, however, when the Papal Nuncio at Paris requested Ben Franklin to persuade Congress to jointly, with France, appoint a French superior for American Catholics. Franklin dutifully referred the request to Congress which rejected it spuriously with the explanation that such action was "purely spiritual" and outside "the jurisdiction and powers of Congress, who have no authority to permit or refuse it, these powers being reserved to the several states individually."[12]

A signal beneficiary of Congressional action was the church of the Moravian Brethren, which was extraordinarily successful in evangelizing the Indians. After the war was over and peace with England secured, Congress continued to demonstrate an interest in civilizing the Indians and promoting Christianity among them.

On at least three different occasions, May 20, 1785, July 27, 1787, and September 3, 1788, the records of Congress document the granting of lands to the Moravian Brethren for the purposes of propagating the gospel among the heathen. On the first request, the towns of Gnadenhutten, Schoenbrun, and Salem in Pennsylvania were set aside for this purpose. Some two years later, the Society initiated another request, with Congress responding by granting an additional 10,000 acres. Still unable to meet the demands of their unique calling, the Moravians requested even more land one year later and again met with favorable response. (For more detail, see "An Act of Congress," Appendix F).

The Northwest Ordinance of 1787

The conclusion of the war in 1783 did not leave the United States devoid of internal difficulties. The economy was in a shambles, with both Congress and the states printing almost worthless paper money with which to pay their staggering war debts. Families had been torn asunder by divided loyalties and also by battlefield casualties. Industries which had geared up for production of war materials suddenly found their shops idle. The most pressing problems of peace, however, were the displacement of unpaid troops returning from war and the need to govern the vast expanses of Western territory which had been won from Britain.

The millions of acres which comprised the territory west of the Demarcation Line had early proved to be more bane than blessing to the British. In order to secure the territory and to control the Indian inhabitants, England had found it necessary to raise taxes and to quarter troops on colonial soil. Their futile efforts at governance had finally culminated in the cries of "taxation without representation" and in the war of revolution. Rid finally of the albatross beyond the Alleghanies, numbers of Britishers smiled in derision as the Continental Congress set out to tame the frontier which was now theirs to govern.

In June, 1783, before the peace treaty with Britain was signed, George Washington and Alexander Hamilton began making suggestions to Congress concerning the governance of the Northwest Territory. Central to their plan was the reservation of 10% of the land for federal purposes. By holding out 10,000 acres of every 100,000, they reasoned, Congress could make payment to the soldiers, build forts, establish schools, and strengthen the fledgling navy. Rufus Putnam, in a separate petition to Congress, amended their plan by recommending the division of the entire territory into townships and reserving within each township 3040 acres for the ministry, schools, and a variety of other civic needs.[13]

Plagued by doubts concerning the extent of federal authority, the necessary legislation dragged through Congressional committees during 1783, 1784, and 1785. With pressure mounting from companies of unpaid militia, a new ordinance was finally reported out of Committee on April 14, 1785. Influenced heavily by Rufus Putnam, who served as lobbyist for the still disgruntled veterans, the law stipulated that, "There shall be reserved the central section of every township for the maintenance of public schools, and the section immediately adjoining for the support of religion, the profits arising therefrom in both instances to be applied forever according to the will of the majority of male residents of full age."[14] With a complex array of political pressures coming to bear on the issue, Congress passed the ordinance on May 20, 1785, but deleted the clause referring to religion.

Congress had passed an ordinance for the governance of territories northwest of the Ohio River, but major stumbling blocks effectively deterred them from enacting it. In the first place, individual states still had unsettled claims to much of that land, which needed to be resolved before the territory could be opened to settlers. An equally pressing problem was the attitude of the military petitioners from New England, who insisted that the governance of the Territory be structured along the lines of the Massachusetts and Connecticut constitutions. The question of setting apart lands in each township for education and religion was settled in their minds, for such values were deeply entrenched in New England society.

While state governments reluctantly were agreeing to cede their land claims to the federal government, Generals Rufus Putname and Benjamin Tupper were actively martialing support for their cause in the Northeast. Finally, on March 1, 1786, the Ohio Company was formed, with the stated purpose of buying tracts of land in the Ohio Territory. Among the directors was Rev. Manasseh Cutler, a Congregational minister and eloquent spokesman for the Puritan way of life. Although some of the Congressional delegates did not share his enthusiasm for religion, morality, and knowledge, his insistence that "the only conditions on which the company would purchase the lands" were the reservation of sections for schools and the ministry carried considerable weight.[15] George Washington endorsed the idea as "the most rational and practicable scheme which can be adopted."[16]

The Congress which met during the summer of 1787 was materially affected by the sessions of the Constitutional Convention. A number of the outstanding leaders from both North and South had been selected as delegates and were then busily engaged in Philadelphia. While the process of drafting the Constitution moved ahead in Philadephia, such delegates as Madison and Washington maintained a keen interest in various bills as they worked their way to the floor of Congress for final vote. The "Ordinance for the Government of the United States, Northwest of the River Ohio" was one of particular interest, for Washington had actively promoted it and Madison had served on the committee which drafted it. Framed very closely on the model of the Massachusetts Constitution, the law passed through second and third readings with only minor revisions in wording. Finally, in early July, 1787, the ordinance was taken up by the full Congress assembled in New York.

Intended "for the prevention of crime and injuries, and for the execution of process, criminal and civil,"[17] the law required that all of the lands north and west of the Ohio River be surveyed and divided into townships of 36 square miles each, with each township assuming the basic governmental functions for the people residing in it. Article one guaranteed religious toleration, specifying that "No person, demeaning himself in a peaceable and orderly manner, shall ever be molested on account of his mode of worship or religious sentiments."[18] The most far-reaching section, though, and the one most often quoted, was the third article, which began,

> Religion, morality and knowledge, being necessary to good government and the happiness of mankind, schools and the means of education shall forever be encouraged. The utmost good faith shall always be observed toward the Indians; their lands and property shall never be taken from them without their consent; and in their property, rights, and liberty, they never shall be invaded or disturbed.[19]

In the wholistic fashion which had characterized the governments of Massachusetts and Connecticut, Congress combined into one article their concerns for religion, knowledge, morality, civil government, and the welfare of the native peoples. Recognizing the legitimacy and necessity of such or ordinance, the vote on final passage was recorded as "unanimous," with all states present casting their votes in the affirmative. Amongst the individual delegates, Yates of New York was the only person to vote negative, but since voting under the Articles was done by states, his ballot did not influence the outcome. With Washington and Madison both favoring its passage, the delegates from Virginia cast a unanimous affirmative vote and were touted by some as being "the backbone and energy of the whole body."[20]

Ten days after Congress legislatively approved the Northwest Ordinance, they met again to vote on ennabling legislation which would define the terms of sale, for offers of purchase had already been received from the Ohio Company. On July 23, 1787, Congress approved "Powers to the Board of Treasury to Contract for the Sale of Western Territory," in which they stipulated various responsibilities and contractual obligations. Section 16 in each township was "to be given perpetually for the purposes contained in the said ordinance," defined there as being "religion, morality, and knowledge," the coterminous tasks of the school. Of equal import was the requirement that section 29 in each township must "be given perpetually for the purposes of religion," in order that churches might be established and pastors' salaries paid.[21] In addition, Congress stipulated that sections 8, 11, and 26 needed to be reserved for future disposition by Congress, and "not more than two complete townships be given perpetually for the purposes of an university." (For details, see Appendix E).

Within the next three months Congress negotiated the sale of millions of acres of land in what later was to become the states of Ohio, Indiana, and Illinois. The first contract was made with Manasseh Cutler and Winthrop Sargent on July 27, 1787. On behalf of the Ohio Company, these two men purchased 1,500,000 acres in the area of Ohio at a price of $1 per acre. With payment arranged as one-third down, one-third at the completion of the surveying, and the balance in six equal installments, Congress acquired not only much needed cash, but also the assurance of highly reputable developers.[22] On August 29, 1787, John Cleve Symmes of New Jersey petitioned Congress to sell another large tract of land and to draw up a contract "in all respects similar in form and matter, to the said grant made to Mssrs. Sargent and Cutler, differing only in quantity and place."[23] On October 2 the sale was approved in Congress and another large band of townships opened to westward expansion. A short time later, with homestead fever running high in the northern states, another petition was received in Congress, this time from Royal Flint and Jos. Parker, who wished to purchase 2,000,000 acres of what is now Indiana and an additional 1,000,000 acres in what is southern Illinois. When it was verified by the Board of Treasury that Flint and Parker's proposal was "founded on the same principles as have been agreed to"[24] in the earlier contracts, Congress approved the sale, thereby opening vast new territories and establishing state-financed religion as a prerequisite for settlement. No denominational or sectarian preferences were specified, with each township allowed to select their own teachers and pastors according to the will of the majority. Following on the heels of the Constitutional Convention, Congress implied that their action was consistent with the new constitution which had been drafted and thereby reaffirmed their common belief that "religion, morality, and knowledge" (were) necessary to good government and the happiness of mankind.

Washington's Leadership

As the ratification process drew to its favorable conclusion in 1789, it became apparent to most Americans that George Washington should become the first President of the United States, for he, more than anyone else, personified the republic. When he formally announced that he would consent to candidacy for election, ecclesiastical officers and synodical bodies promptly expressed their delight and that of their denominational members. The General Assembly of the Presbyterian Church incorporated into their Acts and Proceedings, and forwarded to Washington, an address which said in part,

> We are happy that God has inclined your heart to give yourself once more to the public. And we derive a favorable presage of the event from the zeal of all classes of the people, and their confidence in your virtues; as well as from the knowledge and dignity with which the federal councils are filled. But we derive a presage, even more flattering, from the piety of your character. We esteem it a peculiar hap-

piness to behold in our chief magistrate a steady, uniform, avowed friend of the Christian religion; . . . and who, in his private conduct, adorns the doctrines of the gospel of Christ; and on the most public and solemn occasions, devoutly acknowledges the government of Divine Providence.[25]

Other denominational pledges of support and approbation came from a variety of quarters, with the Coetus of the German Reformed church promising "to pray that it may please God to bless you in your person, in your family, and in your government, with all temporal and spiritual blessings in Christ Jesus."[26] The Roman Catholics in the United States, while reminding the President that they had not yet achieved equal rights of citizenship, warmly endorsed his selection and recommended his "preservation to the single care of Divine Providence."[27] From the Committee of the United Baptist Churches of Virginia came an address which reminded Washington of the deep-seated political divisions in his home state, as well as the "unusual strugglings of mind" which the Baptists had experienced. In a concluding paragraph of support, they acknowledged him as a "tried, trusty friend," and acknowledged that, "if religious liberty is rather insecure in the Constitution, the administration will certainly prevent all oppressions, for a Washington will preside."[28]

The new nation which unanimously elected George Washington as their first president was not disappointed. Eschewing the party politics and the rampant individualism which Jefferson so vigorously tried to initiate, Washington maintained a deliberate attitude of statesmanship which was intended to promote unity and avoid the divisiveness of party allegiance. In his first proclamation setting aside a national day of Thanksgiving, he called on all the people to devote themselves "to the service of that great and glorious Being who is the beneficent Author of all the good that was, that is or that will be . . ." and to beseech Him "to enable us all, whether in public or private stations . . . To promote the knowledge and practice of true religion and virtue."[29]

Later Developments

The deliberate and specific legislation to promote religion, morality, and knowledge, which Congress enacted on July 13, 1787, was not a one-time action to placate the Congregational zealots from New England. The Northwest Ordinance and its provisions for schools and the support of religion were deeply entrenched principles which later generations and other legislative bodies would follow.

When North Carolina ceded the territory of Tennessee to the United States in 1790, their legislature specifically stipulated in the act of cession that the inhabitants of the new state "shall enjoy all the privileges, benefits, and advantages set forth in the Ordinance of 1787." Furthermore, they stipulated that Congress "shall execute in a manner similar to that which they support in the territory west of the Ohio."[30] In 1800, Congress passed an act to divide the Northwest Territory into two separate governmental units and declared that "there shall be established within the said Territory a government in all respects similar to that provided by the ordinance of Congress"[31] on July 13, 1787. Two years later, in an act enabling Ohio to graduate from territorial status to statehood, Congress again made the clear stipulation that any constitution or laws enacted by Ohio might not be "repugnant to the ordinance of the thirteenth of July, one thousand seven hundred and eighty-seven."[32]

Sometime later, when conditions indicated the need for a university, the Ohio legislature reminded the people that, whereas Congress had "made grants of lands for the encouragement and support of a University, for schools, and for the purposes of Religion, . . . Therefore: Be it enacted by the General Assembly, That there be a University instituted and established . . . for the promotion of good education, piety, religion, and morality."[33] Within the charter that was drafted, the legislature further specified that the Board of Trustees should have the power "to let, lease, or cause to be improved, . . . the lots number sixteen, given by Congress for the use of schools, and the lots number twenty-nine, appropriated by Congress to the purposes of Religion,"[33] thereby retaining the practice of local control and avoiding the pitfall of a national establishment.

When the original ordinance was passed, during that historic summer of constitution-making, Congress had declared that sections 16 and 29 shall "be given perpetually" for the causes specified. Morally and ethically, subsequent legislative assemblies were obligated to perpetuate such enactments, especially since the legislation had no expiration date. Barring a ruling from the

Supreme Court that the ordinance was unconstitutional, for which no serious attempt was ever made, later Congresses were legally tied to a code which mandated the establishment of religion without designating any denomination as the exclusive beneficiary of tax benefits.

As the religious character of later assemblies fluctuated with the tenor of the times, more or less attention was focused on the specific demands instituted in 1787. In 1809, under James Madison's administration, Congress specified that "all the requirements"[34] of the Northwest Ordinance shall apply to the territory of Illinois. Eight years later, however, under the presidency of James Monroe, Congress proclaimed that the government of Mississippi should be both "republican" and "not repugnant to the principles of the ordinance."[35] Similar language was incorporated into the Enabling Act for Alabama (1819), but references to the Northwest Ordinance were politely omitted when the controversial case of Missouri came before them one year later. In 1836, when Wisconsin applied for statehood, and in 1848, when Oregon became a Territory, Congress again mandated that the peoples in those regions "shall be entitled to, and enjoy, all and singular, the rights, privileges, and advantages granted and secured to the people of the territory of the United States northwest of the river Ohio."[36]

In subsequent years, no particular reference to section 29 and the "purpose of Religion" can be found in the Enabling Acts for other states. In every piece of legislation, though, there was provision for setting aside section 16 in every township for the support of schools. Henceforth, congregations of church members would have to pass the collection plate if they wished to construct a house of worship or pay their pastor a salary. Reliance on tax monies and profits from land grants was terminated, for the public school had become the nation's officially established church.

End Notes

1. Humphrey, *Nationalism and Religion*, p. 410.
2. Ibid., p. 411.
3. *Journals of Congress*, July 12, 1775. Also quoted by Albert Menendez in "The President as Preacher," *Church and State*, Vol. 35, No. 5, May, 1982, p. 13.
4. *Journals of Congress*, Dec. 11, 1776.

5. Humphrey, *Nationalism and Religion*, p. 408.
6. For defense of this judgment, see Hilldrup, *The Life and Times of Edmund Pendleton*, p. 115.
7. *Journals of Congress*, Nov. 28, 1775, quoted also in Humphrey, pp. 424-5.
8. *Journals of Congress*, October 12, 1778.
9. Humphrey, p. 421.
10. Ibid., p. 428.
11. Ibid., p. 429.
12. Ibid., p. 432.
13. Barrett, Jay A., *Evolution of the Ordinance of 1787*, New York: G.P. Putnam's Sons, 1891, pp. 11-13.
14. Knight, G.W., *History and Management of Land Grants for Education in N.W. Territories*, New York: G.P. Putnam's Sons, 1885, p. 12.
15. Ibid., pp. 15-17. Quotation from p. 17.
16. Barrett, p. 14.
17. Preamble to the Northwest Ordinance, *Journals of Congress*, July 13, 1787.
18. Northwest Ordinance, Article the First.
19. Ibid., Article the Third.
20. Barrett, p. 78.
21. For the complete original text of this act, see the *Appendix*, Journals of Congress, July 23, 1787. The text is also included as Appendix E at the end of this book. Note here that the ordinances used the word "lot," whereas modern usage is "section." Both terms represent one square mile equalling 640 acres. The crops or profits from these sections were to be used to fund the causes designated.
22. *Appendix, Journals of Congress*, July 26, 1787.
23. Ibid., Aug. 29, 1787.
24. Ibid., October 18 and 22, 1787.
25. Humphrey, *Nationalism and Religion*, pp. 505-6.
26. Ibid., pp. 504-5.
27. Ibid., pp. 503-4.
28. Ibid., p. 507.
29. Presidential proclamation, October 3, 1789.
30. Poore, Vol. II, p. 1666.
31. Ibid., Vol. I, p. 434.
32. Enabling Act for Ohio—1802, in Poore, Vol. II, p. 1454.
33. "The Charter of American University in Ohio," contained in Taylor, Howard, *The Educational Significance of Early Federal Land Ordinances*, pp. 135-8.
33. Ibid., p. 137.

34. Poore, Vol. I, p. 435.
35. Enabling Act for Mississippi—1817, Sec. 4. In Poore, Vol. II, p. 1053.
36. "An Act establishing the Territorial gov't. of Wisconsin—1836," Sec. 12 (Poore, Vol. II, p. 2024) and "An Act to establish the territorial government of Oregon," Poore, Vol. II, p. 1489.

CHAPTER VII

The Unholy Alliance: Religion and Politics in Virginia 1775 to 1788

When Thomas Jefferson was elected President, after the most fierce and intense political election in American history, an exuberant celebration broke out among the parishioners of the Baptist church in Cheshire, Massachusetts. Pastor John Leland proposed to his congregation that they should celebrate this momentous victory by making for the new Chief Executive the largest cheese that the world had ever seen. After committees were appointed and plans approved, a special cider-press was outfitted, and the parishioners given their instructions.

The cheese-making party was festive and gay, the men and boys coming in their Sunday coats and clean shirt-collars, and the women donning their best gowns and ribbons. With all due solemnity, including prayer and hymn-singing, the cheese was put to press. After it was well dried, the 1600 pound cheese was loaded onto a sturdy sleigh for its three week journey to Washington.

On the morning of January 1, 1802, the Rev. John Leland made the formal presentation of the gift to an awed and delighted President. Later that morning, a number of Federalists went from the Capitol in coaches to pay their respects to the new President and "wait upon him, with the compliments of the season." After the customary pleasantries were dispensed with, Jefferson invited them to "the mammoth room to see the mammoth cheese." The Reverend Manasseh Cutler, newly elected to Congress from Massachusetts, viewed "this monument of human weakness and folly" with disgust and desire for an early termination to his viewing privileges.[1]

Later that same day, the ebullient President penned a reply to his political allies in the Danbury Baptist Association in Connecticut. Their earlier memorial of congratulation, coupled with the visit from his old friend John Leland and the receipt of such an extra-ordinary gift, prompted him to write,

> Believing with you that religion is a matter which lies solely between man and his God, that he owes account to none other for his faith or his worship, that the legislative powers of government reach actions only, and not opinions, I contemplate with sovereign reverence that act of the whole American people which declared that their legislature should "make no law respecting an establishment of religion, or prohibiting the free exercise thereof," thus building a wall of separation between church and State.[2]

One hundred and forty-five years later, in the 1947 Everson case, Justice Hugo Black revived Jefferson's political promise, making "the wall of separation" a permanent plank in American jurisprudence.[3] In numerous respects, this opinion signaled the final triumph for the alliance between the Baptists and the Deists which had been molded and nourished in Virginia from the early 1760's through the opening decade of the eighteenth century. To trace the roots, the character, and the strength of that unholy alliance is our purpose.

That the relationship between religion and politics in the early national period has not been adequately treated should be obvious to the knowledgeable historian. Rhys Isaac, in his sundry pieces, has directed his attention at what he calls "the evangelical revolt," but he has restricted himself severely to the sociological and moral dimensions of the conflict.[4]

The lack of clarity and insight into the relationship between politics and the church can be attributed to a number of factors. Sidney Mead has insisted for years that church membership during the Revolutionary era totalled no more than 7-8%. William Warren Sweet, writing much earlier than Mead, has stated that "in Virginia at the opening of the eighteenth century no more than one in twenty were church members, and the proportion was undoubtedly smaller in the other southern colonies."[5]

Figures such as the above either are built on or contribute to the widely held notion that the Great Awakening died of exhaustion somewhere on either side of 1750. That it may have simply changed places and continued with unsuspecting strength has not been sufficiently explored.

If we are to see more clearly the relationship between the

various churches and the state in the early national period, we must recognize that religion and politics are not pieces apart, but threads in the wholistic fabric of life.[6] When the Revolutionary War broke out, people did not stop living their lives in the social-political-religious web of interrelationships which typified their pre-1775 existence. Granted, some of them were jerked out of their routines by conscription of military service. Some of them, like Jefferson, were forced temporarily to leave the comforts of their homes and flee into the mountains for temporary safety. The vast majority of the populace, however, stayed at home, attended their churches, served as vestrymen or elders, were elected to synodical assemblies, raised their families, educated their children, and planted their crops. People like Rev. John Witherspoon, for example, not only helped to forge the Declaration of Independence, but he also preached frequently in the churches of his area and served as the president of the Presbyterian Synod of 1789.

This blending of life as one seamless fabric is illustrated clearly in the Delaware Constitution of 1776. Article 22 specifies,

> Every person who shall be chosen a member of either house, or appointed to any office or place of trust, before taking his seat, or entering upon the execution of his office, shall take the following oath, or affirmation if conscientiously scrupulous of taking an oath, to wit:

> I, (......), do profess faith in God the Father, and in Jesus Christ His only Son, and in the Holy Ghost, one God, blessed for evermore; and I do acknowledge the holy scriptures of the Old and New Testament to be given by divine inspiration.[7]

The National Context

Such constitutional requirements were not unusual in 1776 or 1786. Since nine of the thirteen colonies had established state churches when the Revolutionary War broke out, it is not to be expected that a series of somewhat unpopular military engagements would suddenly remove all the established religious practices or drastically alter the theological commitments so long held. The War was a Revolt against the King of England, not against God.

When the Continental Congress issued a call shortly after July 4, 1776, to all the newly independent states, requesting that they draw up constitutions for their continued operation, everyone except Rhode Island complied. The rest of the states, however, were more conventional and anxious to designate Christianity as the only acceptable religion. New Hampshire, Connecticut, New Jersey, the two Carolinas, and Georgia insisted on adherence to the Protestant faith. Pennsylvania and South carolina insisted on belief in the divine inspiration of the Bible, the reality of heaven and hell, and belief in one Triune God. Seven states, New Hampshire, Massachusetts, Connecticut, Maryland, South Carolina, Georgia, and Virginia chose to adhere to the practice of religious establishment.

At a time when most of the states adopted a policy of persistent conservatism and orthodoxy, Virginia seemed to assume a public posture of toleration and accommodation. Instead of stipulating an adherence to the Christian religion, as did the other states, Virginia constitutionally declared:

> That religion, or the duty which we owe to our Creator, and the manner of discharging it, can be directed only by reason and conviction, not by force or violence; and therefore all men are equally entitled to the free exercise of religion, according to the dictates of conscience.[8]

A first reading of Virginia politics after 1775 gives one the uneasy sensation of trying to capture an enigma in a pool of quicksilver or trying to determine the color of a chameleon in a quaking aspen. Edmund Randolph, James Madison, Patrick Henry, and Edmund Pendleton frequently took actions which appear to fluctuate 180 degrees on issues of religious establishment and toleration. Theirs was not a case of cognitive confusion, but rather one of survival in a political jungle in which religious persuasion was the most important ingredient.

Notable exceptions to this political inconsistency were Thomas Jefferson and Richard Henry Lee. Although the Deists comprised only a small handful of the total populace in either Virginia or the colonies as a whole, Jefferson as the most eminent Deist could rise to national prominence by 1776 and continue in a variety of distingushed offices until his retirement in 1808. To most orthodox church people, in 1776 and as late as 1800, Deism seemed "the major threat to organized religion."[9] Jefferson, although knowing the Scriptures well,[10] viewed the Bible as an error-filled product of misguided humans. In addition, he rejected the divinity of Christ and viewed the universe as under the control of natural forces unaffected by divine involvement.[11] Adhering strongly to the doctrine of free will, he argued that "the care of every man's soul belongs to himself . . . and God himself will not save men against their wills."[12]

The Rise of the Baptists

The Baptists who came to Virginia originated from three sources. In 1714 a small contingent had emigrated from England and settled in the extreme southeastern part of the state. Later, in the early 1740's, another handful had entered from Maryland and had started a settlement in the northwest. The third migration beginning in the 1750's, began in the New England states and continued for at least three decades.[13]

During the early part of the Great Awakening, the "Separate Baptist" cause surfaced significantly in Massachusetts. For a time the movement flourished there, with 125 Separate Baptist churches reported in 1754. Because of double taxation, highly restrictive laws, and various forms of harassment by the Massachusetts authorities, "only about a dozen remained by 1776."[14]

The first recorded migration of Separate Baptists from New England to Virginia occurred in 1754, when Pastor Shubal Stearns and his congregation moved to Opeckon in Berkeley County. Their settlement in that place was not satisfactory, however, so one year later they again packed their belongings and moved further south to Sandy Creek, North Carolina.[15]

It was not until after 1765 that the Baptists really began to flourish and grow in Virginia. In May, 1771, when the first meetings of the Separate Baptist Association were held in Orange County, 17 churches were represented, with a reported 1,335 adult members "now under care." By May, 1774 their figures had mushroomed to 51 and 3,954 respectively, with representatives coming from Albermarle, Culpeper, Hanover, Goochland, Spotsylvania, and numerous other countries both north and south of the James River. By 1775 they numbered from 15% to 20% of the total white population, often holding mass revival meetings with up to 5,000 people in attendance.[16]

The growth of the Baptist movement, both nationwide and particularly in Virginia, was one of the truly remarkable phenomena in the late colonial and early national period.

Virginia, although it was the last of the thirteen original colonies in which the Baptists gained a permanent footing, provided such a haven for them that some of their leaders could boast "a membership nearly, if not quite, as large as that of all the other colonies combined."[17]

The Legal Framework

The Baptist enlargement in Virginia was not without its complications and difficulties. By various acts of the Virginia Assembly and supporting legislation from England, the only legitimate, legally approved religious practice was that of the established Anglican church. Ever since 1705 it had been stipulated that,

> if a person brought up in the Christian religion denies the being of a God, or the Trinity, or asserts there are more gods than one, or denies the Christian religion to be true, or the scriptures to be of divine authority, he is punishable on the first offence by incapacity to hold any office or employment ecclesiastical, civil, or military; on the second by disability to sue, to take any gift or legacy, to be guardian, executor, or administrator, and by three years' imprisonment without bail.[18]

Other laws by which the purity of the Anglican faith might be kept unsullied by heresy were well known. Throughout the state taxes were assessed on all residents for the purchase of glebes and the annual support of churches, clergy, and the College of William and Mary.[19] Ever since 1662, no one was allowed to assume the office of minister unless he had received ordination from some bishop in England. Semple tells us,

> If any person without such ordination attempted to preach or perform the services of a minister, the Governor and the Council were empowered to suspend and silence them. If they refused to comply with the laws of the Crown, the colony had the right to deport them. Persons could be fined in either sterling or in tobacco if they failed to attend church every Sunday.[20]

Although the Baptists complied with most of the doctrinal specifications, they exemplified an extreme dissonance with the purpose, tenor, and practical application of the law. Knowing full well the legal prohibitions, "many a rude arbor and shaded grove and private dwelling, *unlicensed by the general court* as places for preaching, *yet used as such by the Baptist preachers,* became witnesses of the stand which they took."[21]

To complicate matters and further to incite the authorities, most of whom were well-bred gentry, "the evangelists appealed to the slaves, received them at the Lord's Supper, and refused in some instances to cooperate with the masters in keeping order among them. With half of the population black, the planters naturally lived in daily dread of a slave insurrection."[22]

Educational Qualifications

Within the established church there were numerous prerequisites for ordination as a minister of the gospel. Not only was there an examination as to confessional and doctrinal matters, but an advanced level of schooling was assumed. "Most of the ministers of the Establishment were men of classical and scientific education, patronized by men in power connected with great families, supported by competent salaries, and put into power by the strong arm of the civil power."[23]

In sharp contrast to them were the Baptist preachers who, in almost every respect, were the opposite of the Anglican clergy. Robert Semple, who was a trained lawyer and later served as a Baptist minister, was a notable exception. He described his colleagues in the clergy as follows:

> The Baptist preachers were without learning, without patronage, generally very poor, very plain in their dress, unrefined in their manners, and awkward in their address.[24]

The only college in the colonies of Baptist persuasion was the College of Rhode Island, founded and chartered by the Rev. James Manning in 1764. Within Virginia itself, of the forty-five educational institutions incorporated prior to 1810, not one of them had been chartered by a Baptist Association.[25] The Baptists, with very few exceptions, simply were not interested in education, with their historical attitudes ranging from passivity to total indifference, and open hostility.

With remarkable honesty and candor, Semple tells us that when James Read "first began to preach he was entirely illiterate, not knowing how to read or write. His wife became his instructor, and he soon acquired learning sufficient to enable him to read the Scriptures."[26]

Throughout the Great Awakening the primary focus of religion had shifted away from the centrality of sanctification to a sharp focus on the importance of conversion. This concentration was nowhere more marked and noticable than among the Baptists. To bring a person to conversion was the chief end of gospel preaching. The chief means to reaching such an end, consequently, was the revival meeting. Risjord describes one such gathering:

> A unique feature of this western revival was the cap meeting which lasted for days on end while thousands were exhorted by itinerant preachers, rotating on shifts, for twenty-four hours a day. Mass hysteria led individuals to collapse with the 'jerks,' bark like dogs after the Devil, or dance themselves into exhaustion. One meeting at Cane Ridge, Kentucky, in 1801 attracted more than 10,000 persons. Forty ministers conducted services day and night without intermission for a week; at one point more than a hundred 'sinners' were laid out unconscious in orderly rows.[27]

Theological Distinctives

On October 14, 1774, the Reverends James Manning and Isaac Backus led a Baptist delegation before the Continental Congress, at which time they presented a memorial, which read, in part,

> . . . but two things are worth contending for, —Religion and Liberty . . . . The free exercises of private judgment, and the unalienable rights of conscience, are of too high a rank and dignity to be submitted to the decrees of Councils, or the imperfect laws of fallible legislators . . . . Men unite in society, according to the great Mr. Locke, with an intention in every one the better to preserve himself, his liberty and property.

> The care of souls cannot belong to the civil magistrate, because his power consists only in outward force . . . . Religion is a concern between God and the soul with which no human authority can intermeddle.[28]

Appealing to the "great Mr. Locke" gave them a measure of respectability, but nothing could hide the Baptist's wholesale rejection of the covenant, infant baptism, and the magistrates' responsibility to protect and promote Biblical Christianity. At the October 1783 meeting of the Separate Baptist Association, the delegates had voted to adopt the Philadelphia Confession of Faith. But, true to their character as the apostles of independence, they had appended the following conditions to their acceptance:

1) every person is not bound to a strict observance or adherence to it;
2) it is not to be considered as equal or superior to the Scriptures in matters of faith and practice; and
3) the confession shall be subject to alterations and amendments whenever the General Committee of the Association shall see fit.[29]

Without due regard for the inconsistency of their actions, they practiced ecclesiastical discipline with a fervor untypical of other denominations. Between October, 1770 and May, 1771, for example, the Lower Church in Spotsylvania reported 103 conversions and adult baptisms, but also reported 57 persons "dismissed," 3 "excommunicated," and 3 "under censure." Their total membership "under care" was listed as 253.[30] The Spotsylvania church was not alone in such practices, for part of the agenda for the First Separate Baptist Association dealt with discipline matters. Among their decisions was one that ruled that "the doctrine of the non-eternity of hell-torments . . . was heretical, and all persons holding it ought to be purged out of their churches."[31]

Persecution

In reflecting back upon the years just described, Robert Semple, the officially designated Baptist historian, concluded,

> It should not excite great surprise that when the Baptists arose in Virginia with principles so antagonistic to the union of church and State, so clamorous for a regenerate church-membership, for the baptism of believers only, for independence in church government, and the voluntary principle in support of religion, they should have met with determined opposition, and that all the machinery of the law and the courts should have been employed to restrain and silence them.[32]

That the law was brought to bear on the illegal activities of the Baptists is well documented in the historical record. In some cases, especially during the war years, Quakers, Mennonites, and Methodists were imprisoned and in other ways harassed by the law, but their offenses were usually connected with their loyalist or Tory leanings and not with their mode of worship or their offenses against ecclesiastical regulations.[33]

The Baptists' sin can best be summed up as deliberate civil disobedience on all matters religious. In some counties the sheriffs hauled them to court on charges of disturbing the peace, holding night meetings beyond posted hours, failing to obtain licenses to preach, and being a public nuisance. One of those who felt compelled to uphold the law was Edmund Pendleton, the chief magistrate of Carolina County, later to be appointed as chief justice for the state. On one occasion, Pendleton brought in Lewis Craig, John Burruss, John Young, Edward Herndon, James Goodrich, and Bartholomew Chewning, "all of whom were arrested because they had no license to preach and were allegedly disturbing the peace . . ."[34]

In spite of such difficulties, the Baptists persisted. They were willing to endure abuse, suffering, loss of freedom, and humiliation, for theirs was, at least in their estimation, a holy cause. They were on a mission. They were at war with the enemy, identified as the Anglican-State of Virginia complex. As Semple later saw it,

> In the contest which ensued, . . . it is but simple justice to say that no other parties in Virginia, religious or political, saw so clearly as the *Separate Baptists* the stand which it was necessary to make, in order to secure perfect religious equality and freedom.[35]

The jails in many of the county seats, consequently, housed not only common criminals, but also varying numbers of Baptist preachers. One of the men who was incensed at such enforcement of the law was young James Madison. Schooled in both theology and law at Princeton, he had developed a sympathy for the revivalists as well as a commitment to Federalist ideology. Writing to a college classmate in 1774, he complained,

> . . . There are at this time in the adjacent county not less than five or six well-meaning men in close jail for publishing their religious sentiments, which, in the main, are very orthodox . . . . I have squabbled and scolded, abused and ridiculed, so long about it, to little purpose, that I am without common patience.[36]

In Albemarle County, located in the west central part of the state, there was another observer to all these proceedings. When his father passed away at an early age, the young intellectual not only inherited a large tobacco plantation, but his father's position as justice of the peace for Albermarle County. Assuming the office in 1767, shortly after the Baptist influx into the area, he had the responsibility of enforcing the laws of Virginia. There is no indication that he did. On the contrary, the brash young lawyer built a political base from which he was to vault rapidly from county to state and from thence to national office. Somehow endearing himself to the Baptist cause, he so enamoured them that in 1773 the Jeffersonton Baptist church in Culpeper County was named after him.[37] The young man's name, of course, was Thomas Jefferson.

The Political Arena

In an era when most of the Virginia gentry and the majority of the House of Burgesses remained loyal to the Anglican Church,[38] a few Enlightenment lawyers could hardly be expected to overturn the Establishment. The lawyers might make the speeches and grab all the headlines, but the impetus and the political power rested squarely in the Baptist Associations and constituency which by 1775 had come to dominate the central and southern parts of the state. To read the history of Baptists in Virginia is to read a litany of litigation against the state's government. At almost every meeting of their Associations or of the Baptist General committee, the primary business was that of applying political pressure on the General Assembly. The typical procedure, or ritual, to be followed was: 1) hear a report from the delegates to the last Assembly, 2) select a "political grievance" which was currently most offensive, 3) draft a petition, or memorial, or remonstrance outlining that grievance, 4) select one or more delegates to present their case, and 5) go home and wait for the next session.

Prior to 1771, the dissenters had rarely filed protests or complained of mistreatment. With the formalization of the Association meetings in that year, however, the petitions from Baptists became very frequent and very specific in their charges. Typical of them was the one presented by the Baptists of Lunenberg County on February 12, 1772. "They asserted that they were restricted in the exercise of their religion, their teachers imprisoned under various pretenses, and the benefits of the toleration act denied them. They requested that they might be treated with the same kind of indulgence as Quakers, Presbyterians, and other Protestants."[39] Among all the petitions presented between 1771 and 1775, not one asked for the abolition of the established church and not one protested the state taxation for the support of religion.[40]

By late 1774, however, the political climate began to change along with the ascending aspirations of the dissenters. The

Separate Baptist Association considered prospects of victory to be so favorable that "they began to entertain serious hopes, not only of obtaining liberty of conscience, but of actually overturning the Church Establishment. Petitions for this purpose were accordingly drawn and circulated with great industry.[41]

The State Constitution

On May 6, 1776, two months before the Continental Congress adopted their Declaration of Independence, a forty-five member constitutional convention began meeting in Williamsburg, Virginia.[42] By June 12 they had not only hammered out their famous Bill of Rights, but had also declared themselves to be a free and independent state, with a government based solely on their rights and not on the authority of the King of England.

When the first legislative session under the new constitution convened on October 7, 1776, the Assembly was greeted with a flood of petitions from every quarter. Since the constitution had not been submitted to the people for ratification, the Anglicans and Methodists howled in protest against the tenor of the Bill of Rights, especially Section 16, which declared that "religion . . . and the manner of discharging it" was simply a matter of individual conscience and not to be governed by the magistrates.[43] Equally unhappy were the Baptists, Presbyterians, Lutherans, and other dissenters who realized, belatedly, that the Anglican church was still established.

Because of the flood of petitions which had been received, on October 11 that Assembly appointed a newly created standing committee on religion. Jefferson was made a member, but not chairman. As soon as the committee met, they were handed a petition from Prince Edward County, requesting that, "without delay, all church establishments might be pulled down, and every tax upon conscience and private judgment abolished."[44] On October 16 an almost identical petition was received from another county. On October 22 similar petitions were received from Albemarle, Amherst, Buckingham, Culpeper, and Richmond Counties. Two days later the Presbyterians from Hanover County followed suit, with "more extensive arguments," and others still to follow.[45]

Later, when reflecting on this crisis, Jefferson commented, "These petitions of the dissenters brought on the severest contests in which I have ever been engaged."[46] "After desperate contests in that committee almost daily from the 11th of October to the 5th of December, we prevailed so far only as to repeal the laws which rendered criminal the maintenance of any religious opinions (other than those of the Episcopaleans), the forebearance of repairing to (Episcopal) church, or the exercise of any mode of worship."[47]

The opposition was adamant and ably led by the venerable Edmund Pendleton. On October 28 he received a petition from the Methodists, which was addressed "to the House," and not to the committee now dominated by Jefferson. Proclaiming clearly that the Methodists were a society in communion with the church of England, they pledged "that they would do all in their power to strengthen and support that church."[48] In support of that action, "a considerable number of the clergy of the established church" presented their memorial, also "to the House," in which they set forth the arguments for continuance.[49] By November 9 the entire House had become keenly interested in the disputes going on within the Committee on Religion. Unable to restrain themselves any longer, the House passed a resolution taking "all present and future petitions" away from the special committee and bringing them before the House as a committee of the whole. The alliance of Jefferson and the Baptists had lost, although winning a few minor concessions. The Church of England, in spite of the Revolution and the Declaration of Independence, had prevailed.

Beaten but undaunted, the Deist Baptist alliance kept chipping away at the foundations of the established church. "Too powerful to be slighted, and . . . too watchful to be cheated by an ineffectual sacrifice, . . . nothing less than a total overthrow of all ecclesiastical distinctions would satisfy their sanguine hopes."[50] In the war years that followed, both the General Assembly and the Baptist Associations kept on meeting, but the Assembly's interest, of necessity, focused on such things as the militia, finances, and battlefield successes. The Baptists, meanwhile, were faced with the prospect of continuing their civil disobedience or going out of business. Turning to Patrick Henry for advice, he counseled them to proceed with their worship services and marriage ceremonies, even if the law did not permit it. Proceeding illegally, he said, would be "the most certain method of obtaining" a change in the law.[51]

Jefferson apparently was undeterred by repeated defeats, for in 1779 he submitted to the legislature his famous Bill for Establishing Religious Freedom. It was quickly pigeonholed in the Assembly, but Jefferson had the political foresight to give a copy of it to his Baptist friends, who reviewed it carefully at their Association meeting in October. They then unanimously passed the following motion:

> On consideration of the bill establishing religious freedom, agreed: That the said bill, in our opinion, puts religious freedom upon its proper basis; prescribes the just limits of the power of the State, with regard to religion; and properly guards against partiality towards any religious denomination; we, therefore, heartily approve of the same, and wish it to pass into law.[52]

Then, true to form, they instructed their officers to have their motion printed, transmitted to the public, and inserted in the Gazettes. With the military war intensifying in Virginia, however, little headway was made on this issue during the next four years. When the revolution was finally over and peace restored, the Baptists redoubled their efforts. Temporarily shunting aside their radical individualism and independence, four different Associations combined in October, 1784, to organize the Baptist General Committee. This political arm of the Baptist Associations was to be composed of no more than four delegates from each Association, and was formed for the singular purpose of acting on "all the political grievances of the whole Baptist Society in Virginia. All petitions and memorials were to originate with the General Committee, thereby presenting a unified front."[53]

The General Assessment Bill

But the Baptists were not the only ones who had been politically active. When the Virginia Assembly convened in October, it was met "by a flood of petitions" calling for a return to state-supported religion, broadened now to include all denominations, with each church to share proportionately in the tax receipts. The Methodists, who had grown from 1166 to 14,998 members in the last ten years,[54] and the Presbyterians formed a solid phalanx with the Anglicans in support of the measures.[55] Even Patrick Henry, swayed by such sentiment, offered a resolution proposing a general assessment "for the support of the Christian religion," and argued strongly for it.[56]

But Jefferson and Madison, noting that "not a solitary opposing position lay on the table,"[57] were less than pleased. With Patrick Henry against them, and their Baptist constituency caught unprepared, they clearly needed to buy time. During the subsequent meetings it became apparent that the Anglican-Presbyterian-Methodist forces had a majority of votes. By a 47 to 38 vote, the House of Delegates passed an act incorporating the Protestant Episcopal Church, thereby protecting the property and privileges of the old established church.[58]

Amongst the associates of Madison and Jefferson strategy was planned whereby the general assessment bill might be defeated. Hopes for such defeat, they all agreed, must arise from the fears and suspicions of the general populace. It was decided, furthermore, that "identical petitions, from all parts of the state,"[59] would defeat the measure. Obviously, too, a petition was needed to incite the people. James Madison was chosen to write it, and soon produced his "Memorial and Remonstrance Against Religious Assessments." George Nicholas endorsed it exactly as written and got 150 freeholders to sign it in a single day. George Mason took a copy to Alexandria and got enough prints made for statewide distribution.

Madison's Memorial was a masterpiece of deceit. Beginning with quotations from Section 16 of the Bill of Rights and earlier Baptist memorials, he moved quickly into insinuations and falsehood designed to alarm the uninformed. The bill, he said, "violates that equality which ought to be the basis of every law." Appealing to their memories of imprisonment and beatings, he argued, "Instead of holding forth an asylum to the persecuted, it is itself a signal of persecution . . . Distant as it may be, in its present form, from the Inquisition, it differs from it only in degree." In addition, "it will have a like tendency to banish our Citizens," and "torrents of blood" would be spilled if it were enacted.[60]

Jefferson, Madison, Mason, and Nicholas, the co-conspirators in this religious warfare, were almost immediately successful. Cloaking their real intent in the complaint that this "bill is adverse to the diffusion of the light of Christianity,"[61] they were able to quickly raise a storm of protests. Circulated throughout the state, the "petitions rolled back upon Richmond like a crunching avalanche, each copy bearing a dozen to a hundred signatures."[62] Although the bill had passed its first reading in the House by a vote of 47 to 32, it was now clearly in trouble. In order to protect its intent, the measure was drastically altered so as to become a "provision for teachers of the Christian religion," but even that would not appease the aroused Baptists.[63] George Washington, whose support was also mustered in defense, "could see no harm in the bill . . . I am not among the number of those who are so alarmed at making men pay toward the support of that which they profess."[64]

On third reading, nevertheless, the bill was postponed for one year by a vote of 45 to 38. As soon as the vote was counted, the following resolution was moved and adopted:

> Resolved, that the engrossed bill establishing a provision for the teachers of the Christian religion, together with the names of the ayes and noes on the question of postponing the third reading of the said bill to the fourth Thursday in November next, be published in handbills, and twelve copies thereof delivered to each member of the General Assembly, to be distributed in their respective counties, . . .[65]

The Baptists were overjoyed at the turn of events and praised Madison's Memorial as a most distinguished piece. "For elegance of style, strength of reasoning, and purity of principle, it has, perhaps, seldom been equalled; certainly never surpassed by anything in the English language."[66] The General Committee, however, could not rest on its laurels or bask in the support of the Deists, for the bill was only postponed. Meeting in Powhatan County on August 13, 1785, the delegates urged every county which had not yet presented petitions to do so as soon as possible.

When the Assembly reconvened in October, 1785, the Baptist-Deist alliance had enough votes to assure passage, for the intensive petition drive had resulted in the defeat of some pro-assessment candidates, just as they had hoped. Calling the bill to a vote before its scheduled time, the Assembly defeated the bill by a slim margin of three votes.[67] With that accomplished, Jefferson's "Bill for Establishing Religious Freedom" was dug out of committee, where it had lain since 1779, and passed on December 17, 1785. Jefferson, who was the United States Minister to France at the time, received the news in Europe with exhileration. He promptly had copies printed in both French and English and distributed throughout France.[68]

Tempestuous, turbulent Virginia was not yet destined for peace and harmony. Much of the legislation which had given direction to religious affairs was still in the statute books. The victory which had been gained by the Baptists was only a close and temporary loss for the Episcopaleans, Methodists, and Presbyterians. The state was and would remain almost equally divided.

The Federal Constitution

During the years following the war it became increasingly apparent that the Articles of Confederation was not an adequate instrument for governing the affairs of the new nation. Domestic affairs were at a low ebb, with inadequate provision for solving the problems of worthless state currencies, huge war debts, an open rebellion in Western Massachusetts, and increasing interest in westward expansion. In foreign affairs, the fledgling nation soon realized that the world was a hostile place, not inclined to treat a new, rebellious nation with kindness and courtesy.

In the face of such difficulties, a call went out to the states for a constitutional convention, with delegates to be chosen from each state. Rhode Island, the stronghold of the new England Baptists, refused to comply and did not send any delegates. The convention met, nevertheless, with fifty-five delegates slated to begin their important task in Philadelphia on May 25, 1787.

Virginia's delegation was unevenly divided, with the balance tipped in favor of the anti-establishment, weak government camp. Elected to represent them were George Mason, Edmund Randolph, Patrick Henry, Richard Henry Lee, Thomas Nelson, and James Madison. Politics, however, is a strange business, for Henry, Nelson, and Lee refused to serve when the convention met.[69] Madison, too, became an enigma, for he not only sided strongly with the Federalists during the secret sessions of the convention, but also co-authored the Federalist Papers with John Jay and Alexander Hamilton under the pseudonym of Publius.

Representing the traditional establishment side of Virginia politics were John Blair, George Wythe, James McClurg, and George Washington, who was chosen quickly as president of the convention. As the proceedings dragged on for nearly four months, with detail after detail carefully hammered out, it became apparent that not all was harmony and peace. A number of the delegates walked out and returned to their homes. George Mason and Edmund Randolph stayed until the end of the convention, but refused to sign the constitution.[70]

In spite of such obstinacy amongst a number of delegates, the thirty-nine signers recommended the new constitution to Congress, who unanimously voted to transmit it to the states for their approval and ratification. But George Washington was apprehensive about the outcome from the start. Well before the Convention met, he had angrily expressed concern for the "thirst for power, and the *bantling, I had like to have said monster, for sovereignty*" which had taken such fast hold in some of the states.[71]

During the months that followed the Congressional action, the fate of the document was of almost constant concern and a prominent topic in much of Washington's correspondence. The Constitution, he said, was "now before the Judgment Seat . . . (and) its adversaries . . . probably will be most active, as the major part of them will . . . be governed by sinister and self-important motives." "It is highly probable that (their) reasons will be clothed in most terrific array for the purposes of alarming; some things are already addressed to the fears of the people."[72] The final outcome in his home state of Virginia was uncertain. With the area around Mt. Vernon endorsing it beyond his expectations, he correctly predicted that "the great opposition . . . will come from the Southern and Western Counties."[73]

Instead of ratifying the Constitution in the General Assembly during the fall of 1787, the delegates voted to call for a special ratifying convention to be held the next June. The key figure in arguing for the delay was that flamboyant orator, Patrick Henry. In response to his persistent demand that the Assembly had no authority to decide a federal matter, and that such power resided only in the people, the Assembly ordered that 5,000 copies of the Constitution be printed and dispersed by the members in their respective counties. Patrick Henry was delighted, for time was essential for oiling and gearing up the political machinery. But George Washington was not. The grand old statesman abhorred politics, sharing his loathings with a suddenly trustworthy Madison. After complaining about a falsified and misleading let-

THE UNHOLY ALLIANCE   115

ter from Richard Henry Lee to Governor Randolph, currently circulating around the state, Washington concluded, "The enemies to the Constitution leave no stone unturned to increase the opposition to it."

If the enemy was going to play a dirty game, the Federalists might have to resort to similar tactics. Edmund Randolph, they knew, had refused to sign the Constitution, not out of conviction, but out of political expediency. Randolph's home county was openly hostile, and his political career would reach a dead end if he openly favored a Federalist position. Such concerns, however, could be allayed if a high ranking appointment in the new national government were to be assured.[75]

The Baptists, meanwhile, called a special meeting for all state Associations to be held on March 7, 1788, in Goochland County. Six Associations responded, forming a temporary union which they called The United Baptist Churches of Christ in Virginia. The only way to guarantee the total separation of church and state was for the church to intensify its involvement in the state.

At the same meeting, the Baptists also laid plans for conducting a national correspondence campaign against the Constitution in states which had not yet ratified. Letters of correspondence were drawn up and sent to the various Baptist Associations. In addition, Mr. John Leland was commissioned to visit as many of the associations as time would allow.

The election process in Virginia was as heated and bitter as anything that tempestuous state had recently experienced. The contests were particularly fierce in Carolina, Hanover, Henrico, Orange, and Spotsylvania Counties, all of "which were full of dissenters, particularly of the Baptist faith."[76]

Orange County meanwhile, had grown suspicious of James Madison, who was reputedly (and actually) in New York campaigning in favor of the Constitution. Although Madison had filed for election, when he returned home he found that Rev. John Leland had been nominated to oppose him.[77] Madison knew he would be defeated unless he practiced the art of compromise, for the Baptist strength in Orange County "could not have been offset by the influence of the Episcopaleans, who favored the Constitution almost to a man."[78] Early on the day of the election, Madison arranged a meeting with John Leland and promised him certain concessions, which were to become apparent in the latter days of the convention. John Leland responded by withdrawing his name and Madison was elected.[79]

The election contest in Henrico County was just as tense. Patrick Henry had stumped the area and had also forayed into the western regions, trying to build a solid bloc of Baptists and other dissenters in opposition. Resorting to the strategy of alarm and fear which Washington had predicted, Henry told his audiences that ratification would bring about the loss of the Mississippi and the re-establishment of the Episcopal Church.

From all indications, though, the Federalists had emerged from the election with a slight majority. The counties north of the Rappahannock River, in the Shenandoah Valley, and in the Northwest had gone strongly federalist, while those between the Rappahannock and the James were evenly divided. South of the James River, from the Piedmont to the border with Tennessee, the vast majority of the victors were anti-federalists.

On June 1, 1788, the 170 delegates to the ratifying convention arrived in Richmond, prepared for high drama. The principals were clearly known, with Edmund Pendleton the acknowledged leader of the Federalists and Patrick Henry the leading spokesman for the anti-federalists. These two political heavy-weights had opposed each other in many important debates, "but none of their contests was to have a more profound influence upon posterity than the one they were about to engage in now."[80] Since Virginia was the largest and most populace state, and since eight states had already ratified the Constitution, the ninth state's decision was crucial.

In the election for a presiding officer, Pendleton was given a majority. In an attempt to allay the fears and worries of the weak government advocates, he gave an address that sounded strongly like the language and philosophy of the Enlightenment. The second speaker scheduled to have the floor was Governor Edmund Randolph. To almost everyone's surprise and the complete consernation of the anti-federalists, the governor came out strongly in favor. A promise of job security had produced a convert, which was nothing short of a political coup.

By twisting Randolph's arm, the federalists may have overplayed their hand and given new fuel to the fires of the demagogues. For twenty-three days Patrick Henry had them worried. Speaking two and three times a day, he appealed to the delegates' fears, passions, prejudices, and principles. Near the end of the convention, however, news came in that New Hampshire had ratified, thus assuring the operation of the federal government, and making all of the harangue in Richmond little more than an academic exercise.

On June 25, as the debates began to wear down, the opponents of the constitution moved that, prior to ratification, a bill of rights ought to be considered by the convention. The motion lost, 80 to 88. The drama should have played its last act, but, in the face of victory, and before the final vote, James Madison promised to present a list of amendments to the Congress as soon as possible. When the final vote was taken later that day, the count had changed only by 1, with 89 favoring ratification and 79 opposed.

The battle should have been over, but in the ring of Virginia politics, the potential knock-out punch was clothed with compromise. A new round in the contest between the dissenting revivalists and the staid establishment could instead begin.

Conclusion

In reading the record, as we have done, it is difficult to conclude that religion had atrophied to the point of national impotence at the time of the American Revolution. It would also be difficult and unwise to consider the research finished. Much work of the same type still remains to be done, not only in Virginia, but also in Rhode Island and North Carolina, where the Federal Constitution met even more strident opposition. Were their Baptist populations even more aggressive than those in Virginia? How does one, then, explain the reluctance in New York, Massachusetts, and New Hampshire, where the votes for ratification were also sharply divided?

In Baptist theology, emaciated as it was on the Virginia frontier, two basic beliefs stand out above all else. The first is the centrality or pre-eminence of conversion. Because conversion was all-important, any means and any methods, even illegal ones, must be employed to bring it about. Once accomplished, once salvation was guaranteed, nothing more needed to be done.

The second core belief of Baptist theology was that espousing the free will of the individual. Man's relationship to God was a totally individualistic one, a relationship that no one but the individual himself could ever dictate. The natural and not illogical conclusion was the total separation of church and state with all its attendant arguments. Their obviously inconsistent practice, then, of becoming so totally involved in the political process could be justified on the pragmatic grounds that the end justified the means.

Without the Baptists on their small farms in Albermarle County, Jefferson might very well have followed in the staid tradition of his Anglican father. And without the Baptists' memorials and petitions to copy and to tout as his own, Jefferson's speeches might have sounded as pedantic and dull as all the other ones which have long since been forgotten. All of that might have been, but in the cauldron of conflict, the young politician picked a winner and forged from that an unholy alliance which would some day make him the biggest cheese of all.

End Notes

1. Cutler, William P., ed., *Life, Journals, and Correspondence of Rev. Manassah Cutler*, Vol. 2. Cincinnati: Robert Clarke & Co., 1888, pp. 54-5. Other details were derived from Semple, Robert B., *A History of the Rise and Progress of the Baptists in Virginia*, Revised edition. Richmond: Pitt and Dickinson, Publishers, 1894, p. 208. Otto Lohrenz reported the cheese at 1,235 pounds, four feet in diameter, and a thickness of 17 inches. (*The Virginia Clergy and the American Revolution, 1774-1799*, Ph.D. Dissertation, Univ. of Michigan Microfilm, 1956), p. 261
2. Letter, Jefferson to Danbury Baptist Association, Jan. 1, 1802, *Works of Thomas Jefferson*, Vol. III, pp. 113-4.
3. Sorauf, *The Wall of Separation*, p. 19
4. See, for example, Isaac's "Evangelical Revolt: The Nature of the Baptists' Challenge to the Traditional Order" in Timothy Breen's *Shaping Southern Society*, pp. 247-265
5. Sweet, William Warren, *The Story of Religion in America*, p. 5
6. The outstanding source for this perspective on the early national period is Edward Frank Humphrey's *Nationalism and Religion in America 1774-1789* (Boston: Chipman Law Publishing Co.) 1924
7. Poore, Benjamin Perley, *Federal and State Constitutions, Colonial Charters*, Vol. I, p. 279

8. "Virginia Bill of Rights," Section 16. Quoted in Poore, *Federal and State Constitutions,* Vol. II, p. 1909
9. Risjord, *Forging the American Republic,* p. 239
10. "Notes on Religion," *The Writings of Thomas Jefferson,* Ford edition, Vol. II, p. 99
11. For a more complete analysis of Jefferson's theological views, see my *Christianity and Democracy,* The Craig Press, 1978, pp. 30-40
12. Jefferson, "Notes on Religion," op. cit., p. 99
13. Semple, *A History of the Rise and Progress of the Baptists in Virginia,* p. 11 (hereafter referred to as History of the Virginia Baptists).
14. McLoughlin, William G., "Isaac Backus and the Separation of Church and State in America," *American Historical Review,* LXXIII, June, 1968. p. 1396
15. Semple, p. 13
16. Isaac, Rhys, "Preachers and Patriots," *The American Revolution,* Northern Illinois University Press, 1976, p. 128
17. Semple, p. 5.
18. Jefferson, *Notes on the State of Virginia,* Torchbooks edition, New York: Harper and Row, 1964, pp. 151-2.
19. Hilldrup, *The Life and Times of Edmund Pendleton,* p. 203.
20. Semple, p. 480.
21. Ibid., p. 3.
22. Hilldrup, p. 92.
23. Semple, p. 43.
24. Ibid.
25. Bell, Sadie, *The Church, The State, and Education in Virginia,* Philadelphia: Univ. of Pennsylvania Press, 1930. p. 209.
26. Semple, p. 17.
27. Risjord, *Forging the American Republic,* p. 240.
28. Humphrey, *Nationalism and Religion,* p. 332.
29. Semple, pp. 92-3.
30. Ibid., p. 70.
31. Ibid., p. 79.
32. Ibid., p. 3.
33. Sweet, *The Story of Religion,* p. 185.
34. Hilldrup, *The Life and Times of Pendleton,* p. 91-2.
35. Semple, p. 3.
36. Letter, Madison to Bradford, Jan. 24, 1774. Quoted in Humphrey, *Nationalism and Religion,* p. 371.
37. Slaughter, *A History of St. Mark's Parish,* p. 41.
38. Hilldrup, p. 90; see also Risjord, *Forging the American Republic,* p. 66.

39. Hilldrup, p. 91.
40. Humphrey, p. 372. For a more detailed accounting and analysis of the various petitions and memorials, see Lohrenz, *The Virginia Clergy and the American Revolution*, pp. 251-403.
41. Semple, p. 43.
42. Poore, *Federal and State Constitutions*, Vol. II, p. 1908.
43. Humphrey, p. 377.
44. Hilldrup, p. 202.
45. Ibid., p. 203. Semple recounts the same debates on p. 51-2 of his *History*.
46. Jefferson, *The Papers of Thomas Jefferson*, Vol. 1, p. 526.
47. *Works of Jefferson*, Ford edition, Vol. 1, pp. 53-54. Also quoted in Humphrey, pp. 378-9.
48. Hilldrup, pp. 203-4.
49. Ibid., p. 204 — their arguments, as well as those of the Methodists, are summarized here.
50. Semple, p. 45.
51. Ibid., p. 89.
52. Op. cit.
53. Ibid., p. 94.
54. Humphrey, p. 169.
55. Brant, *The Fourth President, A Life of James Madison*, New York: The Bobbs-Merrill Co., 1970, p. 126.
56. Ibid.
57. Ibid.
58. Semple, p. 53. Note that the name change now became formalized.
59. Brant, p. 128.
60. James Madison, "A Memorial and Remonstrance," quoted in its entirety in Gaustad, Religious Issues, pp. 72-3.
61. Ibid.
62. Brant, p. 129.
63. Semple, p. 52. See also: Humphrey, pp. 392-402, and Brant, p. 127.
64. Humphrey, p. 402.
65. Semple, p. 52.
66. Ibid.
67. Humphrey, pp. 401-2.
68. Ibid., p. 404.
69. In addition to the three from Virginia who refused to attend, there were five such from Maryland, two from North Carolina, and one from Connecticut. Virginia was entitled to ten delegates because it had the largest population. Patrick Henry excused himself by claiming "that he smelled a rat."

70. Letter, Washington to the Secretary for Foreign Affairs, March 10, 1787, *Writings of Washington,* Vol. 29, p. 175.
72. Letter, Washington to Henry Knox, October 15, 1787, *Writings of Washington,* Vol. 29, p. 288.
73. Letter, Washington to David Humphrey, October 10, 1787, op. cit., p. 287.
74. Letter, Washington to James Madison, Dec. 7, 1787, op. cit., pp. 331-4.
75. Risjord, *Forging the American Republic,* p. 215.
76. Hilldrup, p. 282.
77. Humphrey, p. 471. See also Hilldrup, p. 281.
78. Hilldrup, p. 282.
79. Ibid., p. 281. See also Humphrey, p. 471, and Scott, *History of Orange County, Va.*, p. 188.
80. Hilldrup, p. 283.

CHAPTER VIII

The Constitution of the United States and Separation of Church & State

Constitutional interpretation has a long history in the United States, a history that began as soon as the ink was dry on the signatures of the framers, September 17, 1787. The Constitution, ratified and implemented, has been a flexible framework for both people and laws in the two centuries since them. Constitutional interpretation is a highly developed, if enduringly controversial, art which is pursued according to varying theories. John Hart Ely frames the problem this way:

> A long-standing dispute in constitutional theory has gone under different names at different times, but today's terminology seems as helpful as any. Today we are likely to call the contending sides "interpretivism" and "noninterpretivism"—the former indicating that judges deciding constitutional issues should confine themselves to enforcing norms that are stated or clearly implicit in the written Constitution, the latter the contrary view that courts should go beyond that set of references and enforce norms that cannot be discovered within the four corners of the document.
>
> ... What distinguishes interpretivism from its opposite is its insistence that the work of the political branches is to be invalidated only in accord with an inference whose starting point, whose underlying premise is fairly discoverable in the Constitution.[1]

This discussion will proceed on the assumption that interpretivism should be preferred rather than its opposite. It also assumes the wisdom Ely ascribes to taking account of what the founders meant to do. But note the balanced tone:

> It would be a mistake—albeit an understandable one in light of the excesses one witnesses at the other extreme—to dismiss "the intent of the framers" as beside any relevant point. Something that wasn't ratified

can't be part of our Constitution, and sometimes in order to know what was ratified we need to know what was intended . . . . To frame the issue thus, however, is to bring to the fore what seems invariably to get lost in excursions into the intent of the framers, *namely that the most important datum bearing on what was intended is the constitutional language itself* . . . The debates (or other contemporary sources) can serve the "dictionary function" of resolving ambiguities as (for example,) in the natural born citizen case, but that function fulfilled, the critical record of what was meant to be proposed and ratified is what was proposed and ratified.[2]

The Constitution and the work of the framers is much remarked about. A scholar whose prodigious efforts have established the standard works of this century on the Convention,[3] was also a keen commentator. Max Farrand argued that the compelling feature of the Constitution was its simplicity and practical character. It was a document everyone could understand and it was a solution to the weaknesses of the Articles of Confederation. "The substance of the argument which prevailed was: Reform is necessary; the new constitution proposes remedies with which all are familiar; and if the government does not work well, provision is made for changes at any time and to any extent."[4] Moreover, he adds, "Planned to meet certain immediate needs and modified to suit the exegencies of the situation, it was floated on a wave of commercial prosperity, and it had been adapted by an ingenious political people to meet the changing requirements of a century and a quarter."[5]

From the beginning, constitution-making was a political process. It was carried out by politically chosen men who had great personal stakes in the society of their time. The nation had won independence, but its civil affairs were not in good order. Shays's Rebellion had frightened most men of affairs. Government under the Articles of Confederation was awkward, fragile and ineffective. Greater centralization of power was needed, but the individualism of the times would not tolerate anything approaching unitary government, much less, monarchy. Confederation had to be turned into a union of strength, but not tyranny.

At its founding American society was pluralistic. Then as now rural interests were contrary to urban ones. Debtors were opposed to creditors. Southern agriculture depended upon slaves but Northern enterprise did not. Diverse religious sects were spread across the land. A variety of tongues were spoken and accents differed greatly. Frontiersmen confronted problems markedly different than those in Boston, Philadelphia and Charleston. The small states harbored different fears about union than did the large ones.

If the American Constitution was founded on a theory, it was pluralistic theory. The evidence for that is mostly after the fact rather than before. But the primary draftsman at the Convention, James Madison, crystalized his perceptions of what was done there six weeks after its adjournment in a letter to Jefferson. A "simple democracy, or a pure republic" could only work in a small, homogeneous society—a hypothetical one at that. Certainly that was not an apt description of the new nation. Like all civilized societies, America was marked by distinctions of property, religion, and attachment to leading individuals.

> If, then, there must be different interests and parties in society, and a majority, when united by a common interest or passion, cannot be restrained from oppressing the minority, what remedy can be found in a republican government where the majority must ultimately decide, but that of giving such an extent to its sphere that no common interest or passion will be likely to unite a majority of the whole number in an unjust pursuit? In a large society, the people are broken into so many interests and parties that a common sentiment is less likely to be felt, and the requisite concert less likely to be formed by a majority of the whole. The same security seems requisite for the civil as for the religious rights of individuals. If the same sect form a majority and have the power, other sects will be sure to be depressed. *Divide et impera* (divide and conquer), the reprobated axiom of tyranny, is, under certain qualifications, the only policy by which a republic can be administered on just principles.[6]

The result of this pluralistic thinking was the establishment of a representative government which could act on all the people directly, rather than simply through the states, within the limits of power granted by the Constitution. The legislature, executive and courts were separate in structure, but with overlapping powers. The states and the people were understood to have discretion in matters not assigned to the national government. As Ely notes, "the original Constitution was principally, indeed I would say overwhelmingly, dedicated to concerns of process and structure and not to the identification and preservation of specific and substantive values,"[7] although one value that was countenanced was slavery. But references to it (Art. 1, Sec. 2; Art. 1, Sec. 9; Art. 4, Sec. 2; and Art. 5) were carefully crafted not to express the concept explicitly.

The primary purpose of this chapter is to focus on the proceedings of the Convention and its ratification to see what light may be shed upon the meaning of religious disestablishment and free exercise. How and to what extent were these concepts dealt with in the Convention? Why were they dealt with in the Bill of Rights? How should the First Amendments be understood with regard to religion? To what extent were the politics of religion in the country generalized into the Bill of Rights? My attention is specific to the matter of religion, but it is intended to respect the content of pluralism within which the issue came to expression.

The Convention: Disestablishment and Religious Freedom

Religion, per se, was not an issue in the Convention.[8] There were only four particulars in which religion obtained significant mention.

Substantively it was a part of the question of oaths of office for public officials, but that matter did not even come up until August 20, 1787, less than a month before the Convention's end. After the great compromise between the large and small states, a "committee of detail" drafted a document with 23 articles for review, approval, and polishing by the membership. These were taken up by the Convention on August 6 and were the object of careful debate for five weeks. The committee of detail draft on the oath provided:

> The members of the Legislatures, and the Executive and Judicial offices of the United States, and of the several states, shall be bound by oath to support this Constitution.[9]

By August 20th, when the Convention was plodding through Article VII, Charles Pinckney, from South Carolina, submitted numerous proposals to be referred to the committee of detail. Included was the item, "No religious test or qualification shall ever be annexed to any oath of office under the authority of the U.S."[10] His proposals were referred without debate.

Article XX was not taken up in debate until late in the day

on August 30. After the word "oath" was added "or affirmation." Pinckney moved to add, "but no religious test shall ever be required as qualification to any office or public trust under the authority of the U. States." One member, Roger Sherman from Connecticut, "thought it unnecessary, the prevailing liberality being a sufficient security agst. such tests,"[11] according to Madison. However, the proposal then passed unanimously, and it remained in subsequent versions of the Constitution.

The notion that religion should be a province beyond the reach of the national government was not expressed in the so-called Virginia Plan, which was offered to the Convention on Tuesday, May 29. By that time the Convention had only gotten started, and had established its rules of procedure. Governor Randolph, the formal leader of the Virginia delegation, made a lengthy speech followed by the fifteen resolutions of that plan which had been prepared by the Virginians. According to Farrand, "Internal evidence shows much of Madison's handiwork informing these resolutions . . ."[12] It had been anticipated that Virginia would have a proposal and it was expected that the proposal would become the focus of debate and counterproposals. However, late in that day's session Charles Pinckney of South Carolina, apparently only in behalf of himself, offered his own complete draft of a constitution. The hour was late, and Pinckney was not afforded the chance to speak in behalf of his plan. The *Journal* and Madison's *Notes* agree that Pinckney's plan was simply referred to the committee of the whole.

The Pinckney plan did not displace the Virginia Plan. Subsequent conflict and compromises were in relation to the Virginia Plan. But for present purposes mention must be made that in the Pinckney plan, as subsequently published with the *Journal* of the Convention, there was a provision on religious freedom:

> The Legislature of the United States shall pass no Law on the subject of Religion, nor touching or abridging the Liberty of the Press . . . .[13]

However, subsequent scholarship traced out by Farrand indicated that Pinckney's actual draft was a much less elaborate document than the one published with the *Journal*. The Farrand reconstruction does not include the religious and press freedoms statement quoted above.[14] What may be said more certainly is that there was an absence of discussion during the Convention concerning any constitutional provision for disestablishment or religious freedom.

Perhaps a certain sense of the Convention with regard to religion may be inferred from the Franklin motion for prayers in the Convention. Madison records that on June 28, Dr. Franklin complained about the "small progress" of the Convention, and asked, "how has it happened, Sir, that we have not hitherto once thought of humbly applying to the Father of lights to illuminate our understandings?" Citing the success of previous prayers "in this room" during the war with Britain, and making biblical references, he concluded by saying:

> I therefore beg leave to move—that hence forth prayers imploring the assistance of Heaven, and its blessings on our deliberations, be held in this Assembly every morning before we proceed to business, and that one or more of the Clergy in this City be requested to officiate in that service—[15]

Even this motion did not obtain the support of a majority. The responses were that public attention to this might bring blame, it would let people know of dissention within the Convention, there were no funds for this, and the like. "After several unsuccessful attempts for silently postponing the matter of adjourning, the adjournment was at length carried, without any vote on the motion." Farrand's footnote records a notation on the manuscript for Franklin's speech: "The Convention, except three or four persons, thought Prayers unnecessary."[16]

Finally, mention should be made of a provision that was not included in the Constitution. On August 18, while the Constitution was being refined, Madison submitted a series of specific powers for the legislature, including the power to establish a University. Charles Pinckney offered a different list including one to "establish seminaries for the promotion of literature and the arts and sciences."[17] On September 12, when the Committee of style reported, neither of these provisions were in the draft. On September 14, as the Convention toiled through the language concerning the powers of Congress, Madison and Charles Pinckney together proposed a power—

> "to establish an University, in which no preferences or distinctions should be allowed on account of religion."

Debate was brief. Wilson, from Pennsylvania, supported the motion, but Gouverneur Morris, also from Pennsylvania, said it was unnecessary, and the motion was defeated with six states against, four in favor, and one divided.[18]

This examination of the records fits well with the more encompassing comments of Clinton Rossiter. In his description of the Convention members he says:

> Although it had its share of strenuous Christians . . . , the gathering at Philadelphia was largely made up of men in whom the old fires were under control or had even flickered out. Most were nominally members of one of the traditional churches in their part of the country . . . and most were men who could take their religion or leave it alone . . . . The Convention of 1787 was highly rationalistic and even secular in spirit.[19]

Intentionally or not, the matters of religious establishment and religious freedom were not dealt with at length by the Convention. Its most definitive action was to bar any religious test from preventing a person from public office at any level.

Religion and the Bill of Rights in the States

Convention delegates were familiar with the notion of a Bill of Rights. Some state constitutions had one, most notably the Virginia Constitution of 1776. But the matter did not come up in the Convention until September 12. During a discussion of juries in civil court cases, Mason of Virginia

> . . . wished the plan had been prefaced with a Bill of Rights, and would second a Motion if made for the purpose—It would give great quiet to the people; and with the aid of the State declarations, a bill might be prepared in a few hours.[20]

But the proposal was quickly voted down with ten states opposed and none in favor. The members were anxious to be done with their work in Philadelphia.

However, the absence of a Bill of Rights quickly obtained much more attention when the proposed Constitution was made public. Rossiter observes that four decisions of the Convention drew fire in every state—and at the top of the list was the decision not to include a Bill of Rights.[21] This concern became so commonplace, it gave even some friends of the Constitution something negative to say about it without the need to in any way condemn the substance of the proposal.

When the Convention transmitted its product to Congress,

ten Convention delegates hurried to New York to resume their positions as members of Congress. Thirty-three Congressmen voted to transmit the proposed Constitution to the States, "in order to be submitted to a Convention of Delegates chosen in each state, by the people thereof . . . ."²² So the states elected their own Conventions to review the proposed Constitution, in the manner recommended by the Philadelphia convention.

Propagandizing for and against the proposed Constitution began immediately. George Mason, the Convention member who asked for a Bill of Rights, wrote objections which were widely disseminated. The first sentence said:

> There is no declaration of rights: and the laws of the general government being paramount to the laws and constitutions of the several states, the declarations of rights, in the separate states, are no security."²³

Responses were prompt, stating that no Bill of Rights was necessary because the national government had no power but those expressly assigned in the Constitution. One respondent answered,

> To have inserted in this cons(t)itution a bill of rights for the states, would suppose them to derive and hold their rights from the federal government, when the reverse is the case.²⁴

However, such arguments were not persuasive, and the demands for a Bill of Rights were insistent. Delegates to state conventions took up the task of specifying powers the national government had and did not have, as well as what the states could and could not do *apart* from what was already in the proposed Constitution.

Mention should be made that records of the debates in the state conventions are not complete. None exist for Delaware, New Jersey, and Georgia, but they ratified the Constitution unanimously and promptly without urging any amendments. Pennsylvania was early, but divided, and defeated a bill of rights proposed by a minority in its convention. However, the minority composed a document with 15 proposed amendments which were exemplary for the other state conventions. The first is as follows:

> The rights of conscience shall be held inviolable, and neither the legislative, executive nor judicial powers of the United States shall have the authority to alter, abrogate or infringe any part of the constitutions of the several States, which provide for the preservation of liberty in matters of religion.²⁵

However, there was no exposition of what such an amendment would mean. Pennsylvania never had an established church, but other states certainly did. Would a state constitutional provision that established a religion or church be safe from abrogation by Congress had this language been adopted? No answer can be given. This language was rejected in Pennsylvania.

Connecticut ratified the Constitution. Its fragmentary record reveals one Oliver Wolcott, who did "not believe that the United States would ever be disposed to establish one religious sect, and lay all others under legal liabilities."[26] Certainly his understanding of this issue was that establishment had to do with selecting a specific denomination, but as he understood American pluralism of the time, accompanied by the contemporary knowledge and liberty then prevalent, he was content with an unamended Constitution.

Massachusetts, the home of the Puritans, made constitutional provision in the Massachusetts Declaration of Rights of 1780 for religious establishment. That had been part of a larger issue of state constitutionalism. A proposed state constitution from the legislature had failed to win popular approval in 1778. Some towns formulated "declarations" on that proposed constitution calling for a bill of rights.[27] The subsequent Declaration of Rights, adopted in 1780, gave the legislature authority to tax "for the institution of the public worship of God, and for the support and maintenance of public protestant teachers of piety, religion and morality, in all cases where such provision shall not be made voluntarily." But it also provided that "no subordination of any one sect or denomination shall ever be established by law."[28]

Despite having labored long over the establishment and religious freedom article during state constitution making, there is not much evidence of those concerns in the Massachusetts debates. On January 19, 1788, delegate Singletary, apparently concerned about the absence of religious test for office, is recorded as follows:

> The Hon. Mr. Singletary thought we were giving up all our privileges, as there was no provision that men in power should have any *religion*; and though he hoped to see Christians, yet by the Constitution, a Papist, or an Infidel, was as eligible as they."[29]

No one picked up on Singletary's implied religious preference.

The subject came up again on January 30, 1788, in comments by Dr. Jarvis. Concerning the absence of any religious test,

> ... several gentlemen urged that it was a departure from the principles of our forefathers, who came here for the preservation of their religion; and that it would admit deists, atheists, etc., into the general government.... Gentlemen on the other side applauded the liberality of the clause ....[30]

Col. Jones (of Bristol) favored a requirement that rulers "believe in God or Christ," but a very generous argument opposing a religious test was made by Rev. Mr. Shute, who argued that a religious test "would be attended with injurious consequences to some individuals, with no advantage to the *whole*." He said further,

> Far from limiting my charity and confidence to men of my own denomination in religion, I suppose, and I believe, sir, that there are worthy characters among men of every denomination — among the Quakers, the Baptists, the Church of England, the Papists; and even among those who have no other guide, in the way to virtue and heaven, than the dictates of natural religion.[31]

When Col. Jones persisted, another proponent of the proposed Constitution was Rev. Mr. Payson, who insisted that religious belief was a matter of conscience, and that a religious test for office would be a "great blemish" in the Constitution.[32] On February 4, Rev. Mr. Backus also spoke against any religious test for office, arguing that "the imposing of religious tests hath been the greatest engine of tyranny in the world." Applauding the Constitution, he argued, "But it is almost certain that no such way of worship can be established without any religious test."[33]

The Massachusetts ratification is noted for the fact that it was the first accompanied by amendments which the Convention requested to be made to the Constitution.[34] Nine were requested. The first was to reserve all the powers not expressly delegated to Congress to the States. There was, however, no action on establishment or free exercise of religion. It is noteworthy that on the final vote in the Massachusetts convention on the Constitution, its passage was close: 187 to 168. Among the membership, seventeen members were recorded with the title, "Rev." Of those 17, three opposed and 14 favored. Levy observes that, "No person in the state convention or in antiratificationists tracts alluded to an establishment of religion. This would be an astonishing fact, considering the opposition within the state to the establishment there existing, *unless there was an undisputed understanding that Congress had no power over religion.*"[35]

Records of action in Maryland are fragmentary. The Constitution was endorsed emphatically by a vote of 63 to 11. Although the convention adopted no amendments, during its proceedings many were considered. In fact, 13 were adopted in committee. Another 15 were not. In the latter group was this proposal:

> 12. That there be no national religion established by law; but that all persons be equally entitled to protection of their religious liberty.[36]

The most popular item in the former group was this:

> 1. That Congress shall exercise no power but what is expressly delegated by this Constitution.[37]

Despite consideration of these ideas, internal politics led to the decision that no proposed amendments would be made. Maryland's state constitution allowed religious establishment and permitted its legislature to tax "for the support of the Christian religion;" it specified as a test of office holders "a declaration of a belief in the Christian religion." Maryland's action should be understood as action by a Federalist majority to pass the proposed Constitution which would have no authority to intervene with national authority on the arrangements of the states with regard to denominations and sects of the Christian religion.

South Carolina took the consideration of the proposed Constitution so seriously it was literally considered twice. First, in January, 1788, it was thoroughly reviewed in the state House of Representatives in three days of debate. The notes of the first exchange are brief. Member Arthur Simkins asked "whether Congress had a right to interfere in religion." Charles Cotesworth Pinckney, previoulsy a Convention delegate, answered, "they have no power at all and explained this point to Mr. Simkin's satisfaction."[38] The next day Patrick Calhoun, from the same constituency as Simkins, raised the same point, which was followed by a lengthy objection from a third member from that constituency, James Lincoln. Lincoln emphasized "a total silence with regard to the liberty of the press," and concluded by asking "why was not this Constitution ushered in with a bill of rights? Are the people to have no rights?" Again C.C. Pinckney responded with the standard Federalist answer. "The general government has no powers but what are expressly granted to it; it therefore has no power to take away the liberty of the press . . . . For the same reason, we had no bill of rights inserted in our Constitution . . . ." He then went on to point out that the South Carolinian delegation to the Convention "weighed particularly" against a bill of rights the fact that, "Such bills generally begin with declaring that all men are by nature free. Now, we should make that declaration with a very bad grace, when a large part of our property consists in men who are actually born slaves."[39] The legislature than voted unanimously to refer the proposal to a state convention.

The convention convened the next May. Its records are more brief than those for legislative consideration. The bill of rights question was raised again, but without specific concern about religion. The proposed constitution was approved by a two to one margin. The ratification message contained several resolutions on the meaning of the constitution and future amendments, including an addition to the religious test provision: add the word "other." It would read, "but no other religious test shall ever be required . . . ."

South Carolina's action on the national Constitution should be understood along side of its actions within the state. In March, 1778, the state General Assembly formulated a state constitution. Article 38, the longest of the document, stated that "The Christian Protestant religion shall be deemed . . . the established religion of this State." To participate in this establishment congregations would have to assent to five standards in the Constitution. Moreover, ministers were required to subscribe to a detailed declaration as well, to assure their orthodoxy as Protestant Christians.[40]

New Hampshire's state bill of rights, adopted in 1783, provided for religious establishment as well as free exercise. Its debates on the Constitution were lost, but it ratified the document, recommending twelve amendments. The essentials of the 10th Amendment came first. Near the end of the list was, "Congress shall make no Laws touching Religion, or to infringe the rights of Conscience."[41]

The New York convention occurred at the same time as the one in Virginia (whose politics was discussed in Chapter 7). It was a political donnybrook in which Hamilton and Jay, publicists for the Constitution, fought vigorously. Antifederalists included concern about protection from a religious establishment by the national government,[42] which was not allowed in New York under its state constitution of 1777. The state constitution had, in fact, disestablished the Church of England, and provided for "free exercise and enjoyment of religious profession and worship, without discrimination or preference . . ."[43] The records of the debates on recommended amendments in the ratifying convention are sketchy. However, its ratifying document contained a series of statements of right that "cannot be abridged or violated." One was as follows:

> That the People have an equal, natural and unalienable right, freely and peaceably to Exercise their Religion according to the dictates of Conscience, and that no Religious Sect or Society ought to be favoured or established by Law in preference to others.[44]

North Carolina actually refused to ratify the new Constitution because of the lack of a Bill of Rights. Its state declaration of rights, formed in 1776, was silent on establishment, but allowed the "right to worship Almighty God" according to conscience.[45] Debate on the Constitution did concern both establishment and free exercise. One delegate expected a religious establishment, preferred Episcopal, and feared that without a religious test, "pagans, deists and Mahametans might obtain office among us, and that the senators and representatives might all be pagans."[46] Fears were expressed about the Pope, Jews, and heathens from the eastern hemisphere. Governor Johnston responded by reciting the religious heterogeneity of the states, and mistakenly argued that there were "but two or three states where there is the least chance of establishing any particular religion." Therefore he inferred that there were no grounds to fear "that any one religion shall be exclusively established."[47] Ratification with amendments was defeated in North Carolina. It then adopted a Declaration of Rights for consideration by Congress which had as its final article one declaring the "unalienable right to the free exercise of religion" and "that no particular religious sect or society ought to be favored or established by law in preference to others." These declarations, with 26 proposed amendments, were transmitted to Congress.[48]

The legislature of Rhode Island did not call a Convention until a good deal later. Thus it is appropriate to assess sentiments at the time that political questions had to go to the new Congress, which could be organized now that eleven states had actually adopted the Constitution. Five inferences may be made. (1) The Constitution would have to be amended with a Bill of Rights. (2) One broad amendment would limit the national government to its delegated powers. (3) Several freedoms would need to be specified. One in particular would concern the right to religious freedom in worship and conscience. (4) The establishments of religion in the states were acknowledged and unopposed. (5) Of those concerned about religious establishment, the fear was of national establishment of a particular sect or religious denomination.

In retrospect it is plausible to suggest that a national establishment something on the order of South Carolina's might have been popularly acceptable and feasible throughout the states. While many leading people were chary of any particular denomination or sect, the South Carolina criteria would have allowed privileged status for all the major Protestant denominations—Presbyterians, Congregationalists, Episcopals, Methodists, Baptists. However, no ecumenical religious coalition emerged to give positive substance to constitutional action. The religiously pluralistic states only agreed on the necessity of a free exercise provision. In the more homogeneous states, the preservation of particular state religious establishments could be assumed to be protected by an amendment that would limit the national government to its delegated powers. There was never any public consideration of what would have seemed a far-fetched idea—that a Constitutional prohibition of establishment would erect a wall of separation between orthodox Protestant churches and the Republic or the republican states. (For a chronology of Ratification, see Appendix G).

Framing the Religion Clauses of the First Amendment in Congress

Eleven states, having adopted the Constitution, now sent their quotas of Members to the House and Senate of Congress, and, of course, George Washington was President. Of the members of the philadelphia Convention, many of whom were active in the state ratifying conventions, nineteen now became members of Congress.[49] Most of them accepted the idea that it was their responsibility to amend the Constitution and establish the freedoms so often referred to as a bill of rights. However, this would be no mean task. It is estimated that the states proposed 210 amendments.[50] The "gun behind the door" was a proposition to call a second constitutional convention to do the job—a notion not welcome among Federalists who believed that the general government had come a long way in less than three years.

Madison took the lead in the amending process. As a congressional candidate he had sought to dispell reports that he opposed amendments. Rather, he argued that Congress should propose changes, "providing additional guards in favour of liberty."[51] After Congress convened, Madison initiated proposals which were sent to committee, debated, amended, sent to the Senate, amended further, revised by a conference committee, and finally adopted as a conference report. Madison was involved at every stage except consideration in the Senate. The various versions of the religious amendment are given below with fragments of the debate. It must be recalled, however, that there was a broad range of issues under consideration; the give and take with regard to religion occurred within a larger context.

Madison's first formulation was part of a series of changes to the body of the Constitution. He proposed that revisions would be inserted at various points in the Constitution, beginning with the Prologue. Stated in nine points, they covered a wide range of proposals. Point four contained ten major provisions, all of which was to be placed in Article 1, Section 9, between clauses 3 and 4. The first provision was:

> The civil rights of none shall be abridged on account of religious belief or worship, nor shall any national religion be established, nor shall the full and equal rights of conscience be in any manner, or on any pretext, infringed.[52]

Article 1 is the legislative article. Section 8 assigned Congress its powers. Section 9 listed the forbidden actions. Presumably this placement of the above amendment would be a bar on Congressional infringements. Further, Madison proposed that in Section 10, which contained prohibitions on states, this addition:

> No State shall violate the equal rights of conscience, or the freedom of the press; or the trial by jury in criminal cases.[53]

Referred first to a committee of the whole, then to a select committee, action was not rapid. When formed, the select committee consisted of eleven members, one from each state, and Madison was one of the members. The select committee was to consider not only Madison's proposals, but all those that had been sent to Congress by the states. A week later the select committee had its report ready, but it lay on the table until Thursday, August 13. The report was taken up in the Committee of the whole, section by section. On Saturday, August 15, attention focused on the proposal, "no religion shall be established by law, nor shall the equal rights of conscience be infringed." This would be in Article 1, Section 9, between paragraphs two and three.

Debate was broadranging, but does not necessarily clarify the meaning.

> Mr. Madison said, he apprehended the meaning of the words to be, that Congress should not establish a religion, and enforce the legal observation of it by law, nor compel men to worship God in any manner contrary to their conscience.[54]

One member feared that such would endanger existing state establishments. Madison was willing to insert the word "national" before "religion," but that aroused a whole different genre of concerns. Substitute language then passed: "Congress shall make no laws touching religion, or infringing the rights of conscience."

After treatment in the Committee of the Whole, the House took up the Committee's report. But Roger Sherman objected to the amendments as supplementary language to be interspersed throughout the Constitution. He wanted the amendments appended to the Constitution, and this proposal carried with a two-thirds vote. The House then returned to the amendments. On Thursday, August 20, the religion amendment was altered so as to read,

> Congress shall make no law establishing religion, or to prevent the free exercise thereof, or to infringe the rights of conscience.[55]

and in this form it was adopted. In like manner, the House accumulated a list of seventeen amendments which were approved by two-thirds of its members, and these were sent to the Senate.

The Senate took up the House amendments seriatim. On the religion article, the Senate Journal records:

The first motion to amend this article was by striking out these words: "Religion, or prohibiting the free exercise thereof," and inserting these words: "One religious sect or society in preference to others." This motion was negatived. A motion for reconsideration then prevailed, and it was moved to strike out the third article all together; but this motion was decided in the negative. An unsuccessful attempt was then made to adopt, as a substitute for the third article, the following: "Congress shall not make any law infringing the rights of conscience, or establishing any religious sect or society." The question was then taken on the adoption of the third article, as it came from the House of Representatives, when it was decided in the negative. Finally the words, "Nor shall the rights of conscience be infringed," were stricken out; and, in this form, the article was agreed to.[56]

A week later the Senate amended the article and combined it with the one following:

> Congress shall make no law establishing articles of faith, or a mode of worship, or prohibiting the free exercise of religion, or abridging the freedom of speech, or the press, or the right of the people peaceably to assemble, and petition to the government for the redress of grievances.[57]

The House received a request for concurrence from the Senate on the amendments as the Senate had made them. The House agreed with some, but not all, and requested a committee of conference. Madison was one of the three House conferees.[58] After doing their work, the conferees reported to their respective chambers. Madison brought a proposal back to the House which recast the language of the religion amendment again:

> Congress shall make no law respecting an establishment of religion, or prohibiting the free exercise thereof; or abridging the freedom of speech . . .

On September 25 the Senate concurred with the actions of the House.

Historical records of debates in the states to ratify the amendments are practically nonexistent. Congress recommended twelve. Two were not approved by the states. North Carolina, Rhode Island, and Vermont acted on the amendments, but Connecticut, Georgia, and Massachusetts did not do so officially until 1939. Ratification became official on December 15, 1791, when Virginia approved.[59]

Religion, "Separation" and the Intent of the Framers

The Constitution was formed through a long, represenational process. It is not fair to try to put in an unambiguous statement what was the "intent of the framers." Different ones had different intentions. It is difficult even to crisply sum up Madison's intentions about religion and separation in the Constitution because he formulated his proposals out of a personal conception of good government, with a regard for what would satisfy constituents, sensitive to what could pass under given political circumstances, and mindful that accommodation in one area could obtain advantage in another. Constitution making was always a political process and Madison, for one, was significantly involved at every stage.

Many framers were enamored of natural law and viewed people as inheritors of unalienable rights. The compact which allowed government, they believed, should minimize the potential for government to abuse those rights. But experience under the Articles of Confederation and in the states led different framers to conflicting conclusions about the relative importance of what, and how firmly, provisions had to be put into the Constitution. Framers obviously differed about how to state the freedoms in which they believed—speech, press, religious expression, participation in politics, conscience.

Religion was especially difficult to deal with constitutionally because, while freedom had to be assured, existing establishments had to be protected. If these two concepts might be ultimately contradictory, the contradiction would have to be compromised. The first solution—to only bar religious test for public holders—was insufficient. The arguments for a Bill of Rights precluded ignoring religion. However, because free exercise and establishment both needed protection, religion usually was dealt with separately from the other matters of liberty.

Sherman convinced his colleagues that, Madison not withstanding, the amendments should not be inserted into the various sections of the Constitution. Thus the amendment now known as the First is very specifically limited by its beginning: "Congress shall make no law . . . ." It is noteworthy that "Congress shall make no law . . . abridging" speech, press, assembly, and petitioning. It is true to the language to infer that Congress *could* pass laws to enlarge these freedoms.[60]

But religion needed special treatment, different from the other freedoms. Religious freedom was commonly exercised in worship; in modes of action that exceeded speech, press, assembly and petitioning. At the same time, in varying legal formulation, establishments in several states had to be protected. Disestablishment of state arrangements with churches was not politically feasible. To the contrary, a frontal attack on state establishments could have endangered the whole Constitution. At the same time fears were easily aroused in major denominations and sects lest any one become established for the whole nation. For leaders "in whom the old fires . . . had . . . flickered out," such as Madison, Washington, and Jefferson, the notion that mainline, Protestant denominations might ally themselves to obtain some kind of establishment was clearly threatening.

The result was an amendment by which Congress has no power for making a national establishment, broad or narrow, and no power to deal with an establishment in or by any state. Certainly Congress had no power to make laws prohibiting free exercise. But the language does not forbid Congress to make laws to enlarge free exercise or to protect free exercise from prohibitions by the states.

How should the word "respecting," as in "respecting an establishment of religion" be understood? The usage in 1789 is the same as in our day; it is the equivalent of *concerning, about, and regarding*. It was not used in the sense of *honoring*. No specific attention was given in the debates to this choice of words. It only appears in the final version. Clearly, however, those who had to that time preserved establishments in the states, who were represented in Congress, and who would be in the amendment ratifying processes, could not endorse an asymetical amendment. An asymetical amendment would disallow Congress from *honoring* and establishment, while allowing Congress to *dishonor* an establishment. Such a reading of the amendment simply does not fit the facts of how it was developed. That word is best understood as *about* or *concerning*.

So the First Amendment, as written and adopted, is entirely clear about establishment. Congress shall make no law concerning an establishment of religion. What the states shall or shall not do on the matter of establishment would be up to them. Moreover, Congress could not prohibit free exercise. It could assist free exercise. The first amendment is open to the interpretation that Congress could prohibit the states from prohibiting free exercise. But if and when that gray area would lead Congress to actions against state establishment, Congress would have to give way. The first amendment absolutely forbids Congressional enactment about any such state establishment.

The interpretivism and, indeed, the noninterpretivism of the Constitution which had taken place in the years since 1790 has rendered quite a different meaning from the words of the First Amendment that are justified by history. But that is a story that goes beyond this chapter.

End Notes

1. John Hart Ely, *Democracy and Distrust: A Theory of Judicial Review*. (Cambridge: Harvard University Press, 1980), pp. 1,2.
2. Ely, *Democracy and Distrust*, pp. 16 and 17; emphasis by Ely.
3. Max Farrand (ed.), *Records of the Federal Convention of 1787*. Revised Edition (New Haven: Yale University Press, 1966). Published in four volumes, subsequent references will be to this edition, cited as Farrand, *Records*, followed by the volume and page numbers.
4. Max Farrand, *The Framing of the Constitution of the United States*. (New Haven: Yale University Press, 1913), pp. 207 and 208.
5. Farrand, *The Framing*, p. 210.
6. Madison to Jefferson, who was then in Paris, October 24, 1787. With the letter, Madison enclosed a copy of the then unratified Constitution. Commentators note how the perspectives expressed in this letter foreshadow the arguments made later in The Federalist, No. 10. Reprinted in *The Annals of America* Volume 3 (Chicago: Encyclopedia Britannica, Inc., 1968), pp. 145-149: quotation on p. 149. For an earlier rendition of these ideas, see Madison's notes of his own address to the Convention on June 6. See Farrand, *Records*, Vol. 1, p. 134-36.
7. Ely, *Democracy and Distrust*, p. 92.
8. Farrand, *Records*, Vol. 4, contains a general index of 105 pages covering all the relevant documents. There are only a few references for "religious liberty" and "religious test." The same is true of Elliot's index of the Conventions. See Jonathon Elliott,

Debates in the Several State Conventions on the Adoption of the Fedeal Constitution Second edition, 1836 (New York: Burt Franklin; Research and Source Works Series 109, from the edition of 1888). Five volumes; see Vol. 5, p. 632. Cited hereafter as Elliot, *Debates* by volume and page.

9. Farrand, *Records,* Vol. 2, p. 188. This was Art. XX, although it was mistakenly printed as Art. XIX in the Convention's documents. See Farrand, *Records*, Vol. 2, p. 181.
10. Ibid., p. 342.
11. Ibid., p. 468.
12. Farrand, *The Framing,* p. 68.
13. Farrand, *Records*, Vol. 3, p. 599.
14. Ibid., pp. 605-609. See also the discussion on pages 601-604.
15. Ibid., Vol. 1, pp. 451-52.
16. Ibid., p. 452 and 452n.
17. Ibid., Vol. 2, p. 325.
18. Ibid., Vol. 2, p. 616.
19. Clinton Rossiter, *1787: The Grand Convention.* (New York: The Macmillan Company, 1966), pp. 147-148.
20. Farrand, *Records,* Vol. 2, p. 587-88.
21. Rossiter, *1787*, p. 284. The others, in Rossiter's order, are: too powerful a chief executive, an aristocratic upper house, and the narrow scale of representation in the lower house.
22. Elliot, *Debates*, Vol. 1, p. 319.
23. Reprinted in Bernard Schwartz, *The Bill of Rights: A Documentary History* (New York: Chelsea House Publishers in association with McGraw Hill Book Co., 1971), p. 444. Published in two volumes, pagination is continous. Here and future references are by page.
24. Schwartz, *The Bill* p. 461. The respondent is Oliver Ellsworth, Convention delegate and later, Cheif Justice of the U.S. supreme Court.
25. Ibid., p. 658.
26. Elliot, *Debates*, Vol. II, p. 202.
27. See the "Essex Result," in Schwartz, *The Bill*, pp. 344ff. See also the earlier discussions in Chapter 14.
28. Article III in the Declaration of Rights; Schwartz, *The Bill*, pp. 340-41.
29. Elliot, *Debates*, Vol. 2, p. 44.
30. Ibid., p. 118.
31. Ibid., pp. 118-9.
32. Ibid., p. 120.
33. Ibid., pp. 148-9.

34. See Schwartz, *The Bill*, pp. 674, ff.
35. Leonard W. Levy, *Judgments: Essays on American Constitutional History*. (Chicago: Quadrangle Books, 1972), p. 175. Emphasis added.
36. Elliot, *Debates*, Vol. 2, p. 553.
37. Ibid., p. 550.
38. Ibid., Vol. 4, p. 300.
39. Ibid., pp. 312-316.
40. See Schwartz, *The Bill*, especially pp. 333-335. The five standards are as follows: (1) That there is one eternal God, and a future state of rewards and punishments. (2) That God is publicly to be worshipped. (3) That the Christian religion is the true religion. (4) That the holy scriptures of the Old and New Testaments are of divine inspiration, and are the rule of faith and practice. (5) That it is lawful and the duty of every man being thereunto called by those that govern, to bear witness to the truth.
41. Schwartz, *The Bill*, p. 761.
42. See Tredwell, in Elliot, *Debates*, Vol. 2, 399.
43. Schwartz, *The Bill*, pp. 311-312. Quotation from p. 312.
44. Ibid., p. 912.
45. Ibid., p. 287.
46. Elliot, *Debates*, Vol. 4, p. 192.
47. Ibid., p. 199.
48. Schwartz, *The Bill*, p. 968.
49. In the Senate: Langdon, Strong, Ellsworth, Johnson, King, Paterson, Robert Morris, Read, Bassett, Butler and Few—actually half the Senate Membership. In the House: Gilman, Sherman, Clymer, Fitzsimmons, Carroll, Baldwin, Gerry and, of course, Madison. See Rossiter, *1787*, p. 301.
50. Schwartz, *The Bill*, p. 983.
51. Madison to George Eve, January 2, 1789. Reprinted in Schwartz, *The Bill*, pp. 996-7.
52. Schwartz, *The Bill*, p. 1026.
53. Ibid., p. 1027.
54. Ibid., p. 1088.
55. Ibid., p. 1126.
56. From the Senate Journal, reprinted in Schwartz, *The Bill*, p. 1148.
57. Schwartz, *The Bill*, p. 1153.
58. With Madison were Sherman and Vining. Senate conferees were Oliver Ellsworth, Charles Carroll, and William Paterson. Madison, Sherman, Ellsworth, and Paterson all had been Convention delegates.
59. Schwartz, *The Bill*, p. 1172.

60. It may be argued further that Madison and others intended that Congress and the other branches could prevent the states from abridging these freedoms. See William Winslow Crosskey, *Politics and the Constitution in the History of the United States* (Chicago: University of Chicago Press, 1953), Vol. 2, pp. 1049-1082.

CHAPTER IX

The Presidential Election of 1800: Thomas Jefferson's Second Revolution?

For many Americans, images and recollections about Jefferson are hazy. Pictured as robust and handsome on the nickel, he is usually remembered as the draftsman of the Declaration of Independence, Washington's appointee as Secretary of State and the third President of the United States, but after that his accomplishments are a bit vague to the memories of most. Still, his image is a positive one. His name was in the news recently because an enterprising political writer published a new ranking of 38 Presidents by 49 present day scholars and biographers. Jefferson rated fifth place, after Lincoln, Washington, F. Roosevelt and T. Roosevelt.[1]

However, to contemporary scholars, as well as to people of his own time, Jefferson is and was an enigmatic figure. After 20 years of scholarship and more than 1500 published pages focused on Jefferson, Merrill Peterson wrote:

> (My earlier book) suggested that the historical Jefferson could never be truly discovered. The point strikes me even more forcibly now after more years of research and reflection. Jefferson became so much a part of the nation's ongoing search for itself, so deeply implicated in the whole epic of American democracy, that succeeding generations were unable to see him clearly and objectively.
>
> . . . the biographer must also contend with the obstacle of the man himself. He was so closely identified with the first half century of the nation's history that the human figure fades into the events massed around it. His life exhibited seemingly bewildering conflicts and contradictions and it is not easy to resolve these elements in the flow of experience . . . . Although he left to posterity a vast corpus of papers, private and public, his personality remains elusive. Of all his great

contemporaries Jefferson is perhaps the least self-revealing and the hardest to sound to the depths of his being. It is a mortifying confession but he remains for me, finally, an impenetrable man.²

Thus, the events of Jefferson's life, and the political implications that accompanied those events, are kaleidoscopic. With each change of vantage point, they present a different image. Although Jefferson was a man of action in various positions of authority—Virginia governor, Member of the Continental Congress, emissary to France, Secretary of State, Vice President, President—he was more significantly a man of ideas. He wrote voluminously, and he was the intellectual father of Jeffersonian Republicanism. But the ambiguity of his ideology frequently made subsequent actions and ideas vulnerable to the charge that he was inconsistent; if inconsistent, insincere; if insincere, scheming; if scheming, deceptive. The shades of approval and disapproval for his ideas varied hugely during his lifetime. Some of the other leading figures of his day consistently supported or opposed him, while others responded differently at different times. It is in this context of ambiguity that the question of Jefferson's "revolution of 1800" is set.

Jefferson did refer to the revolution of 1800 in correspondence of his later years.³ Certainly one of the dramatized issues of the contest between John Adams and Thomas Jefferson was their differences over religion. The *Gazette of the United States,* a Federalist paper from Philadelphia, often cruelly critical of Jefferson, framed the election contest in these terms:

THE GRAND QUESTION STATED

At the present solemn moment the only question to be asked by every American, laying his hand on his heart, is "Shall I continue in allegiance to

GOD—AND A RELIGIOUS PRESIDENT;
or impiously declare for
JEFFERSON—AND NO GOD!!!⁴

Jefferson's well known epitaph, chosen for his own tombstone, was "Author of the Declaration of Independence, of the Statute of Virginia for Religious Freedom, and Father of the University of Virginia." In none of these accomplishments did the orthodoxy of major Christian churches have a place. The Declaration was remarkably secular; the Virginia statute was arguably to obtain liberation from religious orthodoxy, and the University of Virginia was to displace the eminence of William and Mary, the Episcopal college of the previous establishment (Jefferson's own alma mater).

This chapter focuses upon religion as an issue in the election contest of 1800. Could it in any sense be viewed as a national referendum on whether or not to erect a wall of separation between the Church and State? Did the election constitute a fork in the road for the new nation, and with what consciousness of the implications did the second revolution move America's people toward a secularized community?

Jefferson's Victory: A Sketch of Events

The figure who towered over the deliberations on a new constitution and the initiation of the new government was George Washington, from Virginia. The first Vice President to "balance the ticket" was John Adams of Massachusetts. But the major infighters during Washington's tenure of office were Hamilton, the New York advocate for a strong central government, and Jefferson, the Virginian who wished to minimize governments' intrusions upon the liberty of ordinary citizens.

Following Washington's remarkable precedent in retiring from the presidency after two terms in office, the position passed to the former Vice President, Adams. Typically unremembered about that election is the fact that when the electoral votes were counted, Adams headed Jefferson with 71 votes to 68. Thomas Pinckney was third with 59; Aaron Burr fourth with 30, and a scattering of other votes went to additional names. According to the original provisions of the Constitution, Adams was thereby elected President, and the second place candidate was named the Vice President.

Much of the maneuvering among and between political leaders in the Congress and the states during 1796 prefigured the issues and alliances of 1800. For example, there were the beginnings of two political "parties," really coalitions of leaders and officials who previously held state or national offices. The central figure among the Federalists was actually Hamilton, but for Democratic-Republicans it was Jefferson. In unrecorded meetings and negotiations within the rival elite factions, Federalists agreed to back Adams for President, and General Charles Cotesworth

Pinckney from South Carolina for Vice President, while the Democratic-Republicans slated Jefferson, with Aaron Burr from New York for Vice President.

It must be recalled that there was not nearly the public campaigning for the presidency that is familiar to contemporary Americans, nor was there a national day of voting. Concerning the latter, citizen participation was indirect. Electors were chosen according to state law: in a few states electors ran at large; in a few others, they ran in electoral districts; but in most states they were named by the state legislature. The dates for the election of legislators and electors varied from state to state. The notion that electors had the duty to exercise wise discretion was conspicuous, so any inferences from electoral vote results must be cautiously drawn. In 1796 Virginia's Presidential electors were popularly chosen by districts, and an excerpt about the campaign is illustrative:

> So unpopular was Adams in Virginia that Federalist candidates for Presidential elector did not dare mention him by name. In Alexandria, a Federalist stronghold while Washington was in office, lawyer Charles Simms, a candidate for the electoral college, refused publicly to endorse either candidate. He promised only to vote for the best man available. Leven Powell, . . . Loudoun County, was bold enough to undertake a defense of Adam's career and a critical review of Jefferson's, but he hedged by announcing his intention to vote for Patrick Henry if he would agree to serve. If Henry declined, Powell would take the "least exceptionable" among the remaining possibilities. Farther to the south Federalists adopted similar nonpartisan stances.[5]

The partisanship of 1796 was developmental. The contention between proponents of Adams and supporters of Jefferson nationalized the incipient divisions of state and local levels. The caucusing of leaders to make slates of presidential electors, slates of congressional candidates and slates of candidates for state and local assemblies was advanced, and linkages were formed up and down the levels of government. So, too, there was growing partisan coherence in legislative bodies.

> Formerly hampered in their opposition to the administration by the widespread respect for Washington, Republicans now became an unhesitant party of opposition. The retirement of Washington cleared the way for uninhibited party development, and the history of the next

four years is the story of the struggle between two opposing parties for the control of the government.[6]

Adams led an administration of Washington holdovers. Unfortunately for him, several cabinet members felt more allegiance to the brilliant Hamilton than to their President. But the first two years of the term produced a political windfall for Adam's party. France, in the venal hands of the Directory, played the XYZ affair for a bribe from the United States. Revealed as French corruption in the American press,

> In the congressional elections of 1798-99 the Federalists won a strong majority . . . . Jefferson and his party appeared to be utterly discredited by their pro-French leanings, but time was preparing for their revenge. A rift appeared in the Federalist party between the President and Hamilton . . . .[7]

During its ascendency the Federalist-dominated Congress adopted restrictive legislation in the Naturalization Act, Alien Act and Sedition Act. The first two were especially negative toward French, Irish and other immigrants, many of whom sought the frontier, and were inclined toward Republican, rather than Federalist, political sympathies. The Sedition Act allowed the government to fine or imprison persons for speaking or writing against the President or Congress. Never broadly implemented, it was, nonetheless, used to arrest Republican editors, printers and publicists. Federalist partisanship was taking an ugly direction, one that viewed the Democratic-Republicans not as a "loyal opposition", but as potential domestic traitors.

Jefferson and Madison led the Republican response, but by means of the state governments. Within the close circle of political friends Jefferson and Madison drafted resolutions to challenge the legality, legitimacy, constitutionality and morality of the Alien and Sedition Laws. Jefferson's nine resolutions, which he thought to direct to the North Carolina legislature, were passed along instead to John Breckinridge of Kentucky, where they were adopted in late 1798. Madison, with suggested alterations by Jefferson, drafted the Virginia resolutions which were sponsored by John Taylor in the Virginia House of Delegates.[8] For the election of 1800 the importance of these steps was in the active leadership Jefferson took to counter the Federalists.

In 1800 the candidacy of Jefferson for President by the

Democratic-Republicans was a foregone conclusion. A caucus was more for the purpose of affirming unity on the support of Aaron Burr for Vice President. Federalists, despite having an incumbent President, were not unified. Some Federalists sought to bring General Washington out of retirement. He would not, and shortly thereafter he died. By mid-1800 they had agreed to support a ticket of Adams and Charles Cotesworth Pinckney; but there was plotting among the Hamiltonians that Pinckney would get more electoral votes than Adams, and thus not only defeat Jefferson, but displace Adams from the presidency.[9]

The campaign was long, and filled with suprises. As in 1796, there were elections within the states at different dates, for legislative slates of electors. Part of the contest was in altering the rules of the game. The first election significant to the presidential outcome was in New York in April, 1800. Aaron Burr arranged a slate of candidates for New York City for "a member of Congress, senators and members of assembly."[10] Polls were open for three days, and when they closed Burr and his associates had defeated Alexander Hamilton and his lieutenants, leading to great despair that this would signal a presidential turnover. Federalists considered convening the Federalist dominated, lame duck legislature to change the rules for choosing presidential electors, but Governor John Jay thought such a measure "would not become me . . ."[11]

If not quite as close, the final electoral vote outcome was clearly much more partisanly cohesive than in 1796. Only a single vote went to anyone but the party nominees, and that was a Rhode Island vote for Jay, a venerable Federalist. All of New England was solidly Federalist. The South and West were strongly for Jefferson, while the Middle States were divided. A legislative compromise in Pennsylvania resulted in a nearly equal division of electors by the legislature. In Maryland, electors were voted on by the people according to districts and the outcome was split. North Carolina also had district elections, and Federalists won a third of those.[12] Because selections and elections occurred in the states on different dates, it was well appreciated on both sides in late 1800 that the electoral votes from South Carolina could turn the contest, and the electors would be chosen by the legislature.

The Electoral Vote in the 1800 Election

States	Jefferson	Burr	Adams	Pinckney	Jay
New Hampshire	-	-	6	6	-
Vermont	-	-	4	4	-
Massachusetts	-	-	16	16	-
Rhode Island	-	-	4	3	1
Connecticut	-	-	9	9	-
New York	12	12	-	-	-
New Jersey	-	-	7	7	-
Pennsylvania	8	8	7	7	-
Delaware	-	-	3	3	-
Maryland	5	5	5	5	-
Virginia	21	21	-	-	-
North Carolina	8	8	4	4	-
South Carolina	8	8	-	-	-
Georgia	4	4	-	-	-
Kentucky	4	4	-	-	-
Tennessee	3	3	-	-	-
	73	73	65	64	1

South Carolina was considered the most Federalist of the Southern states, and it was the home of Adams' running mate, Charles Cotesworth Pinckney. But the Republican campaign was led for Jefferson by Charles ("Blackguard Charlie"[13]) Pinckney, cousin to Adam's running mate, and at the time one of the state's U.S. Senators. He managed the legislative selection of a slate that unanimously supported Jefferson and Burr. Actually, it had been expected that the South Carolina electors would cast 8 votes for Jefferson, 7 for Burr and 1 for George Clinton, precluding the tie between Jefferson and Burr.[14]

When the electoral votes were counted, the embarrassing result was that the outcome was still in doubt. Despite universal understanding about who was the Democratic-Republican presidential candidate and who was nominated for Vice President, the matter had to be determined in the U.S. House, with each state delegation entitled to one vote, and a majority of states needed to win. The critical question to be resolved was whether or not Federalists in Congress could obstruct a majority of states from voting for Jefferson. The following excerpts from Cunningham describe the outcome:

> Although Federalists had a majority, they did not control a majority of the state delegations; but neither did the Republicans. Two states were divided, and the Republicans needed 1 of these to command the 9 states necessary for a majority. The Federalists were thus in a position to block the election of Jefferson or prevent a decision before Adams' term of office ended on March 4. From the beginning of the contest, Hamilton urged the Federalists to support Jefferson rather than Burr, whose "public principles have no other spring or aim than his own aggrandizement." But the Federalists in Congress ignored Hamilton's advice and threw their support to Burr. They did not have the votes to elect Burr, but by supporting him persistently enough they might persuade some Republicans to switch from Jefferson to Burr . . . .[15]

Balloting began on February 11, 1801, with 8 states supporting Jefferson, 6 for Burr, and the delegations in Vermont and Maryland divided. Quoting Cunningham further:

> As tensions mounted, the Federalists yielded. On February 17, on the thirty-sixth ballot, Jefferson received the votes of 10 states and was elected President. This resulted from the Federalist members of Vermont and Maryland either not voting or putting in blank ballots so that those 2 states which had previously been divided went to Jefferson.[16]

So the crisis was past and succession was determined. On March 4, 1801, Thomas Jefferson took the oath of office from Federalist Chief Justice of the Supreme Court, John Marshall. It was an event as remarkable as Washington's voluntary retirement on the completion of two terms. Here the incumbent Federalist President, John Adams, stepped down after the election of his rival Republican in a disputatious contest marked not only by issue differences, but serious contentions over the rules of the game.

Religion and the Election of 1800

The switching of a handful of electoral votes might have reelected Adams to the presidency. Alterations in a couple of state delegations could have put Burr into the highest office instead of Jefferson. Because the contest was so close, did it in fact turn on the question of religion? A definite answer could only be given carelessly, while a definitive answer might well turn out to be indeterminant.

The most commonplace debate among historians concerning the election of 1800 is the extent to which this should be understood as a partisan election or even the establishment of a partisan system.[17]

For Risjord,

> The basic theme is the evolution of political parties after the Revolution. I am not concerned with the subtle distinction between "party" and "faction"; nor am I concerned with pinpointing a moment when a modern "party" can be said to exist. I feel that party development was an evolutionary process . . . . These were various elements or stages . . . (including the following):
>
> -The perception, at least among party leaders, of an interrelationship among various issues, leading to a public announcement of a program or platform.
> -Appeals to the public for support, based upon a candidate's or a party's stand on certain issues, followed by efforts to influence public opinion and mobilize voters.
> -The appearance of a party apparatus: legislative whips, nominating committees, or "juntos" that coordinate statewide activities.[18]

Unquestionably these circumstances did prevail in the election of 1800. On the other hand, there was a good deal of fluidity during that period. Scholars cannot identify all the candidates for Congress, for example, as either Federalists or Democratic-Republicans. In fact, the use of words like Federalist, Republican, Democrat and others were both confusing, and used to confuse. Perhaps most significant is the fact that many citizens lacked what political scientists now refer to as "party identification." Although few Americans could today thoroughly distinguish Democrats from Republicans, a majority *do* know to which party they feel closer. They know which party their parents preferred. They have some traditional associations with the parties and political figures who carried party colors in previous elections and administrations. But in the post-Revolution era those delineations were obviously new and often vague.

If Jefferson's interest in the presidency was casual in 1796, it was calculated thereafter. According to Cunningham, Jefferson penned "his best expression of the Republican platform" in a letter to Elbridge Gerry in January, 1799.[19] It affirmed his attachment to the Constitution, and gave a Republican view of state's rights, the legislature, the executive, national debt, the militia, the navy, international trade and relations, and domestic liberty. In particular, "I am for freedom of religion, and against all maneuvers to bring about a legal ascendency of one sect over another . . . ."

There were no official party platforms in 1800, but Cunningham has reprinted a summary of Republican campaign arguments as published in the Republican paper of Philadelphia, the *Aurora*, on October 14, 1800. Statements were set in a comparative format, with two of the eleven propositions setting forth religious stands.[20]

ATTENTION
Citizens of Philadelphia
Take Your Choice

	FEDERAL Things as They Have Been		REPUBLICAN Things as They Will Be
	. . . .		. . . .
7.	Priests and Judges incorporated with the Government for political purposes, and equally polluting the holy alters of religion, and the seats of Justice	7.	Good government without the aid of priestcraft, or religious politics, and Justice administered without political intolerance
	. . . .		. . . .
11.	An established church, a religious test, and an order of Priesthood.	11.	Religious liberty, the right of conscience, no priesthood, truth and Jefferson.

Unquestionably there was a distinguishable religious issue. One of the standard sources, written to chronicle the secularization of American Society, assesses the beginning of the 19th century in these terms:

It is difficult for us at this distance of time to appreciate the alarm felt in conservative Church circles over the re-entrance of Thomas Jefferson into public life . . . . This was especially manifest in the New England states of Connecticut and Massachusetts, where the Congregational Church was still established and where Jefferson was looked upon as representing the ideals of the French Revolution—radicalism in matters political and social, and atheism, or at least agnosticism in religion.

. . . .

Next to the orthodox Congregationalists of New England the Episcopal leaders in Virginia were among Jefferson's most bitter opponents, although after the first decade of the nineteenth century the Episcopal clergy of Connecticut supported his party as being the only way they could break the strangle hold of the established Congregational Church, always in close alliance with the Federalists. In other religious bodies there was considerable opposition to Jefferson because of his radical theological and social views, but as he was an ardent advocate of religious freedom, which he had done so much to secure in Virginia, many dissenting sects, including especially the rank and file of Baptists and Methodists, gave him support in the hope of disestablishing the Church.[21]

Much of the campaign rhetoric of the period harshly viewed Jefferson's religious commitments, and associated them with other offensive objects. "A Christian Federalist" warned Delaware voters "that if Jefferson is elected, and the Jacobins get into authority, that those morals which protect our lives . . . which guard the chastity of our wives and daughters . . . (,) defend our property from plunder and devastation, and shield our religion from contempt and profanation . . ." will be trampled, and the worst consequences of the French Revolution would tear up the land.[22] Cunningham notes that Jefferson was repeatedly accused of being a deist, atheist, and enemy to religion. He was charged with disbelief of and disregard for the Bible, and for failure to observe the Sabbath. For a nation to elect him President would be rebellion against God.

The closest scholar of this issue, Charles O. Lerche, Jr., summarized four main avenues of attack on Jefferson as follows:

First, and perhaps most unfair of all, was the accusation of atheism. This, largely the product of New England divines, runs like a leitmotif through nearly all the anti-Jefferson literature. Second in importance was the charge of being an "impractical" dreamer and philosopher, thus unfitted for responsible office. Third, . . . a broad charge of disrespect to Washington. Fourth, Jefferson's attachment to democracy in general and to the French Revolution in particular . . . . An offshoot of this was the accusation that he intended to make himself another Bonaparte. In addition to these four broad accusations, a tremendous variety of miscellaneous dirt was dug up and laid at his door . . . with cowardice both personal and moral, with sexual immorality, with dishonesty in business affairs, with political inefficiency; and with "want of personal firmness" by the specialists in character defamation.[23]

Another way to appreciate the significance of religion as an issue in the campaign is to perceive the revolutionary view of it which Jefferson pursued so diligently. It is helpful to see this through the eyes of a contemporary scholar who contends that Jefferson was *not* a civil liberties champion in both word and deed. Looking at both the words and the actions of Jefferson over his long career, Leonard W. Levy observes, "Thomas Jefferson never once risked career or reputation to champion free speech, fair trial, or any other libertarian value. On many others he trimmed his sails and remained silent." Levy goes on to note several concurrences by Jefferson in which he "chose the easy path of lawful performance of his duties instead of conscientious opposition on the ground that liberty and justice were being victimized."[24] This observant critic of Jefferson's civil libertarianism comes to quite a different conclusion about the relation between Jefferson's preachments and practice concerning religion. Levy insists that, "Between his words and deeds on religious liberty there was an almost perfect congruence . . . ." Levy declares further:

> Jefferson cared very deeply about religious liberty. Diligent study and thought had given him a systematic theory, the most advanced of his age, and he put it into practice. His position was clearly defined, publicly stated, and vigorously defended. Although it exposed him to abusive criticism he carried on his fight for separation of church and state, and for free exercise of religion, throughout his long public career without serious contradictions. In sum his thought on religious liberty was profoundly libertarian, and his actions suited his thought.[25]

It was precisely this "advanced" (or read: deviant, secular, deistic, anti-clerical, disestablishmentarian) theory of religion in statecraft that those with establishment interests in religion feared. Nor were they wrong to fear. He had told Gerry, quoted above, that he was against "all maneuvers" to bring about establishment. In fact he opposed any defense of existing establishments. His devoted biographer, Dumas Malone, infers his perspectives late in 1800:

> He (Jefferson) doubted if it (his views on Christianity, conveyed to Dr. Rush) would reconcile him to the irritable tribe of clergy who were in arms against him—on grounds of their own interest, as he was convinced. He believed that certain groups of them wanted an establishment of their particular form of Christianity. The real danger may have been considerably less than he thought, but, since freedom of the press had been so successfully attacked, there had surely been grounds to fear for freedom of religion. With renewed confidence he now said: "The returning good sense of our country threatens abortion to their hopes, and they believe that any portion of power confided to me will be exerted in opposition to their schemes. And they believe truly. For *I have sworn upon the altar of God eternal hostility against every form of tyranny over the mind of man.*"[26]

One aspect of this issue is remarkable. It is that Jefferson took such pains to make his religious sentiments, and the political strategies to spring from those sentiments, private. To Dr. Rush in 1803, he said:

> I am moreover averse to the communication of my religious tenets to the public; because it would countenance the presumption of those who have endeavored to draw them before that tribunal, and to seduce public opinion into that inquisition over the rights of conscience, which the laws have so justly proscribed.[27]

He cites his fears that public opinion will be seduced into inquisition about his private views. In fact, the private views of a private citizen were not at stake. The privately held premises for public policy intentions of the President were being withheld from the people before and after the election of 1800. His chroniclers often note the pains Jefferson took to keep his religious opinions, especially his few written opinions about religion, private. He used silence as a means to disarm critics about his intentions to displace the political rights of churches. That these churches had rights—constitutional rights, rights asserted through state political processes, and rights to seek redress for grievances—was whisked into the realm of individual rights of private conscience by Jeffersonian political theology.

Jefferson's rival in 1800 was John Adams, a son of the Commonwealth of Massachusetts, which was the second ranking state in population and representation in Congress; second, of course, to Jefferson's Virginia. Adams was part of the establishment of Massachusetts, and a central aspect of that concept was the established societies of Congregational faith. There was an extremely close overlapping of interest within the established church and Federalist orthodoxy in politics. According to Banner, the following are elements:

> Harmony, unity, order, solidarity; these were the basic motifs of Massachusetts Federalist thought . . . . Massachusetts Federalists saw society both as a structure of harmonious and mutually interdependent interests and as a collectivity in which individuals, by occupying fixed places and performing specified tasks, contributed to the health and prosperity of the whole community . . . .
>
> . . . When Federalists envisaged a general equilibrium, they had in mind inequality as well as interdependence, deference and denial as well as agreement and compromise . . . . (T)he social harmony presupposed natural distinctions among men and, what is more, unprotesting submission to one's place in the social heirarchy . . . .
>
> . . . (T)he clergy were expected—and expected themselves—to help maintain the deference and submission. "The business of religious teachers perfectly coincides with the business of civil rulers," declared Nathanial Emmons. "It is the ultimate design of civil magistrates to restrain the external actions of men; and so far as religious teachers restrain their internal corruption, just so far they aid the civil powers, and contribute all their influence to promote the good of civil society." . . .
>
> For their part, the Congregational clerics were not loath to indulge the invitation to support the state that gave them special privileges. They zealously pressed religion into service as the guarantor of stability. Indeed, no one articulated the elitist definition of social harmony better than the ministers of the established church.[28]

So Jefferson and his party, aggressively seeking office (rather than "standing" for election), and courting support from a variety of dissenters, newcomers, westerners, southerners, mechanics and nere-do-wells, were viewed as threatening to normal, good order. Religious orthodoxy was an element in a large constellation of concerns that New England Congregationalists held about the Democratic-Republicans. The Congregationalists saw the Jeffersonians from the vantage point of their own Commonwealth.

Broadly conceived, the Massachusetts religious community was divided by 1800 into two sectors, one incorporating the established Congregational church, the other the dissenting "sects"—a word which in the Federalist-Congregational lexicon embraced all religious and political nonconformists. In the roughest sense, political alignments expressed this central division among the denominations. As defenders of a preferred position, seekers after an ancient exclusiveness, and opponents of all sectarianism, Congregationalists and their Calvinist allies, the Presbyterians, were naturally inclined to identify themselves with the part of stability and tradition. In contrast, members of the dissenting sects generally joined the party which championed an end to all limitations upon the free exercise of religion.[29]

The irony of this Federalist-Congregational union is that the two parts went hand in hand into minority status. In New England the religious dissenters, Baptist and Methodist, grew in number among the frontiersmen and urban immigrants. Internal divisions within the establishment, along side of growth in the dissenter churches, was concurrent with the rising tide of Jeffersonianism.

> Thus the sects' poor and ill-placed members flocked to Jefferson's party, not out of approval of its budgetary policy or its diplomacy, but because of the willingness of local Republican leaders to champion their demands for relief from parish taxes and from obstructions placed in the way of their itinerant and irregular clergy and because the Republicans vigorously besieged the citadels of Federalist strength in governments, the professions and the church.[30]

Fisher has supplied a discussion of the religious patterns in the country at-large in 1800. For the parts outside of New England he says:

> In other parts of the Union, three religious groups were generally Jeffersonian—Baptists, Jews, and Irish Catholics. The Baptist Church in Londonderry, Vermont, which excommunicated four of its members for joining the Washington Benevolent Society, appears to have been representative in its politics if not in its zeal. Even in Virginia it was said that Baptists were "almost universally Republican."
>
> Notice was taken in chapter VIII of Jews in politics, and specifically of Benjamin Nones, who publicly declared, "I am a Jew, and if for no other reason, for that reason am I a republican." There were exceptions—Jacob Henry, the North Carolina Jew who figures in a notable test of religious liberty, had been the victim of discrimination less for his religion, perhaps, than his politics—he was a Federalist. But notwithstanding this and other exceptions, the antisemitism which

appeared in Federalist tracts during the 1790s had effectively alienated another minority group.

The Irish and French voters who supported Jefferson in 1800 were, of course, generally Catholic. Their religion did not cause their political commitment, but a descriptive pattern is clear. On the other hand, English Catholics in Maryland were described as Federalist "almost without exception."

Two other religious groups were generally Federalist—Methodists on the Delmarva peninsula, and Scotch-Irish Presbyterians in Western Virginia and the Cape Fear region of North Carolina. Jefferson himself wrote that "the string of countries at the Western foot of the Blue ridge settled originally by Irish presbyterians (composes) precisely the tory (Federalist) district of the state." Local historians have discussed the relevance of Methodism to Federalist strength in Delmarva, and of Presbyterianism in the Cape Fear region.[31]

Two brief assessments of the significance of religion and establishment to the election of 1800 need to be mentioned. The first is that the election did not divide the religious from the irreligious, the Protestant from the Roman Catholic or the Christian from the non-Christian. There were patterns, and Jefferson was the lightning rod for those patterns. In general he was opposed by churchmen whose church enjoyed or had lost the privilege of establishment. He was supported by churchmen who opposed establishment. However, there was much more than the establishment issue at stake. Fischer's judgment is instructive:

> I have found no single pattern of partisan allegiance in 1800, no magic monism which unlocks the inner secrets of political behavior. There was surely no simple symmetry of political conviction and economic interest, no clean-cut cleavage between wealth and poverty, between agriculture and commerce, between realty and personalty holdings, between city-dwellers and countryfolk, between northern merchants and southern planters, between subsistence and commercial farmers, between hardy frontiersmen and effete easterners, between orthodox Calvinists and other religious groups.
>
> There were many patterns of political allegiance—all of them intricate in the extreme. Taken together, they present a picture of bewildering, disheartening complexity.[32]

So there is no justification for characterizing the election politics of 1800 in stark terms based upon religious identities.

Joined with the first point is the argument that Jefferson's religious positions did not make the difference upon which people supported or opposed him. The point is put most simply by Dumas Malone: "we may safely assume that the overwhelming majority of those who raised the religious issue against him were also Federalists on other grounds."[33]

To this argument the reminder should be added that relatively few popular votes were actually cast for or against Jefferson or Adams. In only five states were electors chosen by the people, and part of the strategy was to name elector candidates who were locally attractive. But the majority of electors were chosen in the legislatures by political participants motivated by a plurality of interests, perhaps including religion, but certainly more than simply religion.

The Revolution of 1800: A Religious Revolution?

In an often cited passage, written well after his presidency, Jefferson responded to an inquiry from Judge Spencer Roane. Roane had sent Jefferson some essays, of which Jefferson approvingly said they contained ". . . the true principles of the revolution of 1800, for that was as real a revolution in the principles of our government as that of 1776 was in its form . . . ."[34] Historians have interpreted the significance and meaning of the "revolution of 1800" rather differently. For Sisson it embodied a plan for "forming the inhabitants of the earth into one vast republic, of rendering the whole family of mankind enlightened, free and happy."[35] Merrill Peterson perceives it as party democracy:

> The development of political parties, which no one had wanted, came largely in response to forces released by the French Revolution; and the party of Jefferson, by assimilating elements of that revolution to the creed of the American Revolution, secured the democratic line of advance. It was the second revolution that made the first a datum of American *democratic* consciousness; but it was the third revolution, "the revolution of 1800," that warranted no further revolution would be necessary. Democracy superceded revolution.[36]

Lance Banning, on the other hand, says "most historians would probably prefer a different phrase. Too little changed—and that too slowly—to justify the connotations of that loaded word."[37] Similarly Cunningham considers the statement an exaggeration, although he counts the transfer of power accomplished by the 1800 election as rendering it as "one of the most significant elections in American history."[38]

Dumas Malone assigns a moderate and time-bound meaning to Jefferson's characterization of the election:

> To him (Jefferson) the word (revolution) had a predominantly political connotation, and if Americans were basically agreed on the principles of the government as he said in his inaugural address, he might just as well have used the word "restoration." The most accurate statement of the matter, it seems, is that in 1801 he was seeking the return to the principles of the American Revolution, especially by recognizing the sovereignty of the people more fully, and that, in the United States, on the political front at least, he checked what he regarded as a counter-revolution . . . . The major change he anticipated was in the spirit of the govenment.[39]

It is noteworthy that none of these varied assessments judge the meaning of the "revolution of 1800" with any reference to the religious predilections of Jefferson or the subsequent impact of this election with regard to the relation of religion with government. It is a figure of speech, a vehicle that different historians have used to carry differing burdens of intellectual weight. I shall not appropriate it to suggest a Jeffersonian implication of turn-over in the relations of religion, politics and government. However, it ought not to be doubted that Jefferson and this election gave impetus to the secularization of politics, and the privatization of religious exercise and expression. In a career of consistent antipathy to religious establishment, Jefferson and his political allies successfully attacked those who would conserve the privilege of establishment. As the central figure of the Democratic-Republican faction-to-party, Jefferson led a political movement that rather consistently worked for freedom of conscience, freedom of religious privacy and the separation of churches from state determined privileges. The effort was not limited to the Virginia Statute for Religious Freedom (how could any legislator or citizen be against religious *freedom*?), but extended to other states in matters such as oaths as conditions for voting or holding office, church incorporations, opening prayers in legislatures, and the sale of lands held by formerly established churches.[40] Madison perceived religious issues in Congressional legislation on the census; the national bank, and the Sedition Act during the 1790s.⁴¹ There was a tumbling of religious requirements in already admitted states of the Union and an absence of such requirements in the new ones. Vermont revised its constitution in 1793. While retaining guarantees of religious freedom, it deleted religious test oaths. Georgia's 1798 constitution forbade compulsory contributions to religion. Delaware's 1792 constitution dropped its previous bar to office for any who would not subscribe to trinitarian Christianity. When Ohio joined the Union in 1802, the first state of the Northwest Territory, its constitution asserted freedom of conscience in religion, but allowed no establishment nor religious tests. Louisiana, purchased during Jefferson's administration, was simply granted religious freedom in the Louisiana Territorial Act of 1804. The "standing order," the established Congregational ministry, was maintained in Connecticut until a new constitution was adopted in 1818. It nominally remained in Massachusetts until 1833, but Republicans, with the help of religious dissenters, passed the Religious Freedom Bill of 1811 which all but finished off establishment in Massachusetts.⁴²

It may even be argued that the Jeffersonians' position more than carried; the issue of establishment was extinguished. New England was the last bastion for establishment, a substantive issue among the Federalists. But the establishment issue died before the Federalists did. In despondency from political and sectional isolation, fearing economic ruin from the War of 1812, and awash in secessionist sentiment, the Federalists, mostly from Massachusetts, Rhode Island and Connecticut, held a secret convention in Hartford at the very end of 1814. The outcome was a set of resolutions calling for amendments to the U.S. Constitution to enhance the status and political influence of the New England states.⁴³ But none of these touched on or implied the matter of religious establishment, or any suggestion to reclaim religious privileges that had been eroded during the rise of Jeffersonian Republicanism.

It is beyond argument that Jefferson was a central figure in the post-Revolution era of social change. It was an era of religious pluralization and dissent which made religious liberty and freedom from orthodoxy much more attractive than establishment and conformity. By the time of his death on July 4, 1826, religious establishment had been almost completely swept away.

Jefferson erected no wall of separation between Church and State, but he laid the political footings for one and he set the terms of consensus on the right to believe or disbelieve. The social and religious diversity fostered in that consensus has rendered establishment irretrievable.

End Notes

1. Steve Neal in *The Chicago Tribune Magazine*, January 10, 1982, pp. 9ff. The poll results are reprinted in *The Presidential Studies Quarterly* 12, No. 2 (Spring 1982), p. 293.
2. Merrill D. Peterson, *Thomas Jefferson and the New Nation: A Biography* (New York: Oxford University Press, 1970), pp. vii-viii; the earlier book by the same author is *The Jefferson Image in the American Mind* (New York: Oxford University Press, 1960).
3. See his letter to Judge Spencer Roane, September 6, 1819. *The Writings of Thomas Jefferson*, collected and edited by Paul Leicester Ford. Vol. X, G.P. Putnam's Sons, 1899, p. 140.
4. Peterson, *T.J. and the New Nation*, p. 638.
5. Norman K. Risjord, *Chesapeake Politics: 1781-1800* (New York: Columbia University Press, 1978), p. 508.
6. Noble E. Cunningham, Jr., *The Jeffersonian Republicans: The Formation of Party Organization, 1789-1801* (Chapel Hill: The University of North Carolina Press, 1957), p. 115.
7. Samuel Eliot Morison and Henry Steele Commager, *The Growth of the American Republic* 4th ed., revised and enlarged (New York: Oxford University Press, 1950), Vol. 1, p. 374.
8. Cunningham, *The Jeffesonian Republicans*, pp. 126-128.
9. See Peterson, *TJ and the New Nation*, p. 632.
10. Cunningham, *The Jeffersonian Republicans*, p. 183; from a quotation in a letter by James Nicholson to Albert Gallatin, May 6, 1800.
11. Cunningham, *The Jeffersonian Republicans*, p. 185.
12. In 1800, Presidential electors were popularly elected in Rhode Island, Maryland, Virginia, North Carolina and Kentucky. Cunningham, *The Jeffersonian Republicans*, p. 176n. In Virginia, the law was changed for the 1800 contest, "providing for the election of presidential electors on a general ticket throughout the state instead of by districts as had been done in the past." (p. 145). In Massachusetts district elections were replaced with legislative appointment of electors, and in New Hampshire a general ticket election was replaced by legislative selection. (pp. 146-147)
13. This according to Paul Goodman, "The First American Party System" in William Nisbet Chambers and Walter Dean Burnham

(eds.) *The American Party Systems: Stages of Political Development* (New York: Oxford University Press, 1967), pp. 56-89; see p. 78.
14. See Cunningham, *The Jeffersonian Republicans* p. 236; and Dumas Malone, *Jefferson and the Ordeal of Liberty* (Boston: Little, Brown and Company, 1962), p. 493. This is Volume Three of Malone's series, *Jefferson and His Time*. Subsequent citation from the series are Malone, *Jefferson,* Volume and page.
15. Noble E. Cunningham, Jr., "Elections of 1800," in Arthur M. Schlesinger, Jr. (ed.) *History of American Presidential Elections* (New York: Chelsea House Publishers, 1971), Vol. 1, pp. 101-155; quotation from pp. 131-132.
16. Cunningham, "Election of 1800," p. 132-133.
17. Prominent authorities in the discussion include Stuart Gerry Brown, *The First Republicans: Political Philosophy and Public Policy in the Party of Jefferson and Madison* (Syracuse: Syracuse University Press, 1954); Noble E. Cunningham, especially in his *The Jeffersonian Republicans;* Paul Goodman, *The Democratic-Republicans of Massachusetts: Politics in a Young Republic* (Cambridge: Harvard University Press, 1964) and his "The First American Party System" (cited above); Ronald P. Formisano, "Federalists and Republicans: Parties, Yes—System, No" in Paul Klepner (ed.), *The Evolution of American Electoral Systems* (Westport, Conn.: Greenwood Press, 1981), pp. 33-76; and Risjord, *Chesapeake Politics.*
18. Risjord, *Chesapeake Politics*, p. viii.
19. Cunningham, "Election of 1800," pp. 118-119.
20. Cunningham, "Election of 1800," pp. 138-139.
21. Anson Phelps Stokes, *Church and State in the United States.* Revised one-volume Edition by Leo Pfeffer, (New York: Harper and Row, 1964), p. 178.
22. Quoted in Cunningham, "Election of 1800," p. 124.
23. Charles O. Lerche, Jr., "Jefferson and the Election of 1800: A Case Study in the Political Smear," *The William and Mary Quarterly* Vol. 5, No. 4 (October, 1948), pp. 467-491; quotation from pp. 470-471.
24. Leonard W. Levy, *Jefferson and Civil Liberties: The Darker Side* (Cambridge: Harvard University Press, 1963), p. 160.
25. Levy, *Jefferson and Civil Liberties,* p. 14-15.
26. Malone, *Jefferson,* Vol. 3, p. 483. Emphasis by Malone.
27. Letter to Dr. Rush, April 21, 1803; reprinted in Merril D. Peterson (ed.) *The Portable Thomas Jefferson* (New York: Viking Press, 1975), p. 491.

28. James M. Banner, Jr., *To the Hartford Convention: The Federalists and the Origins of Party Politics in Massachusetts, 1789-1815* (New York: Alfred A. Knopf, 1970), quoted from pp. 53, 54, and 56.
29. Banner, *To the Hartford Convention*, p. 197. In a footnote, Banner adds the following: "Unlike the Presbyterians outside New England, who joined the party which claimed to have been responsible for disestablishing the Anglican Church, traditional enemy of Presbyterians and Scotch-Irish, the Presbyterians of New England inclined toward the same party as the majority of Congregationalists because of their theological kinship with the established religion, the spread of the consociation principle among the Congregationalists, and a joint interest in limiting the spread of radical dissent." p. 197n.
30. Banner, *To the Hartford Convention*, p. 210.
31. David Hackett Fischer, *The Revolution of American Conservatism: The Federalist Party in the Era of Jeffersonian Democracy* (New York: Harper and Row, Publishers, 1965), p. 225.
32. Fischer, *The Revolution of American Conservatism*, p. 201.
33. Malone, *Jefferson*, Vol. 3, p. 482.
34. Jefferson to Roane, *The Writings of Thomas Jefferson*, edited by Ford, Vol. X, p. 140.
35. Daniel Sisson, *The American Revolution of 1800* (New York: Alfred A. Knopf, 1974), p. 453.
36. Merrill D. Peterson, *Adams and Jefferson: A Revolutionary Dialogue* (Athens: The University of Georgia Press, 1976), p. 93.
37. Lance Banning, *The Jeffersonian Persuasion: Evolution of a Party Ideology* (Ithaca: Cornell University Press, 1978), p. 274.
38. Cunningham, "Election of 1800," p. 101.
39. Malone, *Jefferson*, Vol. 4, p. 27.
40. See, for example, Risjord, *Chesapeake Politics*, pp. 484-489.
41. Brown, *The First Republicans*, pp. 153-156.
42. Stokes, *Church and State in the United States*, pp. 64-82 and 149-158; Banner, *To the Hartford Convention*, pp. 211-212.
43. The primary document of the Hartford Convention is Theodore Dwight, *History of the Hartford Convention: With a Review of the Policy of the United States Government which led to War of 1812* (Freeport, New York: Books for Libraries Press, first published in 1833; reprinted in 1970). Also see Banner, *To the Hartford Convention*, especially pp. 294-350.

CHAPTER X

The Theology of Pluralism

A. In Adam's Fall
We Sinned All.
B. Thy Life to Mend,
This Book Attend.

Enveloped in the above theological perspectives, with appropriate pictures to match, children of the late colonial and early national period were introduced to reading in the opening pages of the *New England Primer*. The letter "A" could have been designated as representational for apples, aquaducts, America, or Africa, but such images and values paled into insignificance before the great and necessary truths of the Christian faith. Learning to read was, by common assumption, not a skill set apart from life, but a necessary tool by which one learned to live as Adam had been created to live before his fall into sin. The alphabet in the context of creation, fall, and redemption, that was the mentality of seventeenth and eighteenth century society.

The intellect of those who drafted state constitutions, established state school funds, enacted the Northwest Ordinance of 1787, and handed down the decision in the Dartmouth case, had been established and directed, down through the decades, by public, Protestant teachers of religion, morality, and knowledge. For them to insist that prospective teachers be interviewed by a committee of local pastors was not an infringement of civil rights, but a necessary precaution for guarding the truth of what was taught and learned. To require, as did the states of Delaware, Pennsylvania, and South Carolina, that all civil officials adhere to the basic tenets of the Protestant faith, was not an infringement of conscience, but a clear expression of the will of the majority. Even in Virginia, where an increasingly raucous minority claimed to be suffering religious persecution, the state assembly demanded that ministers demonstrate literacy as a prerequisite for preaching. In its public documents and in its public actions, the states that were proud to call themselves *United* were also unashamed to be known as Protestants.

Pluralism Within Unity

Although the separate states found it necessary "to form a more perfect union" when the Articles of Confederation proved unworkable, their differences did not dissipate with the ratification of the Constitution. The dissimilarities which had characterized the colonies in the seventeenth century were even more noticeable and intransigent as the eighteenth century wound to a close. Whereas the Puritans of Massachusetts Bay could simply request that Roger Williams and his Arminian followers remove themselves to another place, the luxury of escape-valve politics was not an appealing option until the Northwest Territory was opened and made secure.

Within the established and settled areas east of the Alleghanies, people learned to live with diversity. As most everyone knew, the culture, the economy, the values, and the religious perspectives were vastly different in Georgia, when contrasted with those in New York or in New Hampshire. In Virginia the contrasts between Episcopaleans and Baptists were also pronounced, just as were those between Presbyterians and Quakers in Pennsylvania. In almost every place one could find flaws with his neighbor, for the belief in "one holy, universal church"[1] most often came to imperfect expression in the lives of those who made that profession. While most religious adherents were prone to proclaim their commitments as being more orthodox than the rest, everyone had to admit that the idyllic society of love, truth, and brotherhood had not yet arrived.

The United States in the last quarter of the eighteenth century was tenuously united, but not uniform. Although Protestantism was firmly established, there were Catholics increasingly present. Although many demonstrated a vibrant and personal faith, in others "the fires had gone out," while still others preferred to ignore completely the teachings and demands of traditional religion. The "city on a hill," which the Puritans had earlier envisioned, still struggled with the divergence of competing faiths.

What is notable about the early national period is that,

within a context of ethnic and religious pluralism, the various states and the federal government could produce an array of public legislation that so clearly demonstrated a common faith.

During the early national period the concept of pluralism did not connote religious neutrality or even political compromise. Debates and controversy were the order of the day, with contests on many significant issues decided by close votes, or rejected at the polls. A notable exception was the Northwest Ordinance of 1787, but even there two earlier ordinances were found unacceptable before a workable solution could be found. What was originally proposed in 1784 and revised in 1785, finally found modified acceptance in 1787.

From a political vantage point, pluralism produced satisfying results only so long as there existed a common faith that was still strong enough to withstand the differences that threatened to undo it. Differences there were, certainly, but within the context of Protestant Christianity, the varying theological interpretations could be ignored in political debate and left for the arena of local control. What mattered more were those shared beliefs and assumptions on which agreement was so widespread that they did not even need formal articulation. For purposes of analysis, here, however, we need to identify the basic tenets in that common faith which gave the nation its cohesive religious character.

Their Common Faith

As one reads through the Pennsylvania constitution of 1776 and focuses on the oath required of assemblymen, one is struck by references to eternal rewards and punishment. One might well ask why such were necessary, and why similar language appeared in other consitutions, notably those of Delaware and South Carolina. Implicit in such language was the assumption that heaven and hell were real places, with all men destined for one place or the other. Because of that stark reality, any politician who rejected that belief was constitutionally prohibited from holding office.

But heaven and hell were not important in and by themselves. They were important as places of reward or punishment for the allegiances given in the on-going war between God and Satan. Life was marked by the great antithesis, of which the eighteenth century intellect was perpetually cognizant. Neutrality was nowhere possible, for either one aligned with God and fought with Him in the battle for truth, goodness, beauty, and right, or else one aligned with Satan on the side of falsehood, evil, ugliness, and error. There was no middle ground. The Puritans had indelibly etched that on the colonial conscience already in the 1640's with their "Olde Deluder Satan Laws," in which they had proclaimed education as the essential means of foiling Satan's plan. Such thinking, too, germinated the New England state school funds, the founding of Dartmouth, and the establishment of colleges which had their primary purpose that of training ministers.

The great antithesis was not merely an other-worldly concern, about which one could worry on his death-bed, but a transcendant value which superceded issues of civil rights and temporal justice. With infant mortality rates excessively high and threats of death everywhere present, Americans knew that human life was temporary at best.[2] Painfully familiar with John Bunyan's *Pilgrim's Progress*, they saw themselves as wayfaring strangers in an often hostile land, with eternal reward or punishment awaiting them beyond the portals of death. Since Christ had described Himself as the way, the truth, and the life, as well as the only gateway to Heaven, it was incumbent on them to know the Truth, for the Truth would set them free.[3] At the other end of the spectrum was Satan, who was known as the great deceiver, the father of lies, and the one who specialized in distorting the truth. Reminded by the Mathers, the Edwards, the Witherspoons, and the Muhlenbergs that God was holy and righteous, and not inclined to overlook sin, those who had been reared on a steady diet of Protestant Reformation preaching were compelled to counter sin wherever it occurred. The protagonists in the battle between truth and falsehood did not, therefore, declare a truce in the classroom, anymore than questions of good and evil absented themselves from the constitutional convention.

But not all Christians saw the antithesis in that light, even if they all recognized its reality. In Baptist theology that great conflict between God and Satan took a different turn. Dating back to the Schleitheim Confession of 1526, those in the Anabaptist tradition had cast the antithesis unto the mold of a radical separation between the "Church" and the "World." The "church" was the collection of those who were "called out" from the world, a strictly voluntary, self-initiated association of those who were serious about their discipleship.[4] The "world," by contrast, was all that was not called out, including the state and the civil government. Government, for the Anabaptists at least, was "outside of the realm of grace" and "under the power of the evil one."[5] Rejecting the Calvinists' teaching that God was sovereign ruler over all of life, the Baptists reduced His Kingly rule to the voluntary association of adult believers and consigned everything and everyone else to the dominance of Satan. For summary purposes and human understanding, the great separation was that between the church and the state.

Such an assumption did not sit well with Puritans, Presbyterians, Reformed, Lutherans, or Episcopaleans, although it did find favor with Deists, Quakers, and the handful of Mennonites who had populated Pennsylvania and New York. The alliance of Deists and separatists might have provided formidable resistance had they demonstrated more internal consistency and not permitted such Baptist leaders as Bachus, Leland, Manning, and Ward to be so politically active in the realm of the evil one. As it was, however, the coalition of mainline Protestants could ignore the separatists, except in such Baptist strongholds as Rhode Island and Virginia. Since the Baptists did not consistently practice what they preached, there was little reason to give credence to their sermons.

In the on-going discernment between Truth and Falsehood there was obvious need for a standard or authoritative guide by which Truth could be judged. In the language of the Reformed creeds, the "only rule of faith" and the infallible standard by which all the writings of men must be judged was the Holy Scriptures.[6] Those who adhered to these creeds went on to say that whatever customs, traditions, decrees, or statutes did not agree with this infallible rule were to be rejected, "since the truth is above all."[7] With similar emphasis taught in the Westminster Confession, a creed which graced the pages of every *New England Primer,* the need for such a criterion was inculcated in the mind of most schoolboys in America. Preached relentlessly in the pulpits of Congregational, Presbyterian, Reformed, Lutheran, and Anglican churches, and buttressed by daily reading in the schools, the Bible was given prominent place in the minds of most early Americans. Small wonder, then, that its acceptance became one of the touchstones for eligibility for civil office in most of the states in the union. In the minds of the state constitution drafters, it would have been political folly to allow a candidate for office who did not share the basic beliefs of the constituency to be served.

Whatever did not agree or harmonize with the teachings of Scripture, whether that be in the realm of literature, natural science, or politics, had to be rejected as a perversion of the truth. Again, not everyone of importance was willing to accept the Scriptures as the only authoritative guide for faith and practice. Enlightenment leaders like Jefferson and Paine had long since substituted Reason as their ultimate authority and had replaced truth and righteousness with equality and brotherhood as their highest values. But even Jefferson had his Bible, condensed and edited as it was to eliminate the supernatural and to focus on the democratic faith which he had inherited from his Enlightenment mentors. His infidelity was seen, not in ignoring the Bible, but in superimposing his rational ability on the Bible and thereby making God's Word subservient to his personal judgments.

The Anabaptist tradition, too, had an alternative authority. Schooled for over two centuries on the doctrines of free will and personalized relationships with God, they elevated the individual conscience to the level of final authority. Essentially religious in origin, they were almost inevitably political in effect, disseminating as they did their radical concepts of individualism, equality, and democracy, all of which appeared subversive to the established ecclesiastical order.[8] Fearful of such antinomian philosophy, the New England patriots had memories of the banishment of Anne Hutchinson and Roger Williams during the 1630's and the not unwelcomed exodus of Baptists from Massachusetts in the 1750's. Although desirous of containing their Arminian theology within the provincial boundaries of Rhode Island and Virginia, such was not possible after the states had collectively set about the business of forming a more perfect union. Though there was little love lost between Congregationalists and Baptists in Massachusetts, or between Episcopaleans and Baptists in Virginia, there was no excluding the separatists and dissenters from the new commonwealth, for they, too, were professing Protestants and accepted the Bible as the divinely inspired Word of God.

Another transcendant value which held together the fragile

fabric of national unity was that of evangelism. Recognizing that the common faith which united them was greater than the theological differences that separated them, those who drafted the laws and voted on appropriations were not averse to spending state and federal monies for propagating the gospel, especially when heathen Indians were to be the recipients.[9] Mission emphasis, then as now, was predicated on the assumption that contradictory life-styles, ideas, and religions were not only false, but avenues to eternal perdition. The native Indians, with their pagan rituals, were most obviously in need of the gospel, for they had not even heard of Christ and therefore could not possibly be Christians. All agreed, then, that appropriations for such causes were not only legitimate but necessary, often times without apparent debate and without justifying rationale. In such a mind-set, it was assumed that propagating the Gospel was the proper business of government. Buttressing that assumption was the familiar command of Jesus to "Go therefore, and teach all nations, baptizing them in the name of the Father, and of the Son, and of the Holy Ghost; teaching them to observe all things whatever I have commanded you."[10]

Evangelism, however, was not only directed at the native Indians, although they were the prime concern of the Society for the Propagation of the Gospel, known widely as the SPG. In the Southern states of Georgia and South Carolina, the SPG had directed many of their missionaries to work amongst the black slave population. Such efforts were moderately successful, but often accompanied by the opposition of the white plantation owners. The Baptists in Virginia had also promoted the gospel among the blacks, but had been criticized sharply by some Anglicans for opening the communion sacrament to them.

Among the various denominational groups, it was the Baptists who engaged most vigorously in proselytizing among fellow Protestants. Stridently rejecting such Reformation doctrines as the covenant and infant baptism, the Baptists looked upon Episcopalean congregations as strongholds of the devil in need of salvation. It was said of Isaac Bachus that he looked forward to the day when all Americans would be converted to the Baptist faith.[11]

But it was not only through missionary activity and revival meetings that the gospel was propagated. The primary means for teaching and inculcating religious truths was the school. As noted earlier in Chapters V and VI, the coterminous functions of the school were to promote religion, morality, and knowledge. Throughout the states it was required and almost standard practice to require daily Bible reading and prayer. Without that religious and moral instruction, society could not long remain secure and the youth would degenerate to the level of the reprobate.

This practice of using state tax monies and land grants to finance religious education was so widespread and uncritically accepted that even Thomas Jefferson willingly participated in it. Jefferson no more believed in divorcing religion from public education than did his Federalist opponents in New England. During the time that he served as rector of the State University of Virginia, he enforced compulsory attendance at the Protestant chapel, a practice which continued at least through the Civil War.[12] Although he personally hoped that "Americans would all be deists by 1830,"[13] he was far from being an irreligious leader, sprinkling his letters liberally with spiritual references. Similar practices could be found at most colleges and state universities, with many of them retaining theological seminaries as one of their constituent elements.[14] Present on most campuses, too, was a Protestant chapel, with services regularly conducted by the university chaplain.

In 1851, when Ohio revised its state constitution, they declared that "it shall be the duty of the general assembly to pass suitable laws to protect every religious denomination in the peaceable enjoyment of its own mode of public worship."[15] They also specified that all the monies accruing from the "lands or other property, granted or entrusted to this State for educational and religious purposes, shall forever be preserved inviolate and undiminished; and the income arising therefrom shall be faithfully applied to the specific objects of the original grants."[16] North Carolina further demonstrated a continuing commitment to Protestant public schools by inserting Article III of the Northwest Ordinance into their newly revised constitution of 1868 and followed that with a lengthy section about compulsory, public, religious education, all of which was to be paid with state funds.[17] In his analysis of this on-going practice, Sidney Mead, a Unitarian historian, has argued,

Of necessity the state in its public education system is and always has been teaching religion. The public schools in the United States took over one of the basic responsibilities that traditionally was always assumed by an established church. In this sense the public school system of the United States *is* its established church.[18]

Within the mind of the early national era, it was commonly assumed that religion and education were inextricably linked together both in theory and in practice. Because it was accepted that man was created by God (Charles Darwin did not publish *The Origin of Species* until 1859), each member of the human race was recognized as being incurably or intrinsically religious. Their children and their children's teachers, then, by inclusion in the human race, stood in either a positive or negative relation to God, whose Word had made it abundantly clear that neutrality was impossible in the spiritual warfare between God and Satan. They knew intuitively that all education was religious and that teachers were always selecting, presenting, and interpreting information on the basis of their theological commitments. But they knew, too, that not just any religion would suffice. When the constitution-drafters, the assemblymen, and the voters endorsed the integrated teaching of religion, morality, and knowledge, they expected it to be the Protestant religion which had been passed on from generation to generation. Propagating the gospel through the schools was, for them, as natural and as necessary as teaching the alphabet, an exercise which was never far removed from it.

The Rejection of Errors

When looked at from the negative side, the common faith which held the states together was not only shared beliefs to which they jointly adhered, but also a collection of errors which they commonly rejected. One of the errors which was widely, but not universally, rejected was that of "dualism." Practiced within the Roman Catholic Church since the time of Tertullian, and later cemented into philosophy by Thomas Aquinas, dualists perceived of the church as an exclusively spiritual community of supernatural origin and the state as a secular community of natural origin. Such sacred-secular dichotomies were foreign to those whose creeds taught that the church was the Body of Christ, whose duty it was to be a salting and leavening influence in every facet of society. But the threat of dualism, or "separatism," as it was more commonly known, was present throughout the states and especially so in Virginia. Practiced with varying degrees of consistency by such Anabaptist followers as the Mennonites, Quakers, and sundry strains of Baptists, dualist theology posed serious consequences for patriotic nation builders. During the Revolutionary War patriot fears were so deep-seated as to result in the formation of concentration camps for Quakers and Mennonites. Such concerns were ameliorated by the Baptists, however, who enlisted in the states' militia in unparalleled numbers, thereby suggesting that their dualistic theology would be unevenly applied in the future.

Once the Revolutionary War was finished and independence secured, it became apparent to the majority that force and violence also had to be rejected. Repulsed by the savagery of war and the memories of religious bloodbaths in Europe, the members of almost every religious persuasion became convinced that the gospel should not be propagated at the point of a sword or musket. Painfully aware of such historical events as the St. Bartholomew's Day Massacre of 1572, in which 20,000 French Huguenots were slaughtered as heretics, and the reign of terror conducted by Phillip II in The Netherlands, the citizens of America gradually became sensitized to peaceful evangelism. Goaded on by the criticisms of Jefferson and Madison, who were apalled at the sight of dissenting pastors in jail, even the most tradition-bound Episcopaleans in Virginia soon refused to assess fines and imprisonment for religious offenses. Cognizant also of Jesus' rebuke of Peter for drawing his sword in the Garden of Gethsemane, Christians were persuaded to reject force and violence as being incompatible with the gospel that they preached. Patterned somewhat after Lutheran strategy in post-Reformation Germany, the people of America adopted the policy of local control, whereby each school society or community of believers could select its own teachers or pastors and choose its own curriculum. As along as religion, morality, and knowledge were recognized as the indispensable pillars of society, each new township in the Northwest Territory was free to select its peculiar mode of education and construct the church of its choice.

By continuing the colonial tradition of local control and honoring the wishes of the community, the national government honored its constitution by neither establishing a national religion nor interfering with the established practices which were everywhere present in the states. Distributing state school funds proportionately among denominational groups, supporting seminaries for the training of pastors, and appropriating section 29 in every new township "for purposes of religion" were all harmonious with the First Amendment. Unable to detect any inconsistency with either the Constitution or the peacable character of Christianity, both the federal and the state governments engaged in propagating the gospel, for religion was a corporate as well as an individual concern. Without it, the new nation was not complete and would not long endure.

End Notes

1. The Apostles Creed.
2. For a graphic account of life expectancy studies, see Lorena Walsh's "Till Death Do us Part: Marriage and Family in Seventeenth Century Maryland," *The Chesapeake in the Seventeenth Century*. Chapel Hill: Univ. of North Carolina Press. 1979.
3. John 8:32.
4. For a more complete analysis of Anabaptist theology, see Frank Roberts, *To All Generations*, pp. 152-3, and Paul F. Scotchmer, "Church and State in Western Christendom," *Christian Scholars Review*, 1981, Vol. XI, Number 1, p. 55.
5. Roberts, *To All Generations*, p. 153.
6. Confession of Faith, Article VII; also known as the Belgic Confession.
7. Ibid.
8. For a detailed defense of this assertion, see Cremin, *American Education: The Colonial Experience*, pp. 303-4.
9. In addition to the actions explained in Chapters V and VI, see Evelyn Adams, *American Indian Education*, New York: Arno Press, 1971, and Homer Babbidge, *The Federal Interest in Higher Education*, New York: McGraw Hill, 1962, for detailed accounts of the many federal grants to Indian mission schools.
10. Matt. 28: 19-20 (King James Version)
11. McLoughlin, Wm. G., "Isaac Bachus and the Separation of

Church and State in America," *America Historical Review*, LXXIII, June, 1968. p. 1402.
12. Littell, *From State Church to Pluralism*, p. 15.
13. McLoughlin, *"Isaac Bachus and the Separation,"* p. 1403.
14. Littell calls attention to New Brunswick Theological Seminary at Rutgers University, which prepared pastors for the Reformed Church in America. Until at least 1856 the seminary was receiving state money for its support. He also mentions, on p. 130, that Western Michigan University at Kalamazoo built an impressive Protestant chapel after World War II and installed a Protestant chaplain as Dean of the chapel.
15. Constitution of Ohio—1851, Art. 1, Sec. 7.
16. Ibid., Art. VI, Sec. 1.
17. Constitution of North Carolina—1868, Sec. 1, quoted in Poore, Vol. II, p. 1432.
18. Mead, *The Lively Experiment*, p. 68.

EPILOGUE

Prior to 1947, only four decisions concerning the establishment clause of the First Amendment produced any significant consideration by the Supreme Court of the United States. The first one to be heard, and by far the most distinctive, was the *Dartmouth v. Woodward* case of 1819, which was analyzed earlier in Chapter V. By a 5 to 1 margin, the Court, under Chief Justice Marshall, ruled that the Constitution would protect the right of a state-funded college to retain as its primary purpose the evangelizing of native Indians and the training of missionaries. With that matter unequivocably settled, the opposing Democratic-Republicans not only came to accept the decision, but participated in the practice and helped in the distribution of tax monies for religious purposes.

The issue of establishment lay dormant for most of the nineteenth century, until the case known as *Bradfield v. Roberts* (175 U.S. 291) reached the Supreme Court in 1899. In that decision, the court upheld federal appropriations to a Catholic hospital in the District of Columbia. The majority decided that tax monies could constitutionally be appropriated for ward construction and for the care of indigent patients, because the hospital performed "a public service".[1] In 1908 the *Quick Bear v. Leupp* (210 U.S. 50) decision was handed down, with the Court upholding the federal disbursement of funds, held in trust for the Sioux Indians, to Catholic schools designated by the Sioux for payment of tuition costs. Although the monies were intended for the benefit of the Indian students, the disbursements were made directly to the Catholic schools for their use. In 1930 the court handed down still another decision which ruled in favor of religious establishments. In *Cochran v. Louisiana Board of Education* the Court upheld Louisiana's purchase of textbooks for pupils attending all schools, including private and parochial ones. Reflecting a slight shift in public mentality, the Supreme Court upheld the practice as constitutional on the grounds that the benefits went to the children involved and not to the institutions as such.

In 1947, the United States Supreme Court agreed to hear the case known as *Everson v. Board of Education* (330 U.S. 1, 67 S. Ct. 504). The issue in the litigation was the practice of a New Jersey township whereby they reimbursed, from tax revenues, the cost of sending children "on regular busses operated by the public transporation system" to and from schools, including the private and parochial schools in that township. Everson, a municipal taxpayer, filed a formal complaint charging that payment for Catholic parochial students' transportation violated the establishment clause of the First Amendment. The plaintiff argued that the early Americans "fervently wished to stamp out" all forms of religious establishment and "to preserve liberty for themselves and for their posterity".

If one read only Baptist histories or only the letters of Thomas Jefferson, one could certainly arrive at such a conclusion. It should be obvious, however, in the light of all the evidence submitted in the foregoing pages, that such a selective sampling of the extant literature would do a great disservice to the vast majority of early Americans and would grossly distort the meaning of the First Amendment. Yet Justice Hugo Black, writing the majority opinion in this watershed case, apparently was influenced significantly by the plaintiff's argument and limited himself almost exclusively to the perspective that was promulgated by Thomas Jefferson. In the majority opinion, Justice Black detailed the Virginia practice of paying tithes and taxes "to support government sponsored churches whose ministers preached inflammatory sermons designed to strengthen and consolidate the established faith by generating a burning hatred against dissenters".[2] The abhorrence of these practices, Black argued, "reached its dramatic climax in Virginia in 1785-86" when "Madison wrote his great Memorial and Remonstrance" and "when the Virginia Assembly enacted the famous Virginia Bill for Religious Liberty."[3]

Black's majority opinion argued that "the 'establishment of religion' clause of the First Amendment means at least this: Neither a state nor the Federal Government can set up a church. Neither can pass laws which aid one religion, aid all religious, or prefer one religion over another . . . No tax in any amount, large or small can be levied to support any religious activities or institutions . . . Neither a state nor the Federal Government can, openly or secretly, participate in the affairs of any religious organizations or groups. *In the words of Jefferson,* the clause against establishment of religion by law was intended to erect '*a wall of separation between Church and State*'" (italics added). The First Amendment has erected a wall between church and state. The wall must be kept high and impregnable. We could not approve the slightest breach".[4]

With that pronouncement, a slim majority of the United States Supreme Court substituted myth for historical accuracy, and political wishes for constitutional interpretation. Justice Black and those who concurred were not guilty of not reading, but of not reading enough. Apparently influenced by the plaintiff's arguments, they limited their historical research to Jefferson's biased perspective while ignoring such obvious historical data as the Northwest Ordinance of 1787, the constitutions of the separate states, Madison's notes on the Constitutional Convention, and such well reported practices as the Connecticut School Fund. By focusing excessively on Jefferson's letter to the Danbury Baptists, the court also overlooked the famous *Dartmouth v. Woodward* decision, which should have steered them to more thorough research. A *wall of separation* was erected and placed in the precedent-setting form of a Supreme Court decision. Where the Constitution had never spoken such language, the majority saw fit to substitute. Where the Constitutional Convention had simply decreed that *Congress* might not establish a *national* religion, and might do nothing to prohibit the free exercise of established state churches or tax funding for religious purposes, Justice Black and the concurring majority decreed that the unsuccessful wishes of Jefferson and the Virginia Baptists become the law of the entire land.

One year after the Everson decision, the Court ruled in *McCollum v. Board of Education* (333 U.S. 203) (1948) that a Champaign, Illinois public school released time program violated the establishment clause. Once again Justice Black wrote the majority opinion, arguing this time that the State of Illinois "affords sectarian groups an invaluable aid in that it helps to provide pupils for their religious classes".[5] Justice Frankfurter concurred, but felt compelled to add, "Designed to serve as perhaps the most powerful agency for promoting cohesion among the heterogeneous democratic people, the public school must keep scrupulously free from entanglement in the strife of sects". Whereas Justice Black had interpreted the Constitution selectively in the light of Jefferson's political wishes, Frankfurther now went one step further and interpreted the function of public education in the light of John Dewey's secular philosophy.

In 1952 the Supreme Court upheld a New York City released time program in which the religious classes were held in church buildings. Because the religion classes were held in church buildings and not on public school grounds, the court saw no significant danger in such practice. Yet, the Court was also quick to remind the nation that, "The First Amendment reflects the philosophy that Church and State should be separated (and) within the scope of its coverage permits no exception; the prohibition is absolute".[6] On the heels of such an unconstitutional pronouncement, in a curious and inconsistent rejoinder, the Court went on to add, "The First Amendment, however, does not say that in every and all respects there shall be a separation of Church and State . . . . Otherwise . . . municipalities would not be permitted to render police or fire protection to religious groups. Policemen who helped parishioners into their places of worship would violate the Constitution. Prayers in our legislative halls; the appeals to the Almighty in the messages of the Chief Executive; the proclamations making Thanksgiving a holiday; 'so help me God' in our courtroom oaths—these and all other references to the Almighty that run through our laws, our public rituals, our ceremonies would be flouting the First Amendment".[7]

While substituting Jefferson's wall of separation for the establishment clause, the court still seemed uneasily cognizant of the free exercise portion of the First Amendment. If they had looked around them more carefully, their uneasiness would probably have increased, for numerous other practices clearly indicated a symbiotic relationship between religion and government activity. Not only did the Senate and House require a chaplain paid with tax monies, but so did all the branches of the military. If they had looked into their own pockets, the coins and bills there would have quietly proclaimed, "In God We Trust".

In 1962, when the Court rejected the New York Board of Regents prayer in *Engel v. Vitale,* it was once again Justice Hugo Black who wrote the majority opinion. In concluding his argument, Black asserted that a "union of government and religion tends to destroy government and to degrade religion". In making such a pronouncement, he not only contradicted what the Constitutional framers had repeatedly said about "religion, morality, and knowledge being essential to good government;" he also went well beyond what Madison and Washington had argued when they helped to formulate and enact the Northwest Ordinance of 1787. Instead of following Jefferson's pattern consistently and placing his Deism on the pedestal of prominence, the Court, under the guidance of Justice Black, had entrenched a philosophy of an irreligious state and a secular public school system.

Since 1962 the church-state cases have become almost commonplace on the Supreme Court agenda. The topics have included Bible-reading in public schools, posting of the Ten Commandments, use of university facilities by religious clubs, abortion, and the funding of Christian schools. The issues and the decisions are well known to many of us and will not be analyzed here. Suffice it to say that most of the decisions have served to build and reinforce the "wall of separation" which was not intended or envisioned by the framers of the Constitution or the First Amendment. In the years since the Everson decision, a sacred-secular dichotomy has been imposed on the American republic, not because the Constitution demanded it, but because a myth was substituted for reality and was blessed by the judiciary.

End Notes

1. Sorauf, Frank, *The Wall of Separation*, p. 18-19. See also Lockhart, et. al., *Constitutional Rights and Liberties* Fifth Edition, p. 786. It should be noted here that Sorauf lists only 3 cases, omitting reference to the Dartmouth case, while Lockhart, et al., refer to only 2 cases, omitting both the Dartmouth and the Cochran decisions.
2. Lockhart, et. al., p. 787.
3. Ibid., The reader is reminded here of the earlier discussion, in Chapter VII, of Madison's "Memorial and Remonstrance" and the inflammatory character of that document.
4. Ibid., pp. 787-8.
5. Ibid., p. 790.
6. Zorach v. Clauson, 343 U.S., 306, 72, S. Ct. 679, 96 L. Ed. 954 (1952). Quoted in Lockhart, et al., p. 791.
7. Ibid.

APPENDIX A

Connecticut's Missionary Mandate

In May, 1763, the Rev. Mr. Eleazar Wheelock, pastor of the Second Church in Lebanon, presented a memorial to the Assembly "representing that for some years past he has had under his care and tuition several youths of the Indian tribes, at present increased to more than twenty in number, with a view to their being by proper discipline and instruction fitted for missionaries, schoolmasters, interpreters. & c., among their own people, and that though his past success therein has so recommended his design as to excite the charity and liberality of divers worthy persons in support of almost all the past expenses, yet the present aspect of said undertaking seeming to merit as well as require some further assistance, he was induced to ask the favor and countenance of this Assembly therein." Whereupon the Assembly, "seriously considering the present new and extraordinary prospect (by the blessing of Heaven on his Majesty's arms) doth greatly encourage an attempt to promote Christian knowledge and civility of manners among the Indian natives of this land, . . . grant and order a brief throughout this colony, recommending it to all inhabitants charitably and liberally to their ability to contribute to such pious and important purposes, and that the moneys so collected, be by the persons therewith intrusted, delivered to John Ledyard of Hartford, John Whiting of New Haven, David Gardiner of New London, David Rowland, of Fairfield, Samuel Gray of Windham, and Elisha Sheldon of Litchfield, Esquires, each county's collections to their own respective receivers; which receivers are hereby directed to deliver the same to the treasurer of this colony . . . .

"And it is further resolved, that said Mr. Wheelock do at his discretion, as occasion may be, apply to Jonathan Trumble, Daniel Edwards and George Wyllys, Esquires, for such moneys, parcel of such contributed sum as he shall apprehend to be necessary; which said committee, or any two of them, are hereby appointed, authorized and directed, to draw orders on said Treasurer for such sum or sums thereof as shall be shown to them to be useful and necessary in the then present exigencies of said affair, until the whole is exhausted.

"Provided nevertheless, that if the state and circumstances of said undertaking by any means hereafter become so altered, as in the opinion of said last mentioned committee, to render the further prosecution or support of said affair impracticable or doubtful whether it may answer the good end and design, in such case they are hereby directed to desist drawing as aforesaid, and by the earliest opportunity to advise this Assembly thereof, to the end such further order in the premises be taken as the present emergencies may recommend. Always provided such moneys be ultimately and wholly applied to the pious design of propagating the gospel among the heathen.

"And it is further ordered, that printed copies of this Act be seasonably delivered to the several ministers of the gospel within this colony, who are hereby also directed to read the same in their respective congregations, and thereon appoint a time for making such collection."

In the following autumn, the Assembly ordered the ministers to suspend the publication of the aforesaid brief, having heard that where it had already been published, the collections had been small on account of an outbreak among the Western Indians, and that most of the ministers "apprehensive of the ill success of the charitable design," had appealed, through the Governor, for the advice of the legislature.

In May, 1766, the Assembly complied with a request of Mr. Wheelock and renewed the brief throughout the colony.

From Clews, *Educational Legislation and Administration*, pp. 118-9.

APPENDIX B

Charter of Queen's College

"George the third, by the grace of God, of Great Britain, France and Ireland, King, Defender of the Faith, & c. To all to whom these presents shall come greeting;

"Whereas our loving subjects being of the Protestant Reformed religion, according to the constitution of the reformed churches in the United Provinces, and using the discipline of the said churches, as approved and instituted by the national Synod of Dort in the years one thousand six hundred and eighteen, and one thousand six hundred and nineteen, are in this and the neighbouring provinces very numerous, consisting of many churches and religious assemblies, the ministers and elders of which having taken into serious consideration the manner in which the said churches might be properly supplied with an able, learned and well-qualified ministry; and thinking it necessary, and being very desirous that a college might be erected for that purpose within this our Province of New Jersey, in which the learned languages and other branches of useful knowledge may be taught, and degrees conferred; and especially that young men of suitable abilities may be instructed in divinity, preparing them for the ministry, and supplying the necessity of the churches; for themselves and in behalf of their churches, presented a petition to our trusty and well-beloved WILLIAM FRANKLIN, ESQ., Governour and Commander-in-Chief, in and over our Province of New Jersey in America, setting forth that inconveniences are manifold and the expenses heavy, in either being supplied with ministers of the gospel from foreign parts, or sending young men abroad for education; that the present and increasing necessity for a considerable number to be employed in the ministry is great; that a preservation of a fund for the necessary uses of instruction very much depends upon a charter; and therefore humbly entreat, that some persons might be incorporated in a body politic, for the purposes aforesaid."

Note: Between 1730 and 1740 the Reformed Dutch Church in America became divided on a question of the ordination of clergymen. The party of the Coetus, in opposition to the party of the Conferentia, desired a separate ecclesiastical organization from that of the Classis of Amsterdam with an independent power of ordination. A provincial seminary of the Dutch Reformed persuasion was essential to this purpose; consequently after several vain petitions to the Governor of New Jersey for a charter for such an institution, the ministers of the Coetus finally obtained a charter from the government and, in 1770, Queens College was founded.

From Clews, *Educational Legislation and Administration,* pp. 335-7.

APPENDIX C

Constitution of South Carolina—1778

XXXVIII. That all persons and religious societies who acknowledge that there is one God, and a future state of rewards and punishments, and that God is publicly to be worshipped, shall be freely tolerated. The Christian Protestant religion shall be deemed, and is hereby constituted and declared to be, the established religion of this State. That all denominations of Christian Protestants in the State, demeaning themselves peaceably and faithfully, shall enjoy equal religious and civil privileges. To accomplish this desirable purpose without injury to the religious property of those societies of Christians which are by law already incorporated for the purpose of religious worship, and to put it fully into the power of every other society of Christian Protestants, either already formed or hereafter to be formed, to obtain the like incorporation, it is hereby constituted, appointed, and declared that the respective societies of the Church of England that are already formed in this State for the purpose of religious worship shall still continue incorporate and hold the religious property now in their possession. And that whenever fifteen or more male persons, not under twenty-one years of age, professing the Christian Protestant religion, and agreeing to unite themselves in a society for the purposes of religious worship, they shall, (on complying with the terms hereinafter mentioned,) be, and be instituted, a church, and be esteemed and regarded in law as of the established religion of the State, and on a petition to the legislature shall be entitled to be incoporated and to enjoy equal privileges. That every society of Christians so formed shall give themselves a name or denomination by which they shall be called and known in law, and all that associate with them for the purposes of worship shall be esteemed as belonging to the society so called. But that previous to the establishment and incorporation of the respective societies of every denomination as aforesaid, and in order to entitle them thereto, each society so petitioning shall have agreed to and subscribed in a book the following five articles, without which no agreement or union of men upon pretence of religion shall entitle them to be incorporated and esteemed as a church of the established religion of this State:

1st. That there is one eternal God, and a future state of rewards and punishments.

2d. That God is publicly to be worshipped.

3d. That the Christian religion is the true religion.

4th. That the holy scriptures of the Old and New Testaments are of divine inspiration, and are the rule of faith and practice.

5th. That it is lawful and the duty of every man being thereunto called by those that govern, to bear witness to the truth.

And that every inhabitant of this State, when called to make an appeal to God as a witness to truth, shall be permitted to do it in that way which is most agreeable to the dictates of his own conscience. And that the people of this State may forever enjoy the right of electing their own pastors or clergy, and at the same time that the State may have sufficient security for the due discharge of the pastoral office, by those who shall be admitted to be clergymen, no person shall officiate as minister of any established church who shall not have been chosen by a majority of the society to which he shall minister, or by persons appointed by the said majority, to choose and procure a minister for them; nor until the minister so chosen and appointed shall have made and subscribed to the following declaration, over and above the aforesaid five articles, viz: "That he is determined by God's grace out of the holy scriptures, to instruct the people committed to his charge, and to teach nothing as required of necessity to eternal salvation but that which he shall be persuaded may be concluded and proved from the scripture; that he will use both public and private admonitions, as well to the sick as to the whole within his care, as need shall require and occasion shall be given, and that he will be diligent in prayers, and in reading of the holy scriptures, and in such studies as help to the knowledge of the same; that he will be diligent to frame and fashion his own self and his family according to the doctrine of Christ, and to make both himself and them, as much as in him lieth, wholesome examples and patterns to the flock of Christ; that he will maintain and set forwards, as much as he can, quietness, peace, and love among all people, and especially among those that are or shall be committed to his charge. No person shall disturb or molest any religious assembly; nor shall use any reproachful, reviling, or abusive language against any church, that being the certain way of disturbing the peace, and of hindering the conversion of any to the truth, by engaging them in quarrels and animosities, to the hatred of the professors, and that profession which otherwise they might be brought to assent to. No person whatsoever shall speak anything in their religious assembly irreverently or seditiously of the government of this State. No person shall, by law, be obliged to pay towards the maintenance and support of a religious worship that he does not freely join in, or has not voluntarily engaged to support. But the churches, chapels, parsonages, glebes, and all other property now belonging to any societies of the Church of England, or any other religious societies, shall remain and be secured to them forever. The poor shall be supported, and elections managed in the accustomed manner, until laws shall be provided to adjust those matters in the most equitable way.

XLIV. That no part of this constitution shall be altered without notice being previously given of ninety days, nor shall any part of the same be changed without the consent of a majority of the members of the senate and house of representatives.

In the council-chamber, the 19th day of March, 1778.
Assented to.

RAWLINS LOWNDES

HUGH RUTLEDGE,

Speaker of the Legislative Council.

THOMAS BEE,

Speaker of the General Assembly.

From Poore, *Federal and State Constitutions,* Vol. II, pp. 1626-7.

APPENDIX D

The Constitution of Massachusetts—1780

Part the First

Art. II. "It is the right as well as the duty of all men in society, publicly and at stated season, to worship the Supreme Being, the great Creator and Preserver of the Universe. And no subject shall be hurt, molested, or restrained in his person, liberty, or estate, for worshipping God in the manner and season most agreeable to the dictates of his own conscience, . . . , provided he does not disturb the public peace or obstruct others in their religious worship."

Art. III. "As the happiness of a people and the good order and preservation of civil government essentially depend upon piety, religion, and morality, and as these cannot be generally diffused through a community but by the institution of the public worship of God and of public instructions in piety, religion, and morality: Therefore, to promote their happiness and to secure the good order and preservation of their government, the people of this commonwealth have a right to invest their legislature with power to authorize and require, the several towns, parishes, precincts, and other bodies-politic or religious societies to make suitable provision, at their own expense, for the institution of the public worship of God and for the support and maintenance of public Protestant teachers of piety, religion, and morality in all cases where such provision shall not be made voluntarily.

"And the people of this commonwealth have also a right to, and do, invest their legislature with authority to enjoin upon all the subjects an attendance upon the instructions of the public teachers aforesaid, at stated times and seasons, if there be any on whose instructions they can conscientiously and conveniently attend.

"*Provided, notwithstanding,* that the several towns, parishes, precincts, and other bodies-politic, or religious societies, shall at all times have the exclusive right of electing their public teachers and of contracting with them for their support and maintenance.

"And all moneys paid by the subject to the support of public worship and of the public teachers aforesaid shall, if he require it, be uniformly applied to the support of the public teacher or teachers of his own religious sect or denomination, provided there be any on whose instructions he attends; otherwise it may be paid toward the support of the teacher or teachers of the parish or precinct in which the said money are raised.

"And every denomination of Christians, demeaning themselves peaceably and as good subjects of the commonwealth, shall be equally under the protection of the law; and no subordination of any one sect or denomination to another shall ever be established by law."

Chapter VI

"Article I. Any person chosen governor, lieutenant-governor, councillor, senator, or representative, and accepting the trust, shall, before he proceed to execute the duties of his place or office, make and subscribe the following declaration, viz. "I, A.B., do declare that I believe the Christian religion, and have a firm persuasion of its truth; and that I am seized and possessed in my own right, of the property required by the constitution, as one qualification for the office or place to which I am elected."

From Poore, *The Federal and State Constitutions,* Vol. I.

APPENDIX E

Powers to the Board of Treasury to Contract for the Sale of Western Territory

The report of a committee, consisting of Mr. Carrington, Mr. King, Mr. Dane, Mr. Madison, and Mr. Benson, amended to read as follows, viz:

That the Board of Treasury be authorized and empowered to contract with any person or persons for a grant of a tract of land which shall be bounded by the Ohio, from the mouth of the Scioto to the intersection of the western boundary of the seventh range of townships now surveying; thence, by the said boundary to the northern boundary of the tenth township from the Ohio; thence, by a due west line, to the Scioto; thence, by the Scioto, to the beginning upon the following terms, viz: The tract to be surveyed, and its contents ascertained, by the geographer or some other officer of the United States, who shall plainly mark the said east and west line, and shall render one complete plat to the Board of Treasury, and another to the purchaser or purchasers.

The purchaser or purchasers, within seven years from the completion of this work, to lay off the whole tract, at their own expense, into townships and fractional parts of townships, and to divide the same into lots, according to the land ordinance of the 20th of May, 1785; complete returns whereof to be made to the Treasury Board. The lot No. 16, in each township or fractional part of a township, to be given perpetually for the purposes contained in the said ordinance. The lot No. 29, in each township or fractional part of a township, to be given perpetually for the purposes of religion. The lots Nos. 8, 11, and 26, in each township or fractional part of a township, to be reserved for the future disposition of Congress. Not more than two complete townships to be given perpetually for the purposes of a University, to be laid off by the purchaser or purchasers, as near the center as may be, so that the same shall be of good land, to be applied to the intended object by the legislature of the State.

Ordered, That the above be referred to the Board of Treasury, to take order.

July 23, 1787.

Land Laws, Pt. 1, Chap. 21.

APPENDIX F

An Act of Congress Wednesday, September 3, 1788

Congress assembled, present Massachusetts, Connecticut, New Jersey, Pennsylvania, Delaware, Maryland, Virginia, North Carolina, South Carolina and Georgia and from New Hampshire, Mr. (Paine) Wingate and from New York Mr. (Abraham) Yates.

On a report of a committee consisting of Mr. (Abraham) Clarke Mr. (Hugh) Williamson and Mr. (James) Madison to whom was referred a memorial of John Etwein of Bethlehem, president of the brethrens society for propagating the Gospel among the Heathen.

Whereas the United States in Congress assembled by their Ordinance of the 20 May 1785 among other things ordained that the towns of Gnadenhutten, Schoenbrun and Salem with lands adjoining to the said towns be reserved for the sole use of the Christian Indians who were formerly settled there or the remains of that society; and by an act of the 27 July 1787 directed the board of treasury to except and reserve out of any contract they might make pursuant to an Order of the 23 of the same month a quantity of land around and adjoining to each of the before mentioned towns amounting in the whole to ten thousand acres and ordered the property of the said towns and reserved lands to be vested in the Moravian brethren for civilizing the Indians and promoting christianity (or as they are called The society of the United brethren for propagating the Gospel among the Heathen) in trust and for the uses expressed in the said Ordinance, including others as mentioned in the said act of 27 July 1787; and whereas it has been agreed that the plot of each of the towns should be estimated at 666-2/3 acres so that each town and the reserved land adjoining shall make a tract of four thousand acres; and whereas the remnant of the said Christian Indians are desirous of returning to their towns as speedily as possible, and the United Brethren to facilitate this without loss of time have offered to advance the expenses of surveying the three tracts on condition they be repaid either in Money or land,

Ordered. That the geographer of the United States survey or cause to be surveyed as speedily as possible without interfering with the business he is sent to execute, the three tracts of Gnadenhutten, Shoenbrun and Salem on the Muskingum including the reserved land adjoining each of the said towns and return plats thereof to the board of treasury, that deeds may be issued for the same as is mentioned above; and that he also survey or cause to be surveyed the intermediate spaces, if any there be between the said three tracts and return plats thereof with an account of the expense to the board of treasury and that the said board, provided it can be done without infringing they may have already made, convey the same to the said United brethren or the society of the said brethren for propagating the Gospel among the heathen, upon their paying for the said intermediate space or spaces when the said surveys shall be returned by the Geographer, at the rate at which such lands are granted to others, and also the expenses attending the surveying and plotting the said spaces, deducting the sum advanced for surveying the three tracts, provided that in case any of the abovementioned lands shall fall within the supposed bounds of the millions of acres reserved for the late Army, that the said bounds shall be understood to extend so far to the westward as to include the million of acres exclusive of the above-mentioned lands.

From *Papers of the Continental Congress,* No. 19, II, pp. 229-230, in the writing of Charles Thomson and Mr. Abraham Clark. Read and passed September 3, 1788. This proceeding was also entered by John Fisher in *Western Territory, Papers of the Continental Congress,* No. 176, pp. 67-70. See September 2, 1788.

APPENDIX G

Chronology of Ratification, 1787-88

	Convention Met	Divison*	Final Vote	Division
Delaware	Dec. 3	30-0	Dec. 7	30-0
Pennsylvania	Nov. 21	46-23	Dec. 12	46-23
New Jersey	Dec. 11	39-0	Dec. 18	3 9 - 0
Georgia	Dec. 25	--**	Jan. 2	26-0
Connecticut	Jan. 1	128-40(?)	Jan. 9	128-40
Massachusetts	Jan. 9	170-190	February 16	187-168
New Hampshire	Feb. 13	30-77	June 21	57-47
Rhode Island	(in March towns voted not to call a convention 16-48)**			
Maryland	April 21	62-12	April 26	63-11
South Carolina	May 12	126-98(?)	May 23	149-73
Virginia	June 2	equal	June 25	89-79
New York	June 17	19-46	July 26	30-27
North Carolina	July 21	75-193	Aug. 4	75-193

* Federal strength is given in the first figure here and on the final division. The first vote is approximate. When the figures on the vote are dubious, it has been indicated with a question mark.
** A large Federal majority was reported.
***Rhode Island, threatened with being subjected to tariff duties as a "foreign" country, finally approved the constitution in 1790, by a vote of 34-32.

From Main, Jackson Turner, *The Antifederalists, Critics of the Constitution,* p. 288.

BIBLIOGRAPHY

Adams, Evelyn C. *American Indian Education*. New York: Arno Press, 1971.

Adams, Henry. *History of the United States*, Vol. I, Spectrum edition. Englewood Cliffs, N.J.: Prentice-Hall, Inc., 1963.

Ahlstrom, Sydney E. *A Religious History of the American People*. New Haven: Yale University Press, 1972.

Annals of America (The), Vol. 3. Chicago: Encyclopedia Britannica, Inc., 1968.

Babbidge, Homer D. and Rosenaweig, Robert M. *The Federal Interest in Higher Education*. New York: McGraw Hill, 1962.

Bailyn, Bernard. *Education in the Forming of American Society*. Chapel Hill: University of North Carolina Press, 1960.

Bancroft, George. *History of the Formation of the Constitution of the United States*, Vol. II. New York: D. Appelton and Co., 1900.

Banner, James M., Jr. *To the Hartford Convention: The Federalists and the Origins of Party Politics and Massachusetts, 1789-1815*. New York: Alfred A. Knopf, 1970.

Banning, Lance. *The Jeffersonian Persuasion: Evolution of a Party Ideology*. Ithaca: Cornell University Press, 1978.

Barrett, Jay A. *Evolution of the Ordinance of 1787*. New York: G.P. Putnam's Sons, 1891.

Bean, R. Bennett. *The Peopling of Virginia*. Boston: Chapman & Grimes, Publishers, 1938.

Bell, Sadie. *The Church, the State and Education in Virginia*. Philadelphia: University of Pennsylvania Press, 1930.

Beth, Loren P. *The American Theory of Church and State*. Gainesville: University of Florida Press, 1958.

Brant, Irving. *The Fourth President, A Life of James Madison*. New York: The Bobbs-Merrill Co., 1970.

Breen, Timothy H. (ed.). *Shaping Southern Society, The Colonial Experience*. New York: Oxford University Press, 1976.

Brown, Arlo Ayres. *A History of Religious Education in Recent Times*. New York: The Abington Press, 1923.

Brown, Stuart Gerry. *The First Republicans: Political Philosophy and Public Policy in the Party of Jefferson and Madison*. Syracuse: Syracuse University Press, 1954.

Brown, William Adams. *Church and State in Contemporary America*. New York: Charles Scribners Sons, 1936.

Bryce, James. *The American Commonwealth*, Hacker edition, Vol. I. New York: G.P. Putnam's Sons, 1959.

Butler, Vera M. *Education as Revealed by New England Newspapers Prior to 1850*. New York: Arno Press, 1969, 503 pp.

Campbell, T.E. *Colonial Carolina: A History of Carolina County, Virginia*. Richmond: The Diety Press, 1954.

Cappon, Lester J. (ed.). *The Adams-Jefferson Letters* (two volumes). Chapel Hill: University of North Carolina Press, 1959.

Chambers, William Nisbet and Burnham, Walter Dean (eds.). *The American Party Systems: Stages of Political Development*. New York: Oxford University Press, 1967.

Church and State, Vol. 35, Nos. 4, 5, & 6, April-June, 1982. Silver Spring, Maryland: Americans United for Separation of Church and State.

Clark, Gordon H. *What Do Presbyterians Believe? The Westminster Confession: Yesterday and Today*. Philadelphia: Presbyterian and Reformed Publishing Co., 1965.

Clews, Elsie W. *Educational Legislation and Administration of the Colonial Governments*. New York: The Macmillan Co., 1899.

Cobb, Sanford H. *The Rise of Religious Liberty in America*. New York: The Macmillan Co., 1902.

Corwin, Edward S. (ed.). *The Constitution of the United States of America, Analysis and Interpretation*. Washington, D.C.: U.S. Government Printing Office, 1953.

Cremin, Lawrence A. *American Education: The Colonial Experience, 1607-1783*. New York: Harper & Row, Publishers, 1970, 688 pp.

Crosskey, William Winslow. *Politics and the Constitution in the History of the United States*. Chicago: University of Chicago Press, 1953.

Cunningham, Noble E. *The Jeffersonian Republicans: The Formation of Party Organization, 1789-1801*. Chapel Hill: University of North Carolina Press, 1957.

Cutler, William P. (ed.). *Life, Journals, and Correspondence of Rev. Manasseh Cutler*, Vol. 2. Cincinnati: Robert Clarke and Co., 1888.

de Tocqueville, Alexia. *Democracy in America*. Trans. by Henry Reeve. New York. Vol. 1.

Elliot, Jonathon. *Debates in the Several State Conventions on the Adoption of the Federal Constitution*, second edition, 1836. New York: Burt Franklin; Research and Source Works Series 109.

Ely, John Hart. *Democracy and Distrust: A Theory of Judicial Review*. Cambridge: Harvard University Press, 1980.

Farrand, Max. *The Framing of the Constitution of the United States*. New Haven: Yale University Press, 1913.

Farrand, Max (ed.). *Records of the Federal Convention of 1787*, revised edition. New Haven: Yale University Press, 1966, 4 vols.

Fenton, William N. *American Indian and White Relations to 1830*. Chapel Hill: University of North Carolina Press, 1957, 138 pp.

Fischer, David Hackett. *The Revolution of American Conservatism: The Federalist in the Era of Jeffersonian Democracy*. New York: Harper & Row, Publishers, 1965.

Fleming, Sandford. *Children and Puritanism*, reprint edition. New York: Arno Press, 1969.

Flexner, James Thomas. *George Washington, Anguish and Farewell 1793-1799*. Boston: Little, Brown & Co., 1969.

Force, Peter. *Ordinance of 1787 and Its History*, in St. Clair Papers, ii 610-18.

Gaustad, Edwin Scott (ed.). *Religious Issues in American History*. New York: Harper & Row, Publishers, 1968.

Greene, Evarts B. *Religion and the State, The Making and Testing of An American Tradition*. Ithaca, New York: Cornell University Press, 1941, 172 pp.

Gwathmey, John H. *Twelve Virginia Counties Where the Western Migration Began*. Richmond, Virginia: The Diety Press, 1937.

Hilldrup, Robert Leroy. *The Life and Times of Edmund Pendleton*. Chapel Hill: University of North Carolina Press, 1939.

Humphrey, Edward Frank. *Nationalism and Religion in America 1774-1789*. Boston: Chipman Law Publishing Co., 1924.

Isaac, Rhys. "Preachers and Patriots: Popular Culture and the Revolution in Virginia," *The American Revolution*, Young, Alfred F. (ed.). De Kalb: Northern Illinois University Press, 1976, pp. 125-156.

Jefferson, Thomas. *Notes on the State of Virginia*. New York: Harper Torchbooks, 1964.

Journals of Congress, containing the proceedings from September 5, 1774 to November 3, 1788, 2nd edition, 4 vols. Washington, 1823.

Kelley, Robert. *The Shaping of the American Past*, Vol. 2, second edition. Englewood Cliffs, New Jersey: Prentice-Hall, Inc., 1978.

Knight, Edward W. (ed.). *A Documentary History of Education in the South Before 1860*. Chapel Hill: University of North Carolina Press, 1942.

Knight, G.W. *History and Management of Land Grants for Education in N.W. Territory*, in Papers of American Historical Association, Vol. 1, No. 3. New York: G.P. Putnam's Sons, 1885.

Lerche, Charles O. "Jefferson and the Election of 1800: A Case Study in the Political Smear," *The William and Mary Quarterly*, Vol. 5, No. 4 (October, 1948).

Levy, Leonard W. *Jefferson and Civil Liberties: The Darker Side*. Cambridge: Harvard University Press, 1963.
Levy, Leonard W. *Judgments: Essays on American Constitutional History*. Chicago: Quadrangle Books, 1972.
Littell, Franklin H. *From State Church to Pluralism: A Protestant Interpretation of Religion in American History*. New York: The Macmillan Co., 1962.
Lockhart, Wm. B., Kamisar, Yale, and Choper, Jesse H. *Constitutional Rights and Liberties: Cases and Materials*, fifth edition. St. Paul, Minnesota: West Publishing Co., 1980.
Lockridge, Kenneth A. *A New England Town The First Hundred Years*. New York: W.W. Norton & Co., 1970.
Lohrenz, Otto. *The Virginia Clergy and the American Revolution, 1774-1799*, Ph.D. dissertation, University of Michigan, microfilm, 1956.
Lomask, Milton. *The Spirit of 1787: The Making of Our Constitution*. New York: Farrar Straus Giroux, 1980.
Main, Jackson Turner. *The Antifederalists, Critics of the Constitution— 1781-1788*. Chapel Hill: University of North Carolina Press, 1961.
Malone, Dumas. *Jefferson and the Ordeal of Liberty*. Boston: Little, Brown and Company, 1965.
McLaughlin, Andrew C. *The Confederation and the Constitution, 1783-1789*, J. & J. Harper edition. New York: Harper and Brothers, 1905.
McLaughlin, Wm.G. "Isaac Backus and the Separation of Church and State in America," *American Historical Review*, LXIII, June, 1968, pp. 1392-1413.
McLaughlin, Wm.G. (ed.). *Isaac Bachus on Church, State & Calvinism*. Cambridge: Howard University Press, 1968.
Mead, Sidney E. *The Old Religion in the Brave New World*. Berkeley: University of California Press, 1977.
Moran, Gerald F. and Vinovskis, Maris A. "The Puritan Family and Religion: A Critical Reappraisal," (unpublished paper) 1980, 61 pp.
Morgan, Edmund S. *The Puritan Family*, Harper Torchbooks, new edition. New York: Harper & Row, Publishers, 1966, 196 pp.
Morgan, Edmund S. *The Birth of the Republic 1763-89*, revised edition. Chicago: University of Chicago Press, 1977.
Morison, Samuel Eliot and Commager, Henry Steele. *The Growth of the American Republic*, fourth edition. New York: Oxford University Press, 1950.
Noll, Mark A. *Christians in the American Revolution*. Washington, D.C.: Christian University Press, 1977.

Packard, Frederick A. *The Daily Public School in the United States*, reprint edition. New York: Arno Press, 1969.

The Papers of Alexander Hamilton, Vol. XXV, Harold C. Syrett (ed.). New York: Columbia University Press, 1977.

The Papers of Thomas Jefferson, Vols. 1-18, Julian P. Boyd (ed.). Princeton: Princeton University Press, 1950.

Peterson, Merrill D. *Adams and Jefferson: A Revolutionary Dialogue*. Athens: Univeristy of Georgia Press, 1976.

Peterson, Merrill D. (ed.). *The Portable Thomas Jefferson*. New York: Viking Press, 1975.

Peterson, Merril D. *Thomas Jefferson and the New Nation*. New York: Oxford University Press, 1970.

Poore, Benjamin P. *The Federal and State Constitutions, Colonial Charters, and Other Organic Laws of the United States*, Part I and II. Washington. D.C.: U.S. Government Printing Office, 1877.

Risjord, Norman K. *Chesapeake Politics: 1781-1800*. New York: Columbia University Press, 1978.

Risjord, Norman K. *Forging the American Republic 1760-1815*. Reading, Massachusetts: Addison-Wesley Publishing Co., 1973.

Risjord, Norman K. *The Old Republicans, Southern Conservatism in the Age of Jefferson*. New York: Columbia University Press, 1965.

Roberts, Frank C. *To All Generations: A Study of Church History*. Grand Rapids, Michigan: Christian Reformed Board of Publications, 1981, 309 pp.

Rossiter, Clinton. *1787: The Grand Convention*. New York: The Macmillan Company, 1966.

Schaff, Philip. *The Creeds of Christendom with a History and Critical Notes*, Vol. I, sixth edition. Grand Rapids, Michigan: Baker Book House, 1931.

Schlesinger, Arthur M., Jr. (ed.). *History of American Presidential Elections*, Vol. 1. New York: Chelsen House Publishers, 1971.

Schwartz, Bernard. *The Bill of Rights: A Documentary History*. New York: Chelsea House Publishers; McGraw Hill Book Co., 1971.

Scotchmer, Paul F. "Church and State in Western Christendom: An Historical Typology," *Christian Scholar's Review*, 1981, Vol. XI, No. 1, pp. 49-67.

Scott, S.W. *History of Orange County, Virginia*. Richmond: Everett Waddly Co., 1907.

Semple, Robert B. *A History of the Rise and Progress of the Baptists in Virginia*, revised edition. Richmond: Pitt and Dickinson, Publishers, 1894.

Sisson, Daniel. *The American Revolution of 1800*. New York: Alfred A. Knopf, 1974.

Slaughter, Philip. *A History of St. Mark's Parish, Culpeper County, Virginia*, revised edition. Baltimore: Southern Book Company, 1958.

Sorauf, Frank J. *The Wall of Separation*. Princeton: Princeton University Press, 1976.

Stokes, Anson Phelps. *Church and State in the United States*, revised edition. New York: Harper & Row, Publishers, 1964.

Sweet, William Warren. *The Story of Religion in America*, revised edition. New York: Harper & Bros., Publishers, 1950.

Taylor, Howard Cromwell. *The Educational Significance of the Early Federal Land Ordinances*, reprint edition. New York: Arno Press, 1922, 1969.

Walsh, Lorena S. "Till Death Us Do Part: Marriage and Family in Seventeenth Century Maryland," *The Chesapeake in the Seventeenth Century*, Tate, Thad W. and Ammerman, David (eds.). Chapel Hill: University of North Carolina Press, 1979.

Webster, Noah. *An American Selection of Lessons in Reading and Speaking*, fourth edition. Hartford: Hudson and Goodwin, 1788, 204 pp.

Whitehead, John W. *The Separation Illusion*. Milford, Michigan: Mott Media, 1977.

The Works of Thomas Jefferson, Vol. VIII, H.A. Washington (ed.). New York: Townsend Mac Coun., 1884.

The Writings of George Washington, Bicentennial edition, John C. Fitzpatrick (ed.). Washington, D.C.: U.S. Government Printing Office, 1939.

The Writings of Thomas Jefferson, Vol. I & II, Andrew A. Lipcomb (ed.). Washington, D.C.: The Thomas Jefferson Memorial Association, 1905.

The Writings of Thomas Jefferson, Vol. II, Paul L. Ford (ed.). New York: G.P. Putnam's Sons, 1893.